MICHAEL JACKSON
CONSPIRACY

Other Books by Aphrodite Jones

A Perfect Husband

All She Wanted

Cruel Sacrifice

Della's Web

The Embrace: A True Vampire Story

The FBI Killer

Red Zone: The Behind-the-Scenes Story of the San Francisco Dog Mauling

MICHAEL JACKSON
CONSPIRACY

APHRODITE JONES

FOREWORD BY TOM MESEREAU

aphroditejonesbooks

MICHAEL JACKSON CONSPIRACY

Published by Aphrodite Jones Books,
an imprint of iUniverse,
2021 Pine Lake Road, Suite 100,
Lincoln NE 68512 (800) 288-4677.

The views expressed in this work are solely those of the author.

ISBN: 978-0-9795498-0-9 (cloth)

Printed in the United States of America

For my darling, precious John,

the love of my life.

"To live would be an awfully big adventure."

—Peter Pan

Author's Note

The day Michael Jackson was exonerated, I was asked what I really thought about the verdicts by FOX star Bill O'Reilly. For months, I had been commenting about the trial for *FOX News*, saying many things against Jackson, leading viewers to believe the pop star was guilty. When O'Reilly pressed me for an answer on the "not guilty" verdicts, I was stammering. O'Reilly wanted a straight answer, and I finally said I thought the jury did the right thing.

But part of me was still in shock.

As I made one of my last public comments on the case, I realized that I had become one of the media folks who had predetermined the outcome of the trial, wrongly. Many people around me were so sure of Jackson's guilt. Certain reporters had slanted TV and radio coverage to suit the prosecution, and I was one of the people who followed that dangerous trend.

Somehow, I had missed the truth.

When I read the accounts of the NOT GUILTY verdicts in all the newspapers, I felt ashamed to have been part of the media machine that seemed hell-bent on destroying Jackson. After I thought about it for a few hours, I contacted the jury foreman, Paul Rodriguez, who talked to me about Jackson, who asserted that Jackson had been a target. The jury foreman said Michael Jackson was truly not guilty of the charges. He felt Jackson had been victimized by the media.

Writing a book about Jackson's innocence never crossed my mind, not during the trial in Santa Maria. I respected Tom Mesereau as an attorney, and I came to see why the jury voted not guilty on every charge, but I had no intention of revealing my own slanted news coverage. Beyond that, I certainly didn't want to expose any of my media "friends" as being one-sided and unfair.

To make it clear: there were twenty-two hundred credentialed media people at the trial, and less than a handful of people admitted their deliberate attempts to portray Michael Jackson as guilty. Some of those media folks were a part of my inner circle. I have not named names of any media person in this book, other than Mr. Martin Bashir, because it would be in bad taste to point fingers. Viewers who followed the trial know who the culprits are.

I must admit that there was a point during the trial, toward the end, when I came to feel sad about Jackson, when I felt the whole media world was against him. I wanted the fans to know that I wasn't happy about the media coverage and decided to go down to the gates of Neverland to make peace with his fans. I went to tell people that I wasn't trying to be unfair to Michael, that I was just reporting the facts. I tried to convince them that I didn't have an agenda.

But the fans didn't believe me. They'd seen my newscasts, and many thought I was lying. I stayed for quite a while, trying to tell people that I wasn't out to smear Jackson, but they weren't interested.

As I listened to his fans, who had flown in from places like Spain, Ireland, and even Iran, they told me their side of the story. I heard them insist that the American media was tainted, that Americans hated Jackson for all the wrong reasons. Some people brought up the race card. Others talked about Michael's friendships with children as being acceptable in any part of the world—other than America.

His fans impressed me. Yes, there were a few overzealous people—one woman called me a whore in Spanish—but at the same time, many of his supporters were good-hearted. Some wanted to give me the benefit of the doubt.

I appreciated that.

I took pictures with a few fans at the front gates of Neverland, which was covered in hearts by those who loved Michael. After a while, a small group of us began to laugh about the Arvizo clan and their crazy rebuttal tape. We were mimicking Janet Arvizo, who, on tape, supported Michael Jackson as her only "family." On the rebuttal tape, Janet wondered why, after the airing of the Bashir interview, there were so many people suddenly showing care and concern for her, when really, only Michael was supportive of her family.

In unison, we repeated Janet's lines:

"*Where were they*, when I couldn't feed my children, even a box of cereal?"

"*Where were they*, when my children and I would weep?"

"*Where were they*, when my children and I were lonely?"

"Where were *they*, when I didn't have enough money to pay for bus fare?"

"Where were they?" we asked over and over, and we laughed about Janet's melodramatic rantings.

Because of this visit to Neverland, my reportage took a slight turn. I became more open to the idea that Michael Jackson was not guilty, and I tried to stay away from the negative commentary that filled much of my earlier newscasts. Not only had I been one-sided on TV, I had contributed to Michael Reagan's radio show (the adopted son of President Ronald Reagan) and had spent weeks on Reagan's national program—bashing Michael Jackson.

If there was a media conspiracy, I was guilty.

Some weeks later, as every last TV truck pulled out of Santa Maria, I found myself alone there, lost without the presence of Michael, lost without the comfort of having my media "buddies" to help me through another day. I felt upset.

Santa Maria was a nice place, but it became an empty shell for me. The Jackson "event" was over, and I became a stranger in a small town. I thought about my media friends and realized that many of them weren't my friends at all. They had made use of my input and had already gone off to the next hot story. Some were reporting live from Aruba, in search of a missing teenage girl.

Luckily, I wasn't worried about the next news tidbit. I had a bigger picture in mind and had compiled all kinds of data. I still wanted to write a book about Jackson, because after all, I wasn't at the trial simply to report the news. I was there, primarily, as an author.

Since I was at the trial as a freelance TV reporter, I was left on my own to get myself shipped out, to get everything shipped back home. Sitting in Santa Maria with my thoughts, trying to determine what to do with all the documentation and stacks of notes I'd written about the trial, I decided to ship every last thing, just in case the book materialized.

As I made my journey back to the East Coast, I thought about the financial waste that so many people, especially California taxpayers, had been subjected to. It was impossible to calculate the exact amount of dollars wasted, but the numbers had to be in the millions. The Jackson trial was one of the largest events in U.S. history. The amount of money spent on security alone, was simply outrageous.

I considered the expensive "impact fee" I was asked to pay to Santa Maria, something I never encountered in any trial I attended in the history of my crime-writing career. I wondered why I was asked to pay so much money to be seated at a public proceeding that was supposed to be open to any U.S. taxpayer.

And finally, I wondered why some folks in the mainstream media seemed to think of me as "less than" a reporter, especially when there were people like Marcia Clark, who unsuccessfully prosecuted the O. J. Simpson trial, standing outside the Santa Maria courthouse as a reporter for *Entertainment Tonight*. It was amazing to me that certain network talent saw me as incapable of doing a TV reporting job. Even though I'd been a TV reporter and TV commentator for years, all throughout the Jackson trial, I knew I was being trashed behind my back. Sometimes I was attacked verbally by reporters, even to my face.

I wondered why I had been put through so much drama and expense and agony—all for nothing. When I traveled to New York, I discovered that no American publisher wanted to touch any Michael Jackson book at all—especially one that would be an account of Jackson's side of the story.

I was devastated.

But then I thought about Michael.

I wondered how *he* felt, and realized that he was the one who'd been through hell. He was the one who was subjected to a mainstream media machine that wanted him destroyed. *He* was the one people trashed behind his back.

Less than a month after his acquittal, I learned that Jackson, his three children, and their nanny, had moved to the Persian Gulf Kingdom of Bahrain, and I understood why. At least as a guest of the royal family's Sheik Abdullah, Jackson would have his privacy back, and he could find a way to recuperate, to unwind, and to think about a comeback. Reportedly, the star was being asked to open a vineyard or an amusement park, but Jackson wasn't interested. Michael Jackson had bigger plans, but for the moment, he just wanted the nightmare behind him.

Months later, I contacted Judge Rodney Melville, who wrote a court order allowing me to review and photograph all the evidence from the criminal trial. I spent time making numerous trips to Santa Maria, pouring over documents, taking pictures of Michael's private Neverland, recording all the evidence that I'd seen during the trial, requesting copies of transcripts. Readers should note that all of the quoted testimony in this book comes directly from the trial transcripts.

I had an epiphany when I sat in the Santa Maria Superior Court Complex basement, reviewing hours of never-released footage. With a court clerk monitoring my notes, I paused at that moment when the accuser told police that he "wasn't sure" about certain things. I rewound the tape of the police interview with the accuser, and asked the court clerk what she thought about it. I wanted to know if she had sons, if boys age thirteen already know about their sexuality. The court clerk looked at me and shook her head.

"Of course boys know about that," she said, "certainly by age thirteen."

With that, I had my answer. I decided to contact a Jackson advocate, Pearl Jr., who also covered the Jackson trial, and we had lunch together in Los Angeles.

Pearl Jr. encouraged me to write the book about the Jackson trial, however, I still felt I would be fighting an uphill battle.

A few weeks later, I happened to run into Tom Mesereau, not once, but twice. And I took it as a sign.

I felt that, no matter what the media, the skeptics, and even my friends and family had to say, I needed to stand up for Michael Jackson. As I began to write, I noticed that people everywhere were making fun of me. *A pro-Jackson book?* Impossible.

The more people poked and prodded me, the more I became infuriated. As I struggled through thousands of pages of trial transcripts, with people discouraging me from the start, I began to think the book would never get done. It became my most arduous work, ever, and at times it felt like I had the whole world on my shoulders.

I wondered if Michael lived his life this way.

To keep my spirits up, I kept thinking about the time that Michael said hello to me during the trial. It was in the hallway during a break, and I was staring at him like he was a wax figure. Suddenly Michael looked at me and said, "Hi!"

When he spoke, it startled me.

He was being funny, and I loved it.

People always ask me if I've ever met Michael Jackson, and I tell them yes. But really, I never introduced myself, and he certainly doesn't know me.

Only once did I ask him a question from the media pen. It was early on, when Jackson was still responding to media questions, and I asked him if he was talking to his fans at the gates of Neverland. Michael was already past the media throng, but he turned, and looked back at me and said, "I love my fans, I love my fans!" It was as if they were the only people who mattered.

I hope this book reaches beyond Jackson supporters, and gets to the millions of folks who've been trusting the tabloid media, way too much. If the truth prevails, then one way or another, people will open their hearts.

Aphrodite Jones
March 1, 2007

Foreword

When I first observed journalist Aphrodite Jones at the Santa Maria, California, Courthouse in the Michael Jackson case, I turned the other direction. I wanted nothing to do with Ms. Jones. The first time my eyes met those of Ms. Jones, I threw her a deep, cold stare. If looks could kill, she was buried.

I associated Aphrodite Jones with an international media juggernaut that was heavily invested in seeing Michael Jackson convicted and destroyed. Never in my life or career had I found myself in the middle of such a crazed, dishonest, and manipulative feeding frenzy. Despite the presence of many honorable journalists, the ghost of profit seemed to overshadow much that was truthful, accurate, and careful.

Approximately one year after Michael Jackson was acquitted, I unexpectedly met Ms. Jones at an art gallery in Beverly Hills to celebrate the publication of a series of sketches of high-profile trials. For the first time, I had a candid discussion with Ms. Jones. I told her that I had watched television during the Scott Peterson trial and observed her aggressively place her head on Defense Counsel Mark Geragos' shoulder. This appeared on all of the evening newscasts about the Peterson trial and, in my opinion, looked terrible for the defense. Nothing like this was going to happen to me.

Ms. Jones told me she understood completely and greatly respected my style and approach in the Michael Jackson defense. She claimed she was having second thoughts about the way the media treated and reported on the Michael Jackson trial. She even indicated she felt some guilt for the way she had been caught up in the media frenzy to portray Michael Jackson in the worst light possible. Ms. Jones said she was considering writing a truthful book about the reality of the Michael Jackson trial and the distortion of much of the media reporting.

When Aphrodite Jones asked if she could interview me for this effort, I was skeptical. My law partner and cocounsel in the Jackson defense, Susan Yu, was adamant that I have no part of Ms. Jones' literary efforts. Nevertheless, something told me that Ms. Jones was being truthful, courageous, and professional in her desire to set the record straight about the Michael Jackson defense.

I interviewed with Ms. Jones and reviewed some of the initial drafts of her proposed book. Surprised by her candor and effort to go against the media flow surrounding Michael Jackson and to tell the truth, I agreed to assist, as long the effort came from an honest place. I refused to tell her what to write or how to write it and have no financial or profit interest in this book or foreword. As someone who strongly believes in the power and values of ideas and disagreement, I appreciate views different from my own, as long as they come from a place of integrity, intelligence, and accurate information. In the Michael Jackson case, most media conclusions were shallow, misinformed, and self-serving. I know in my heart of hearts that Michael Jackson was not guilty of any of these grisly charges.

My purpose in writing this foreword is to underscore how important it is to truthfully report the workings of our justice system. For the last fifteen years, American society has been riveted by media treatment of high-profile trials. Television coverage, documentaries, reenactments, television series, movies, and books (both fiction and nonfiction) have found a massive audience when the subject is our justice system. The amount of revenue—literally billions of dollars—that has been generated around the world is staggering. It is critical that professional journalists maintain their values and ethics in the middle of this gargantuan explosion. I believe this did not happen, for the most part, in the trial coverage of Michael Jackson.

When over seventy Santa Barbara sheriffs raided Michael Jackson's home at Neverland Ranch in November of 2003, I was returning to Los Angeles from a much-needed vacation. I was in the final stages of preparation for the defense of actor Robert Blake, who was charged with murdering his wife. Within minutes of activating my cell phone after a nine-day hiatus, it started ringing off the hook with calls from associates of Michael Jackson. They wanted me to immediately fly to Las Vegas and be his attorney.

I declined the offer because I did not feel I could ethically cover both the Blake and Jackson cases at once. The Blake murder trial was set for February of 2004 and would consume all of my time. I had managed to free Robert Blake from jail in a preliminary hearing, during which every American legal expert said obtaining bail would be impossible. I succeeded in having the conspiracy charge against him dismissed in a subsequent hearing and was able to shift public opinion in his favor after cross-examining the prosecution's witnesses at the televised hearing. I was positive he would be acquitted.

Three months after being asked to be Michael Jackson's lawyer, on the eve of the Blake trial, Robert and I had a serious falling out, which the trial judge could not resolve. I removed myself from his defense. Approximately five weeks later, Randy Jackson, Michael's brother, called me and asked if I would reconsider. I had known Randy for many years, and we had gotten together socially from time to time. I told Randy that I was free and willing to meet Michael Jackson. Randy arranged for me to fly to Florida for this purpose and the rest is history. All of our lives were radically changed by Randy's request.

Prior to my entrance into the Michael Jackson case, I was appalled by the theatrics surrounding the Jackson defense. His lawyers were traveling to Santa Maria by private jet and appeared to be having too good of a time. Michael was late for his first appearance, marched on top of an SUV for his fans, and hosted a party for the media at Neverland later that day. A meeting of Jackson's legal and financial advisors, whom local newscasters referred to as Michael's "Dream Team," was held at the posh Beverly Hills Hotel. Michael Jackson and his counsel appeared on *60 Minutes* with disastrous results, and Jackson's Nation of Islam security detail was receiving dramatic publicity in the conservative Santa Maria community. I didn't like any of this.

I chose to tone down everything. I opposed courtroom cameras and supported the trial judge's gag order and sealing of salacious pleadings. I removed provocative individuals from the defense, either immediately or gradually. Certain people I did not trust were frozen out of key meetings or denied access to important information. My focus was on thirteen people—the judge and twelve jurors. I liked the Santa Maria community, who my instincts told me would be fair to Michael.

The Michael Jackson defense had to cope with three primary challenges: the prosecution, the media, and the legion of mediocre advisors surrounding the vulnerable, innocent Michael Jackson. I am happy to say that we successfully coped with all three hurdles.

The prosecution spent more money and time trying to convict Michael Jackson than any prosecution in history. In the early 1990s, District Attorney Tom Sneddon initiated the convening of two grand juries, Santa Barbara and Los Angeles, to investigate and indict Michael Jackson. Both refused to charge Michael with any crime. In the mid-1990s, Mr. Sneddon traveled personally to at least two countries looking for alleged victims of Michael. He couldn't find any.

Mr. Sneddon arranged for a Web site at the Santa Barbara sheriff's department for information on Michael Jackson and hired a PR firm. This was absurd.

In 2004, a third grand jury was assembled in this case, and Michael Jackson was indicted. The prosecution had nine fingerprint experts in this case—more than I have seen in any death penalty case. The fingerprint evidence went nowhere. They recklessly hired every conceivable expert in areas such as accident reconstruction, computer graphics, DNA, forensic accounting, finance, criminal-istics, telephones, acoustics, security systems, child molestation, psychology, pathology, and jury consulting. They pulled out all the stops in an effort to bom-bard the jury with any conceivable fact that might help convict Michael. This included hiring a jury consultant who had successfully helped the prosecutors convict Timothy McVeigh, Martha Stewart, and Scott Peterson.

One will never really know how much money and how many employee hours were spent by the district attorney's office. Numerous mock trials were conducted and law enforcement agencies around the world were contacted. Of course, all of this was at the expense of the taxpayers of Santa Barbara, California.

More accredited media from around the globe covered this trial than the total number of reporters who covered the O. J. Simpson and Scott Peterson trials combined. There has never been a trial covered to this extent, and there probably never will be again. Unfortunately, it was believed that enormous sums of money would be made in films, shows, reenactments, and books about the rise and fall of Michael Jackson. However, a conviction was necessary to successfully complete any of these projects. If Michael Jackson had been sent to prison, it would have generated more media coverage than any event in history. Billions of dollars hung in the balance.

Because he is the world's best-known celebrity, Michael Jackson attracts an endless array of starstruck "wannabes." These include lawyers and non-lawyers alike. He was constantly subjected to mediocre and shortsighted advice from self-anointed experts about how to defend himself. People were willing to say anything they thought would propel them into the event, and dealing with this sea of fools was distracting and dangerous.

As an illustration, consider the role of the accuser's mother in the trial. I decided very early that she was going to be a main target of our attack. During my opening statement, I informed the jury that I would prove that the mother had orchestrated these false allegations. Having examined her for three hours in a pretrial hearing, I knew she would be a disaster for the prosecution on cross-examination. I informed everyone associated with the Jackson defense that no efforts were to be taken that might discourage her from testifying for the prosecution. I specifically forbade anyone from reporting her to the Los Angeles district attorney when I learned she had committed welfare fraud. Under California law, she could have refused to testify.

Despite my clear admonitions, certain lawyers, none of whom were going to examine a single witness in the trial, reported her to Los Angeles authorities. As I expected, she then refused to testify, and it took the prosecutors weeks to convince her to take the stand in their case. Had she hung firm, she could have refused any testimony under the United States and California constitutions. This would have dealt a serious blow to our defense.

I do not believe that the lawyers who reported her intended to hurt Michael Jackson. In my opinion, they simply lacked vision and insight. They wanted to be part of the event and tried to appear strong to a vulnerable client. In reality, they didn't belong anywhere near this case.

Fortunately, I had two exceptional lawyers on my team: Susan Yu and Robert Sanger. Although we all had different backgrounds, styles, and perspectives, we made a good team. Ms. Yu and Mr. Sanger were always focused and driven to see Michael Jackson acquitted. They knew that a team effort was required. No matter what differences we ever had, we always resolved them in a manner which focused on victory. I also regularly consulted with my dear friend Jennifer Keller, a brilliant criminal defense lawyer in Southern California. These are the lawyers who won the case with me.

We also had very professional staffers and assistants. Investigators Jesus Castillo and Scott Ross were outstanding. We kept away from the media and never allowed the lure of stardom to interrupt our focused defense. This was a case where the potential for distraction was everywhere. I had watched lawyers in other cases get carried away with the camera and, in my opinion, they hurt their clients' interests. Fortunately, that never happened with Ms. Yu, Mr. Sanger, or me.

I have reviewed Ms. Jones' book and commend her for her efforts. To anyone who wants to learn what happened in the Michael Jackson courtroom, this is the book to read. It explains in clear and moving detail why an innocent, kindhearted musical genius was acquitted by a conservative jury in Santa Maria, California. Justice was done, and I am very proud to have been Michael Jackson's lead counsel.

Thomas A. Mesereau, Jr.
Los Angeles, California

"ABC ... It's Easy"

It was the final judgment day, one of the biggest verdicts in world history, and thousands of people were flooding the streets around the courthouse. The arrival of Michael Jackson was imminent, and sheriff's deputies treated the crowd like they were in a Nazi boot camp, demanding everyone stand behind strict lines, demanding order out of the chaos. As some of the media stood outside under the main "commander" tent, waiting to see who would be given a seat, people felt exhausted and emotional.

After five months of covering the case for every network under the sun, media folks couldn't agree about what kind of justice was being served in the case of *The People of the State of California v. Michael Joe Jackson*. Throughout the week that the jury deliberated, cable networks were fueling public fire, flashing images of Jackson's potential jail cells. Some people expected the superstar to fail to show up for court, expected that Jackson would try to elude his fate.

It was midday on Monday, June 13, 2005, when final notice was given that the jury reached its verdict. Media from around the world were pumped up, and additional TV people and filmmakers had arrived with new demands and new camera angles to decipher. A mass of Jackson fans had set up various camps surrounding the courthouse: fans with camcorders, fans with cell phone cameras, fans with every conceivable high-tech digital device. People were competing for the best view of Michael, the best photo of Michael, the best T-shirt of Michael, the best poster of Michael. It was madness.

People who camped out in Santa Maria were of every race, size, shape, color, and age. Waiting for breaking news, there was a frenzy among fans, complete with a half dozen Jackson impersonators and a handful of women who wished they were "Billie Jean." Representatives were there from perhaps half of the countries around the world, and they were adamant about Jackson's innocence.

For the Jackson fans who stood outside every day, the trial provided a rare opportunity to put aside differences. People from every corner of the planet became united in their fight for justice. They believed that Michael was a media pawn, and had shown up in droves to support him. People loved Michael as a brother, as an entertainer, as an icon—but to the media, Jackson's fans seemed excessive and eccentric. They were easily dismissed.

As everyone waited for the verdicts to come in, each passing hour seemed like an eternity. Fans were growing antsy. When the gates of the courthouse opened to the public, the crowd came closer to the fences, pressing toward the row of deputies, and a few chosen lottery winners were allowed through the gates. They filed in quietly, the thirty-five members of the public, and were wanded, patted down, and given warnings about outbursts. The lottery winners were escorted inside by armed deputies. They took their seats in the public seating area, barely making a sound.

For each person there, the anticipation of the verdict had grown to mass proportions. Of the twenty-two hundred credentialed media people who covered the trial, only about three dozen would have insider seats. A few dozen producers would watch the verdicts on closed-circuit TV, housed in an overflow room, isolated from fans, but the bulk of the media opted to stay just outside the courtroom doors, guarding their individual tents, with their on-air talent ready to report the "Jackson" news.

The media throng kept looking for any juicy tidbit, anything that might titillate their audience, but all was quiet. And as the world's anticipation for the verdicts kept getting more intense, news producers were suddenly bombarded with a growing number of fans who began to shout, "Michael's innocent!"

And just then, like clockwork, the Jackson family arrived, complete with Katherine and Joe, Janet, La Toya, Rebbie, and Michael's very famous brothers. As his handlers, his bodyguards, and his glamorous family were being greeted by Michael's defense team, one thing stood out clearly: all of these people put together were completely outshined by Michael.

It was Michael, hiding behind mirrored sunglasses and his trademark umbrella, who emerged as the superstar of all superstars. As Michael approached the court, stepping out of his black sport utility vehicle, the wails of screaming and tears of emotion from everyone around him—made it seem like the whole earth stood still.

Whatever his health condition was at the time, whatever toll the trial had taken on him—Michael didn't show it. He waltzed up to his lead attorney, Thomas Mesereau, and, just before he walked behind the closed doors of the court, Michael stood up tall as he waved to his fans, happy to see them out in full force. For the people behind the gates and cyclone fences who were screaming and cheering, there seemed to be a communion. Something about Michael made hearts pound. Everyone in his presence could feel the music. They could feel the dance.

As it happened, just as the last media person was allowed into the tiny courtroom, being wanded and scrutinized by deputies at the metal detector, Michael appeared around the corner, and, for the first time in the proceedings, the superstar looked nervous. His face looked strained. He no longer had a smile. He no longer seemed invincible. In that moment of vulnerability, people could see that the trial had taken its toll on Michael after all. It was obvious that he wanted it to be over.

Michael's attorney later confided that their team felt confident Jackson would be acquitted on all counts, insisting that the subject of prison had not come up very often. Tom Mesereau was unshakable in his belief that Jackson was being prosecuted for crimes he did not commit, and Michael's friends and family certainly believed in him. Still, when Michael was standing at the threshold of the courtroom for those few seconds, being wanded all alone behind the metal detector—the superstar looked scared.

Inside the court, there was an eight-woman, four-man jury who had been presented with six hundred exhibits, who had witnessed what seemed to be a smear campaign launched by the Martin Bashir documentary, who had listened to twelve years of Jackson's private history, all laid bare for them by the Santa Barbara District Attorney Tom Sneddon. In all, Sneddon and his team had presented eighty witnesses in an attempt to portray Jackson as a serial criminal, and had been permitted to delve way back into Jackson's life in an attempt to show the jury a pattern of criminal behavior.

As people inside the courtroom awaited the jury's verdicts, the world seemed incredibly small. Every face was strained, every eye was focused. The Jackson family was only given six seats in the courtroom, and Janet, being gracious, opted to wait outside during the proceeding, allowing brothers Randy and Tito and sisters La Toya and Rebbie, to sit directly behind Michael.

Eleven armed deputies spread out around the room, ready to take care of any outbursts, and at 2:10 PM, Judge Rodney Melville finally began to open up the verdict envelopes. As each envelope slid open, the judge's face remained still. Not a word was spoken in the court, but a few female jurors had tears in their eyes. Time stood still. It seemed like forever. And then, suddenly, the Superior Court Clerk Lorna Ray actually read the words:

"Count One—conspiracy—not guilty."

"Count Two—lewd act upon a child—not guilty"

"Count Three—not guilty."

"Not guilty" were the words being read over and over, fourteen times in all. As the verdicts came down, Katherine, who had never missed a day of the trial, had tears in her eyes. Tito reached over and kissed his mom. The rest of the family hugged and squeezed each other. As the news began sinking in, Michael's fans sobbed quietly in the back rows. And the media crowd, for the most part, sat dumbfounded. They seemed really quite surprised that Jackson hadn't been convicted of anything at all. From the looks on their faces, clearly some media members had been banking on seeing the superstar put behind bars.

Judge Rodney Melville, who had handled the case with such dignity and clarity, who had kept everyone safe and sound, who had not tolerated any disruptions whatsoever, now read a statement to the court:

"We the jury, feeling the weight of the world's eyes upon us, all thoroughly and meticulously studied the testimony, evidence, and rules of procedure presented in this court since January 31, 2005. Following the jury instructions, we confidently came to our verdicts. It is our hope that this case is a testament to the belief in our justice system's integrity and truth."

With those words, Michael, from behind the defense table, resumed his vast composure. In some strange way, Michael seemed to have the appearance of an ancient king. There was something imperial about him. So absolutely commanding with his presence, Michael listened with quiet intent as the statement from the judge was being read. With his head held high, the superstar remained motionless. Only those who could see him close up, could detect a slight tear running down Michael's face.

"Mr. Jackson, your bail is exonerated and you are released," Judge Melville said.

And with that, Michael realized the jury of twelve had rejected the criminal allegations against him on all counts. The King of Pop dabbed his face with a tissue, hugged and thanked his defense attorneys, and slowly proceeded to leave the room. As he walked out of the court, passing Katherine, Joe, and his siblings, he showed little emotion. Michael floated out of the courtroom, as if he were on air, and would soon be gone, like a puff of smoke.

Outside, Michael's fans, who'd heard the verdicts over the live television feed that surrounded every inch of the courthouse, were on the street, dancing and screaming, and going wild. One woman released white doves, others released balloons, some threw confetti, and hundreds of people screamed and cried tears of joy. The Jackson family, now in unity, walked past the thousands of reporters from around the world who were hoping for an interview. With one hand clasped to his heart, Michael Jackson blew a kiss to his fans, then disappeared into a black Yukon SUV—a free man.

As people dispersed, certain folks in the media agreed that after all was said and done, the trial had become yet another hurdle for the pop star—one that might continue to hurt his career. Media folks gossiped about the allegations against Jackson, focusing on hateful rumors—the rumors and innuendos that had millions of people talking trash about the icon.

To his fans, the ugly trial against Jackson just didn't seem fair. But for the majority of the media, the Michael Jackson trial had provided great sound bites. His image was manipulated with a new twist every day, and news reports had gone on *ad nauseam* about Jackson's "special relationships" with children.

The court of public opinion shared the same attitude of many journalists. People were certain that Jackson violated children. It occurred to some media observers that—even after he'd been exonerated—the superstar would forever be defending his private life.

Most people thought Jackson's image had been sacrificed beyond repair.

As the media prepared themselves for their last broadcasts on the case, many wondered if Jackson would recover from this witch hunt. Beyond all else, some folks had to admit that they had unwittingly taken part in the DA's scheme to reduce Jackson's life to a public circus. But rather than feel sorry that they'd been part of a group that was so anxious to ruin the pop star, most reporters seemed to bask in Michael's downward spiral.

People loved to hate him, and, as long as the media could perpetuate the image of Jackson as "weird," their ratings stayed high. It wasn't until after the trial was all over that a few media insiders admitted that Jackson's fans had the last laugh. Throughout the trial, his fans yelled at the media, screaming, "You don't ever report the truth!"

Perhaps they were right.

As select media people began to rethink the five-month trial, re-examining some of the details divulged about Michael's personal life in the courtroom, folks agreed that Jackson was able to withstand a scrutiny that most people could never have survived. Jackson had been through hell, and everything about his life, with the exception of the photos of his private parts, had been sprawled out before God, the courtroom, and all the media in the world.

All along, Jackson fans had insisted that the pop star had fallen prey to a greedy family and an angry prosecutor, but their comments were completely ignored. Instead, the media seemed happy to report allegations from prosecutors, anxious to drag Michael's image through the mud. In the end, a hungry media was unable to see what twelve ordinary citizens had seen all along: there was no proof that Michael Jackson had committed any crimes at all.

Throughout the criminal trial, the media had been called upon to recount the most sordid details, to report the dirty accusations being made against Michael Jackson, many of which had been sold to the tabloids long before they were revealed in court. But it wasn't until the "not guilty" verdicts were being read aloud in the courtroom, that people realized that the icon who stood before them—was a person being charged with criminal acts, without any real proof.

Suddenly, it seemed that the case against Jackson was all smoke and mirrors. It occurred to savvy media folks that the case against Michael Jackson amounted to nothing more than a tax-paid scandal. But of course, that was never mentioned in news reports.

Looking at Michael on that last day of court was like looking at two people. There was Michael the man, in real life, and then all around him was this media image that people were creating, a distorted version of Michael, like a twisted reflection in a "fun house" mirror. The media was selling one thing, and they used specific camera angles and lighting to accentuate his nose, his cheeks, his skin tone. And then there was the real Michael, who was a well-dressed, highly poised man, who seemed to be a humble spirit. In person, he was a shy and quiet guy who had no relation to that tabloid character, whatsoever.

On the day of the verdicts, looking at his face, his body language, and his aura, it was clear that the man known as the King of Pop—was a kindhearted soul who had become a victim of his own fame. There was nothing arrogant about him. There was nothing weird about his facial features, nothing so crazy about his clothing, armbands and all. What was crazy was the mentality of the media who were looking to slice and dice Jackson in every way possible. People were taking shots at Michael. People had no problem ripping Jackson to shreds.

Michael Jackson had become an illusion set by a media machine. It was a machine that made millions by perpetuating the notion that Jackson was a freak. It was a dangerous machine that ultimately tried to bring the icon down, and after all, it was a media effort, the Bashir documentary, that landed Jackson in the Santa Maria court in the first place. Martin Bashir had made a name for himself based on Jackson's goodwill, and somehow Michael Jackson had been brought to face criminal charges because of it.

For people like Martin Bashir, with the bashing of Michael Jackson, a career with *ABC News* was launched. Bashir had promised to tell the truth about Jackson. Bashir played on his candid reportage, and his one-on-one interview with

Princess Diana—in order to get Michael's complete cooperation. Yet Bashir's documentary, which was presented in full at the start of the criminal trial—later appeared to be the cruel and manipulative effort of a self-aggrandizing British journalist who had been officially reprimanded in England for "unfair" journalistic practices.

Nonetheless, once Bashir's "Jackson" documentary had aired around the world, irreversible damage had been done. The exoneration of Jackson didn't seem to matter, certainly not to the mainstream media. For over a decade, the media had built an industry around "the freaky life" of Michael Jackson, and because the Bashir documentary affirmed everyone's suspicions, there was little effort to question the objectivity of the Bashir piece. It seemed most of the media had a vested interest in reporting trash about the pop icon. Trash earned them dollars and won them ratings.

With Jackson walking away triumphant, the media had been trumped.

After the verdicts were reported, the media pulled up their tents and wires, their satellite dishes and campers, and their hair and makeup teams. The town of Santa Maria seemed ghostly. Tabloid media looked for dirt. Some tried to follow Jackson to the hospital to get photos of him looking run down and sickly, but they had no luck.

There was some cursory reportage from the gates of Neverland to show the jubilation of the fans, but in the final analysis, the media was all about the *grit*. The media was all about the *nasty*. With nothing more salacious to report, the media had moved on. For everyone who had access to a microphone, the news about the trial was reduced to a mini-sound bite.

The days of stomping on the King of Pop had come to a grinding halt.

As for the people in the DA's office, they seemed disappointed that the court of public opinion didn't translate into a conviction. In his own press conference, Tom Sneddon blamed Jackson's exoneration on his "star power" and insisted that his fervent pursuit of Jackson in the Santa Maria trial—had nothing to do with his past history regarding Michael Jackson.

Tom Sneddon's innuendo—that Michael Jackson had been cleared because he was a superstar—was coming from sour grapes. The idea that the criminal case had no merit, was something that the DA and his team would never accept. When it came to Michael Jackson, Tom Sneddon had a specific agenda. The prosecutor mistakenly believed that slanted media coverage would further his cause, would help put Jackson behind bars.

But it didn't.

"Music and Me"

Long before there was a trial in Santa Maria, the media seemed to have taken sides, having convicted Jackson for unspeakable acts based on accusations that were floating around the world, all over the Internet, all over the tabloids. Most media reports seemed to revel in the negative cloak which shrouded the pop star, and there was little Jackson could do about it.

In order to sell papers and get ratings, news reports dehumanized him in every way possible, and journalists took every opportunity to report the newest "dirt" about Michael without bothering to corroborate the details. During the trial, even when people took the stand to testify about Michael's good deeds, that side of Michael Jackson was never reported by mainstream media.

Without realizing it, many people in the media had become part of the conspiracy to tear Michael down. People covering the trial seemed to be focusing on the prosecution, telling a one-sided story. And news producers encouraged that. The news machine was interested in ratings, and it seemed TV producers wanted reporters to talk about *anything* that was anti-Jackson. The more negative the commentary, the more attention the story got. It was a vicious cycle that almost everyone in the media got caught up in.

But seeing Michael interact with fans, his family, his attorneys, the law officials, and even the media—one thing was undeniable—the aura of Michael Jackson. The pop star seemed to have a white light around him that transcended all the hoopla. Michael didn't seem the least bit concerned by the lurid allegations being set forth in the courtroom. In fact, his facial expressions inside the court made the prosecutors look like a team of desperate people. The DA seemed to be grasping at straws, and Michael's reaction to their "evidence" seemed to let jurors know that.

As for Michael's fans, who held vigils and camped out around Neverland and at the courthouse, they were irate about the charges and felt Jackson had become the object of an angry mob mentality. Outside the gates of Neverland, some described Michael by making a parallel to Princess Diana, another icon whose every move had been turned against her in an effort to make sensational headlines. Fans felt that the media wanted to use Michael Jackson like a science experiment. To the fans, Jackson had become like an insect caught in a glass jar who could be poked and provoked—never allowed to live freely. Unlike Diana, whose life ended tragically when the media swarmed her, with Michael, the media wanted to keep him alive, to keep their ratings going up forever.

His fans insisted that Michael had become a victim of a media machine that refused to see the truth—even when it was presented in a California Superior Court. Fans talked about the worldwide media appetite that had somehow decided Michael Jackson was "free game" for every rumor and innuendo, for all the mudslinging in the world.

As it turned out, virtually everything that Sneddon and his team had presented in court had been discredited by Thomas Mesereau and his defense team. An imposing figure who was not out for media attention, not a self-promoter in any way, Tom Mesereau had become known as the white-haired defense attorney who meant business. He himself did not want to be the focus of media trial coverage. Unlike other high-profile defense attorneys, Tom Mesereau wasn't interested in the cameras and the bright lights. Mesereau was interested in justice and he believed in Jackson's innocence wholeheartedly.

On the day that Jackson was exonerated, Tom Sneddon became the "Emperor Who Had No Clothes." It was Tom Mesereau who exited the courtroom with humility and grace.

As the truth started to sink in, fans close to Jackson wondered why the public-at-large knew nothing about the actual facts of the case. They wondered why the most significant witnesses had been ignored and passed over by the media. The tabloids were hell-bent on wrapping Jackson in a cloak of vulgarity. They made him out to be almost demonic, accusing him of the worst crime known to man, but no one had proven anything like that in court. Rather than report the details that exonerated Jackson, rather than highlight the specifics from the boys who came forward to say that nothing sexual ever happened in their times spent with Jackson, the media was fixated on trivia. There were major headlines about Jackson coming to court in his pajamas. There were quips about Jackson having a close relationship to his pet chimp, Bubbles. There were endless clips shown of Jackson holding his infant son over a Berlin hotel balcony.

Fans were angry because the media never fully examined the testimony by over a hundred people in the courtroom, testimony which showed that there was no proof about anything sinister in Jackson's personal life. Fans felt that the testimony and photo evidence presented in court—proved that Michael Jackson was more down-to-earth, childlike, and caring—than anyone could have imagined.

But the media wanted to ignore that.

After the trial was over, Tom Mesereau confided that he was informed that Jackson's exoneration actually cost the worldwide media billions of dollars. Apparently, had Michael Jackson been sent to prison, the tabloid business would have started a cottage industry of reports about Jackson's safety in jail, about Jackson's life behind bars, about Jackson's suicide watches, about Jackson's prison inmates, and the feeding frenzy would have continued. Mesereau was told that certain media people had made arrangements to follow Michael's everyday schedule behind bars. Whoever was visiting Michael Jackson—would have created a story a day. Wild rumors would have abounded, selling people on the idea that Jackson was crazier than ever before—fueling supermarket tabloids in perpetuity.

As it was, days after the verdict, *Star* magazine falsely reported that Jackson had plans to throw a party at the Bellagio Hotel in Las Vegas, making it seem like Jackson intended to have a victory celebration with his fans. It was ludicrous. The media reports were based on thin air.

Another tabloid, London's *Daily Mail*, splashed headlines that Jackson was "hiding in the Middle East desert," reporting that "he now faces yet more sex claims." As it turned out, the allegations were made by an unsavory man in New Orleans—and they were completely discredited. The man claimed he had been physically assaulted by Jackson with a razor blade, that Jackson had drugged him, among other things. The court in Louisiana wanted Michael Jackson, or a representative, to show up at a public hearing on August 17, 2005, even though the accuser had a criminal record for harassment and was an admitted bigamist. Some time later, the case was dismissed completely.

It was an example of yet another frivolous case against Michael Jackson, one that would mean more humiliation, more damage to his public image, and more problems in U.S. courts for the King of Pop. Because of his unusual conduct, his tremendous wealth, and the nature of his business, Michael Jackson had become the world's greatest target, and the pop star would find himself in court more and more.

As for the criminal trial, what had come before the court was a case that was actually a result of Michael Jackson trying to help heal a ten-year-old boy with cancer. Jackson became involved with the boy, Gavin Arvizo, after he had been diagnosed with stage-four cancer, and had been given a death sentence by a team of doctors in Los Angeles. Since it was Gavin's dying wish to speak to Michael Jackson, Michael had been calling Gavin's hospital bed from all over the world, holding hours-long conversations with Gavin about video games, toys, and the beauty of Neverland.

It was Jackson who had given the boy a reason to live. It was Jackson who helped the boy find the strength to hang in there, even though the cancer had eaten up a number of the kid's organs, including his spleen and one of his kidneys.

At that point, the sickly boy and the rest of his family had visited Neverland while he was still undergoing chemotherapy treatment. On that first visit, Gavin Arvizo was in a wheelchair, suffering with hair and weight loss. Among other things, Gavin suffered from a lack of self-esteem as well, but it was Michael Jackson who would help transform all that.

In Gavin's own handwriting, this was the note in the guest book after his fist visit to Neverland Valley Ranch:

"Dear Michael: Thank You for giving me the courage to take my hat off in front of people. I love you Michael. Love, Gavin."

It was Michael who gave Gavin and his family the sense of hope they needed. It was Michael who encouraged Gavin to find the strength to leave the sick bed. It was Michael who offered Gavin and his family the thrill of having a stretch limo bring them from an East LA barrio to the splendor of Neverland Valley Ranch. Yet all of Michael's good deeds had been twisted around by the media, had been used against him by a money-hungry family.

Tom Mesereau was miffed that the media spent hours broadcasting damning accusations, never once reporting anything about all of Michael's charity efforts devoted to children. Throughout the trial, Mesereau continually pointed out that Michael was a humanitarian who had helped hundreds of thousands of children around the world, who had never done a concert without visiting a children's hospital first, but no one in the media picked up on that. When the trial was over, Mesereau became vocal about the unfairness of the trial media coverage. To Mesereau, the slanted trial coverage was yet another aspect of the harsh and unusual ways that Jackson had been misrepresented.

Once the criminal trial was over, Tom Mesereau spoke about the approximate $20 million settlement made to Jordie Chandler and his family, and the effect that settlement had on others who were looking for easy money from Jackson. In the case of the Chandlers, Mesereau believed Michael Jackson had been the victim of bad advisors. Mesereau was convinced that Jackson was listening to business associates who were only interested in Jackson making more money. Back in 1993, his business advisors weren't writing the checks, Michael Jackson was, and in comparison to the earning capacity Jackson had at the time, the dollar amount of a settlement didn't seem to matter to those who stood to earn big bucks on future deals.

Back then, as always, everyone around Jackson had a scheme to produce new Jackson products, new Jackson music, new Jackson videos—and they wanted him to go on with business as usual. Jackson's advisors seemed to have had no concern about what kind of effect a settlement of that size would create in the court of public opinion.

On the flip side, many of Jackson's fans had long been convinced that there was a corporate conspiracy to destroy Michael. Fans were certain that powerful people at Sony had helped spread rumors in order to ruin Jackson's career. Some fans believed that Sony executives wanted to force Jackson into the sale of his stake in the SONY/ATV catalogue. Many fans stood outside the courtroom each day, holding up signs about Sony, screaming, "Fight, Michael, fight!"

Fans believed that the campaign to destroy Michael's public image stemmed from corporate greed—which not only fueled the Santa Maria trial—but had been behind the accusations by other young boys and their families as well.

For the record, transcripts of secretly recorded tapes—some of which date back to 1987—hint at dubious conduct by many of the people who'd made lurid allegations against Michael Jackson in the past. Many of these tapes and their corresponding transcripts are now being held by the U.S. federal government for an existing federal case against Anthony Pellicano, the private investigator to the stars, whom Michael Jackson's team once hired to discover the truth about the Chandler family.

As for Michael, the superstar has long been public in his claims that conspirators have been trying to ruin him as part of an attempt to regain control of his large stake in the SONY/ATV music catalogue, which includes songs by Elvis Presley and the Beatles. Jackson made reference to a conspiracy which appeared in a nasty *Vanity Fair* article that hit newsstands just days before the verdicts in Santa Maria. The *Vanity Fair* piece mocked Michael Jackson's alleged belief that the accuser and his family were being paid by "enemies" who wanted to take over the SONY/ATV music catalogue. The vicious article poked fun at Jackson, who believed that former Sony Records president, Tommy Mottola, and the "powers-that-be" at Sony Records—along with DA Tom Sneddon—were the "main conspirators" against him.

About all this, Michael Jackson's defense attorney, Tom Mesereau, has remained somewhat neutral. Though Mesereau had no actual evidence to prove Jackson's theory that he'd been the victim of a corporate conspiracy, the defense attorney agreed that it was perfectly possible that a "subconscious conspiracy" between Sony and the Santa Barbara DA might have existed.

"What Michael said about a conspiracy makes logical sense, but I have no evidence of it," Mesereau confided. "If Michael were in jail or in prison, how would he defend his ownership in the catalogue? How would he defend all these frivolous lawsuits? Sony had so much to gain if there was a conviction, and Sneddon would have gained celebrity status. These people didn't have to actually sit down to conspire together. They might have helped each other on an unplanned level—because they had a common interest."

Ironically, if a conspiracy did exist against Jackson, perhaps it was being led by former employees with personal agendas, fueled by unusual houseguests who wanted to cash in, and fortified by certain members of law enforcement who had their own egotistical reasons for wanting to tear Jackson down.

With Michael Jackson being, perhaps, the most famous person ever to face felony charges, authorities wanted to open up Jackson's eccentric life for public inspection. The Santa Barbara DA took pleasure in trying to shame him.

For obvious reasons, the King of Pop made very few statements and gave very few interviews regarding his criminal trial. Early on, Michael broadcast a statement about his innocence on the Internet. Jackson invited Geraldo Rivera to Neverland for a brief audience, and later an interview with Jackson appeared on *FOX News*, though Geraldo's contention that Jackson was being set up by the Santa Barbara DA—was not well received by the press. During the trial, Jackson spoke to his fans via the radio on a few occasions, but for the most part, the pop star stopped saying much to the media at all, making a single exception for his friend and spiritual advisor, the Reverend Jesse Jackson.

In a one-time radio broadcast, which aired on Easter Sunday, 2005, Michael told Reverend Jackson, "I'm totally innocent, and it's just very painful."

Over the radio, Michael hinted that he was a victim of racism, stating that he was one of many "black luminaries" who had become a victim. Jackson said he found strength in the examples of Nelson Mandela and Muhammad Ali. Jackson said he felt he was being discriminated against as a person of color. When Jesse Jackson asked about a possible Sony conspiracy that might have been behind the allegations in the criminal trial, Michael had very little to say. Reverend Jackson asked Michael to detail exactly what was in the SONY/ATV catalogue, but Michael didn't want to go down that road.

As Jesse Jackson tried to get information about problems surrounding Sony and the pop icon, Michael was clearly afraid to discuss the subject. When asked about the tug-of-war over the Sony catalogue, Michael was cagey. There was only one thing Michael would say about the SONY/ATV catalogue: "It's very valuable. It's worth a lot of money. And there's a big fight going on as we speak about that. I can't comment on it. There's a lot of conspiracy. I'll say that much."

But whether or not anyone at Sony conspired to ruin Michael Jackson (and there is no evidence to that effect) really was not the concern for Tom Mesereau in the criminal case. What Mesereau was sure about—throughout the course of the trial—was that he was dealing with a whole set of people who acted in a joint plan, a conspiracy, to destroy Michael Jackson's image.

These were people, Mesereau would prove, who were out to gain any kind of fame and fortune for themselves—and Michael Jackson was their vehicle. Having made the decision to fight Tom Sneddon and the DA's office once and for all, Mesereau was the first person to see the games being played behind the scenes. He came to consider the entire case against Michael Jackson, in itself, a conspiracy.

According to Mesereau, it was the accuser's family, acting in accordance with DA Tom Sneddon and prodded by certain members of the media, who engaged in a highly thought-out plan to try to bring Michael Jackson to his knees. Attorney Mesereau, who has long been a champion for civil rights in the African American community, confided that when he first looked at the evidence, when he sat down and studied the thousands of pages of discovery, he was able to draw his own conclusions.

"The media was basically saying, 'You can't win this case. There's no hope,' and I didn't really care what they said, to be honest," Mesereau confided. "I just looked at the evidence, as I always do, and I got to know the client. I decided that this was a winnable case, and also decided that we could get a fair trial in Santa Maria."

The public officials never considered the possibility that many people in Santa Maria would have a positive view of Michael Jackson. As it happened, certain residents confided to Mesereau that they felt Tom Sneddon had a serious vendetta against the pop star, though Sneddon consistently denies this. Santa Maria residents felt that Jackson was a great asset to their community, and they expressed a positive sensibility about Jackson. Still, without cameras being allowed into the courtroom, with biased reporting being the only way the public at large could grasp a sense about the trial—the smear factor was inevitable.

At his sensational trial, one hundred thirty-five witnesses testified in all. They ranged from child friends to film stars—from CSI experts to forensic accountants. The amount of experts and staff who testified was enough to boggle the mind. So much money was spent on the effort to place everything about Michael's life under a microscope. Everything he owned was questioned—every book, every piece of art, every item in his laundry. It was all subject to public scrutiny.

By the time all the evidence had been presented, people had proof that Jackson was different—that he led his life in a way that no one would have dreamed possible. More than ever, people saw that Jackson lived in a self-created dream world, in a world where being a child was a part of who Michael was. The jury learned that Michael trusted people too much. Among the details the jury was shocked to discover: Michael had signed over his power of attorney to German advisors apparently without understanding the possible consequences of his childlike actions.

To the outside world, news reports would have people believe that Jackson's Neverland was filled with dark undercurrents, with sinister games to lure children into a trap. However, inside the courtroom, where it really counted, it turned out that the pop icon, through his own privately recorded statements, had convinced the jury that he was an innocent pawn.

"Shake It, Shake It, Baby"

When the Jackson trial first got under way, Michael, wearing an all-white suit with a gold armband, flashed a victory sign toward the crowd outside, who cheered at him vehemently. Jackson was more of a draw than any of the roster of celebrity names who were expected as potential witnesses, from Elizabeth Taylor to Macaulay Culkin, from Stevie Wonder to Larry King. The media wanted to hear from Jackson, and all the major TV networks as well as all the major journals, *People* Magazine, the *New York Times*, *USA Today*, were lined up waiting, fighting for positions among journalists from foreign networks and publications from all around the globe—hoping for a comment from Jackson—a brief glimpse at how the superstar was feeling.

Everyone wanted to report something new about Jackson, and though media people were anxious to see the parade of stars who would be arriving in coming months, everyone was truly focused on Michael, hopeful that the King of Pop would act outrageously, would dance on top of his SUV, would say something crazy to attract more worldwide gossip.

The NBC network and its cable TV subsidiaries had set up a four hundred eighty-square foot platform to hold its giant team of reporters, producers, and cameras. CNN had constructed an elaborate seven-foot platform across from the courthouse on Miller Street, giving them a bird's-eye view of the Jackson spectacle. The rest of the twenty-two hundred credentialed media, FOX, ABC, and CBS included, were relegated to makeshift tents directly facing the Santa Maria Superior Court Complex, tightly slotted in a cordoned-off row. Surrounding the media were bomb squads and arsenals of ammunition hidden in police cars— though no one ever talked about that.

Media members were expert in watching Michael's every move, but knowing this, the pop star was especially quiet as he sat behind the defense table. From the looks on certain faces, media people were disappointed to see that the King of Pop was well mannered, calm, and relaxed, looking fully prepared to face the first group of perspective jurors in the case.

As the morning group of one hundred seventy panelists filtered in, Jackson and his four-member legal team stood at attention. Michael smiled at the group of schoolteachers, football coaches, and students—a cast of "all-American" folks who looked at the pop star with great intent. These were average citizens with families and down-to-earth lifestyles, and they found themselves in the strange position of analyzing Jackson, not as a star, but as a possible criminal. If any of them hoped to see one of Jackson's glassy slides across the room, if anyone thought they might catch a glimpse of one of his motorized robot dances, they were not going to witness that here.

With jury selection in full swing, many citizens came forward with poor excuses about why they didn't have time to serve on a jury trial that would last five months. About this, Judge Melville became somewhat annoyed, making the pronouncement, "Freedom is not free. Jury duty is part of the cost of freedom."

In court, Michael, the entertainer, had nothing to do but sit quietly, watching the proceedings with a steady eye. People who were requesting an exemption from jury duty would look over at the pop star when they approached the podium to ask to be excused, studying Michael's face, as if they were trying to see if he was real. As people from the jury pool explained their personal reasons for being unable to serve, the courtroom became a humdrum place—all the Jackson glitter was gone.

But because a case is thought to be won or lost during jury selection, both sides were fighting, and each had jury consultants, ready to "strike" certain types of jurors. Of the many things each side had to consider: the potential of stealth jurors—people thought to be willing to serve for biased or financial reasons.

Over the course of the next few days, as the jury pool was narrowed, each juror would be individually questioned, asked to disclose information about his or her personal life and ability to be fair in the trial. They were asked questions about their feelings regarding the fairness of law enforcement, and they were asked questions about their own personal experiences with criminal allegations.

News reports would later make fun of the effort to select a jury of Michael Jackson's peers, mentioning the impossibility of finding twelve people who lived in an amusement park, who spent hundreds of millions of dollars, who experienced radical changes in appearance. However, there was one thing that expert commentators agreed on: the jury would *not* be comprised of Michael Jackson fans. If there was going to be a fair trial, the prosecution would be forced to weed Jackson fans out of the jury pool.

Once the jury was selected, the prosecution seemed to have the deck stacked in its favor. Not only were Michael's fans eliminated, but, because of the demographics of Santa Maria, which was comprised mainly of a Caucasian and Latino population, there was little prospect of an African American person being able to serve at the trial. The small town of Santa Maria, with eighty-two thousand residents, was a homogenized community, a place that could have been "Anywhere, USA." With its plethora of franchises, from Toys "R" Us to Applebee's to Home Depot, it was a typical isolated suburban town.

Because it was considered to be a great challenge to find the right jury for the case, Tom Mesereau had spent time in Santa Maria prior to the trial beginning. Dressed in his jeans and a casual shirt, Mesereau sat by himself at some of the local watering holes, and he casually spoke to people to ask them what they thought of the case.

Mesereau had gotten a feel for the town, for the people.

As he spoke to local residents, the defense attorney had the distinct impression that the people of Santa Maria liked having Michael Jackson as a neighbor. Mesereau was told by many folks that Michael was considered a nice person, a good person, who, when he went into local communities, was nice to everyone, particularly creative people. The locals in Santa Maria seemed to find Michael to be a very decent and honest guy.

"They were always white, Caucasian people or Latino people. I don't think I ever saw one African American person in a restaurant or bar," Mesereau recalled. "Although the people there were very conservative, very law-and-order minded people, the media was not reporting how independent-minded they were. These were people who appeared to be somewhat libertarian."

In the end, Mesereau didn't care if he had a jury that was pro-Jackson. He just wanted jurors who would be open-minded and fair. When it came to the case against Michael Jackson, long before jury selection began, Mesereau learned that DA Tom Sneddon was "not necessarily trusted" by the locals in Santa Maria.

"There seemed to be a strong feeling that Tom Sneddon had a vendetta against Michael, which might have clouded his judgment and approach," Mesereau confided. "The word *vendetta* was used a lot. And I felt that when the truth came out, the jury would know that Michael Jackson is a great champion of children around the world. They would know that he has done a lot to further the causes of children around the world. I felt that when the truth about how he approaches children and why he's interested in children came out, people would be very receptive to who Michael is."

For days before the actual jury was seated and the trial would begin, both sides studied facial expressions and had carefully evaluated each juror's life experiences. Mesereau, for instance, questioned jurors about whether they felt children could be manipulated into lying by their parents.

Potential jurors who had been dismissed by the defense included a female teacher who dealt with emotional problems and learning disabilities, as well as a male who, as a researcher for a university, felt defendants at a high-profile trial "might get a better shot at justice" than those in less publicized trials. The DA dismissed a former school attendance officer who said she'd been falsely accused of speeding by California Highway Patrol; however, by far, the most heated dismissals came when the prosecution ousted two potential African American women. Of the entire pool of two hundred forty, only six were African American. For Mesereau, the idea that the panel might not include one single African American juror became a stunning reality.

"I felt the prosecutors were very narrow-minded when it came to race," Mesereau concluded, "they felt the defense was desperate to have an African American juror to hang the jury. They seemed, in my opinion, to very arrogantly believe that this was a case they couldn't lose. While we were selecting the jury, there were two African American women removed, and I went to sidebar and made constitutional objections that these people were being removed because of their race. The judge overruled my objections."

As much as Mesereau would have liked to have had an African American person on the jury panel, the defense attorney really didn't feel it was necessary. Race was something Mesereau had always been concerned about; Mesereau had long been a positive force in the African American community. However, Mesereau wasn't looking for an African American juror who might hang the case. What Mesereau wanted was a complete victory, and when he accepted a jury panel that was missing an African American representative, Mesereau felt he was calling the DA's bluff.

"You ask about African Americans on the jury?" Mesereau explained, "I didn't want race to be an issue in this trial. I feel that Michael transcends race. When I learned about who Michael was, when I learned about his life and his world, I concluded that Michael has a very rare quality, and that is—he brings people of all races together. If you look at paintings in his house, you'll see children from all continents, of all colors, all religions, wearing their native garb."

As the trial began, people of mixed races on the jury panel would become a very close-knit group who felt very protective of each other as they covertly worked their way past the stampede of adoring fans and the raging press. They were a panel of eight women and four men, joined by eight alternate jurors who sat watching the trial—including one young African American man who was selected as an alternate. It was this small group of average American citizens who would decide what the real truth was behind the lurid allegations made against Michael Jackson. A lot was expected of them, and no one was sure that this handful of people would be able to be fair-minded.

"People in the media were very myopic when it came to their view of this jury," Mesereau said. "The media kept asking themselves, 'How is this jury going to judge Michael Jackson?' But they never said to themselves, 'How is this jury going to judge this family of accusers?'"

As it turned out, the jury did make judgments about the accuser's family. When they later held a brief press conference after the verdicts, some of the jurors admitted that Gavin Arvizo's mother, Janet, a key witness in the conspiracy case against Michael, was just not to be believed.

Juror No. 8, a mother of four, hinted that Janet Arvizo's conduct was uncalled for. The mother of four seemed to agree with the defense portrayal of Janet "Jackson" Arvizo as a con artist who schooled her children "to solicit money." The forty-two-year-old juror told the media that she questioned Janet Arvizo's values, stating, "I wouldn't want any of my own children to lie for their own gain."

"The prosecution notion that Neverland was a lure, a monstrous sort of trap set by a pedophile, I thought was ridiculous, and we would disprove it throughout the trial," Mesereau insisted. "In the end, people who care about children, who are interested in children, would see the truth about Michael Jackson and know that his motives were very noble, very honest, very sincerely held."

It was on Monday, February 28, 2005, the day that opening statements began. For the first time, Judge Melville read the ten-count indictment against Mr. Jackson, which included four counts of child molestation, four counts of administering alcohol to commit a felony, one count of attempted molestation, and one count of conspiracy. As each side presented their argument, dueling images of Michael Jackson emerged. The prosecution was calling Jackson a sexual predator; the defense made the argument that Jackson was easy prey. Both sides revealed details and inconsistencies about the case, and ultimately, jurors would hear two completely contrasting accounts about what allegedly happened in the spring of 2003 at Michael Jackson's Neverland Valley Ranch.

Each side was bold and brazen in their claims, and each made a case that seemed plausible. The DA wanted people to believe that Michael Jackson was an evil person who had a sexual agenda lurking behind all of his dealings with the Arvizo children. The defense team wanted to show how Jackson had been a victim of just about everyone around him, to show that families such as the Arvizos, whom Jackson had befriended, always turned out to be underhanded. The defense would argue that there were few people the superstar could trust, insisting that the people he relied upon were often out for the money or a piece of Jackson's fame.

As he began his opening statement, DA Tom Sneddon would do everything in his power to present Jackson as a pedophile who orchestrated an elaborate conspiracy, shrewdly using his fame to woo his friend, Gavin Arvizo, to Neverland where Jackson allegedly plied Gavin with alcohol, "Jesus Juice," in order to molest the thirteen-year-old boy.

The veteran prosecutor recounted how Jackson met Gavin Arvizo in 2000, when the boy was suffering from an aggressive form of cancer, telling jurors that it was during Gavin's initial visit to Neverland that Michael Jackson first showed sexually explicit images of women to the ten-year-old boy and his younger brother, Star Arvizo. Sneddon maintained that nothing sexual occurred on that initial visit, but the DA was attempting to show that a "grooming" pattern existed.

The DA went on to graphically detail the acts of alleged molestation, causing some jurors to appear uneasy. Some folks shot disapproving looks at Jackson when Sneddon said that the pop star showed the Arvizo boys adult Web sites. Among other things Jackson was accused of doing in front of the Arvizo boys: simulating sex with a lifelike mannequin, walking out of the bathroom naked, and telling the Arvizo boys not to be afraid of nudity because "it's natural."

Standing at the podium in front of the jury, Sneddon made his opinion of Jackson clear: "Instead of reading them *Peter Pan*, Jackson is showing them sexually explicit magazines. Instead of cookies and milk, you can substitute wine, vodka, and bourbon."

As the DA began to present his theory about an alleged conspiracy, the courtroom audience heard screeching feedback from the podium's microphone. Sneddon seemed thrown off course for a moment, but went on to describe an elaborate conspiracy theory, which he himself admitted was "hard to follow."

Sneddon told jurors that the documentary by journalist Martin Bashir, in which Gavin Arvizo was shown talking with Michael Jackson about the two of them sharing a bed, created a "firestorm" that threatened the pop star's career, causing Jackson to launch a conspiracy to abduct and extort the Arvizo family.

"Michael Jackson's world was rocked. It didn't rock in the musical sense, it rocked in the real-life sense," Sneddon insisted.

The DA asserted that the Bashir documentary, *Living with Michael Jackson*, prompted Jackson and his "business associates" to conspire to falsely imprison Gavin and his family at Neverland Ranch, asserting that Jackson tried to force the Arvizo clan to tape a rebuttal documentary as an answer to the Bashir piece.

According to Sneddon, the conspiracy further entailed taking the Arvizo family to Miami, allegedly for a press conference that never took place, and also entailed forcing Gavin's mother to sign a blank piece of paper that would later be used by Jackson in a civil suit against Granada TV, the entity that produced the Bashir documentary. (The Granada suit was reportedly settled some time after the criminal trial ended.) Moreover, Sneddon told jurors that one of Jackson's associates had signed Gavin and Star Arvizo out of school, allegedly planning to relocate the Arvizo kids, along with their mother, to Brazil.

As wacky as that might have sounded, what stood out as being the most bizarre claim—was Sneddon's time line regarding the alleged molestation. The DA asserted that Gavin and Star Arvizo each said the acts of alleged abuse occurred *after* the Bashir documentary aired, after the trip to Miami, and after the rebuttal tape for FOX was filmed. In other words, the Arvizos were accusing Jackson of performing lewd acts on a child—not at the time that Bashir taped his damning documentary in 2002—but rather, their claim was that Jackson acted inappropriately in 2003, just weeks after the Bashir piece aired, in the time period that Jackson and his PR people were launching a campaign to battle the very distorted view Bashir had presented about the King of Pop.

It seemed odd.

Tom Mesereau, at the beginning of his opening statement, fiercely attacked Sneddon's theory, telling jurors, "These charges are fictitious. They are bogus, and they never happened."

As Mesereau spoke, he took control of the courtroom, promising that he would prove all the allegations against Michael to be false, and further prove that the boy's mother had fabricated similar allegations numerous times. Mesereau told the jury that Janet "Jackson" Arvizo had perjured herself, had previously alleged sexual molestation, had fraudulently collected welfare funds, had bilked the JC Penney Corporation for a large civil settlement, and had failed to report large sums of money donated for her son's medical expenses.

Everyone's eyebrows were raised when the defense attorney told jurors that Janet Arvizo had solicited donations from celebrities including Adam Sandler, Mike Tyson, and Jim Carrey, all the while knowing that her ex-husband's insurance paid for her son's medical treatments. Mesereau further detailed the strange encounters the Arvizo clan had with Chris Tucker, Jay Leno, and George Lopez, promising to produce testimony that would show how Michael Jackson became the Arvizo family's main target.

"We will prove to you that the best-known celebrity and the most vulnerable celebrity, Michael Jackson, became the mark," Mesereau told jurors. "The molestation allegations started to form after the Arvizo family was unable to get any money for the Bashir documentary or a rebuttal video they made in praise of Jackson."

Mesereau promised the jury that they would hear from Michael Jackson himself, hinting that the pop star might take the stand in order to prove the falsehoods created by the Bashir documentary.

"Bashir wanted to be scandalous, and he wanted to get rich," Mesereau said, telling jurors that he would show the outtake footage of Jackson's interview with Bashir that would clear the icon's name.

"Neverland is not a haven for criminal activity, a lure for molestation, as characterized by the prosecution. It's a Disneyland-like place," Mesereau insisted, "a place for underprivileged and sick children to have a day of fun."

The defense attorney explained that, at their mother's urging, Gavin, Star, and Davellin Arvizo had all turned to a new father—Michael Jackson—as the man who would make their dreams come true. Tom Mesereau pointed out that the Arvizo family came to enjoy vacations, clothes, and gifts, all-expenses-paid by Michael Jackson. Mesereau insinuated that the Arvizos didn't want to lose their meal ticket. As a way to ensure his presence in their lives, Mesereau told jurors, "The Arvizo kids called him 'Daddy Michael.'"

On their first trip to Neverland, Gavin's brother, Star, had written a note thanking Michael for "the time of a lifetime." Gavin's sister Davellin had written a letter saying, "You helped my brother a lot. Without you, I don't know where we'd be. You are so caring and loving. I love you with all my heart."

As Mesereau spoke, jurors discovered that Michael had given the Arvizo family a car, a computer, and various gifts to make their lives a little bit easier. In addition, Michael had allowed the Arvizo kids to visit Neverland on occasions when he wasn't even there—anything to put a smile on young Gavin's face. Michael had hopes that he might help Gavin, that the boy might be able help heal himself.

Among other things, the jury learned that for years, Michael, along with other celebrities, had tried to help the Arvizo family by holding blood drives, by arranging fund-raisers, by doing everything possible to help heal Gavin of a mysterious form of cancer. More than any other celebrity who made attempts to help the Arvizo clan, however, it was Michael Jackson who opened up his home and his heart to this family at a critical time in their lives. To this family of underprivileged Latino American kids, the superstar had become a savior.

"I Wanna Be Where You Are"

The next morning, Tom Mesereau told jurors that he would prove to them, through testimony of staff and visitors of Neverland, that the Arvizo kids had become out of control when they stayed at Michael's ranch. Mesereau wanted the jury to be clear that the alcohol charge against Jackson did not stand alone. He wanted the jury to comprehend the nature of the charge: the DA was claiming that Michael Jackson had given alcohol to the underaged Arvizo kids—specifically for the purposes of molesting young cancer victim, Gavin.

"The alcohol charge is directly tied into allegations of molestation," Mesereau explained. "One doesn't exist without the other in those alcohol charges. And Mr. Jackson absolutely denies this."

As Mesereau detailed the behavior of the Arvizo kids at Neverland, he told jurors that the Arvizo kids broke in to the wine cellar and were caught drinking alcohol by themselves, explaining that Michael Jackson wasn't even present at the time and knew nothing about it. The attorney said the Arvizo kids were also caught breaking into the refrigerator, drinking alcohol in the kitchen, and grabbing alcohol from a cupboard.

"There is one witness who will tell you that Mr. Jackson ordered some alcohol for himself and his guests, and the children stole it," Mesereau said. "They [the Arvizo kids] were caught intoxicated. They were caught with bottles. Mr. Jackson was nowhere around. We will prove to you that they are now trying to say that he was behind all this. And it's false."

The defense attorney described the Arvizo children's behavior at Neverland, stating that at first, they seemed very well behaved, but as time progressed, their actions changed radically. Mesereau gave examples, and he talked about the amusement area at Neverland, and how a worker who was in charge of the rides was "shocked and horrified" to learn that the Arvizo kids had memorized the codes to the rides, had ridden alone to the top of the Ferris wheel, and were seen throwing objects at elephants and people.

"We will prove that they also did this with various codes in the house. They [the Arvizo kids] somehow found a way to roam around the house at will, when Mr. Jackson wasn't even in town," Mesereau said. "They were actually caught in his room. The witnesses will testify to those facts. They were out of control."

When Mesereau made reference to the "girly magazines" found in Jackson's home, he said Mr. Jackson freely admitted that he read *Playboy* and *Hustler* from time to time, asking a staff member to pick them up at a local market. However, Michael absolutely denied showing these magazines to children. In fact, Mesereau said, the magazines that Sneddon mentioned in his opening statement, the "girly magazines" that Sneddon alleged Jackson used to lure the Arvizo boys, were actually in a locked briefcase, hidden in a back closet.

"Mr. Jackson will tell you he found those kids going through his magazines and grabbed them from them and locked them in his briefcase," Mesereau insisted.

As for the Bashir documentary, which would be the first exhibit entered into evidence at trial, Mesereau wanted to emphasize that Michael Jackson had been paid nothing for his participation in that project. The original negotiations between Jackson and Bashir specified that any profit from the project would go to charities in England. In fact, Jackson and Bashir had talked about 250,000 British pounds going to charity.

That charitable donation, according to Jackson's attorney, was the reason that Jackson agreed to do the documentary. If in the past, Michael had been accused of making "statements" that were self-aggrandizing or self-indulgent, that was certainly not the case with the Bashir piece. In his endeavor with Martin Bashir, Michael Jackson's agreement to open up his home was based entirely on Jackson's desire—and Bashir's promise—to produce a film that would help children around the world. Mesereau pointed out that Jackson believed in Bashir so wholeheartedly, the pop icon felt there was no need for negotiations with the unknown British journalist. Jackson was so trusting, he felt no need for intermediaries, for lengthy meetings about schedules or prices.

"Michael trusted that Mr. Bashir was going to present him in an appropriate and honorable and honest light," Mesereau added. "And that's not what happened.

"We will prove to you that Mr. Jackson, because of his presence around the world in the music industry, continually attracts people who seek profit," Mesereau told the jury. "We will prove to you that this creates a problem in his life, and here is the problem that exists: Mr. Jackson is an artist. He's called a musical genius. He's a creative person who dances to the beat of a different drummer.

"Mr. Bashir expressed surprise when Michael said to him, 'I have a tree on my property, and lots of times, I go up and sit in that tree alone, and I'm peaceful and still, and I meditate. And very often, God gives me the creative spark that I need to do the work that I excel in.'

"We will prove to you," Mesereau said, "that Mr. Jackson will often wake up at three o'clock in the morning at Neverland. He will walk out of his house alone, and he will walk under the stars, under the moon, under the sky. He will meditate in his own way, and wait for ideas and inspiration to come."

As the first day of testimony began, Michael, dressed like a military general, wearing gold armbands, a red vest, and a jacket with gold trim, kept completely silent as he sat behind the defense table. Michael was always quiet. He somehow had a quiet command over people. Katherine and brother Jackie were the only family members with him, and that morning, just as Michael approached the defense table, Katherine reached over and pulled a loose thread off her son's jacket. Ever the penultimate mom, Katherine was the essence of grace under pressure.

As he did every day, Michael smiled at the jurors when they filed in, his wire-rimmed glasses making him seem much more serious and adultlike that ever before. Just before the proceedings began, speaking in whispers, people in the media would point out things like Michael's white powder makeup. The media liked to chatter about obscure things, looking for new reasons to pick on the superstar. Media people talked about him like he was a clown. Behind his back, there was incessant gossiping. Even inside a California court of law, where things were serious and real, where Jackson's actions didn't give reporters any reason to say he was wacko or weird, that's all people seemed to hope for.

Media people commented about his skin being light. They wondered about Michael's vitiligo, the skin condition that resulted in loss of pigmentation and white patches of skin. Most felt certain that Michael had chosen to alter the color of his skin. Some people were angry that Michael would never admit to that. Many felt it was their right to judge him.

Even though Michael had explained his skin condition in TV interviews, talking about the emotional pain he suffered from having skin that was spotted, most folks refused to accept his story. Rather than see Michael as a person who transcended race, many Americans seemed perplexed about Jackson's skin—and believed that the superstar had deliberately turned his skin light.

Gary Coleman, a former TV star who was outside the courtroom doing commentary for a comedy show, had already started the public jokes about Michael. Early on, Coleman remarked that Michael Jackson *had* found a jury of his peers: "He hasn't been black since 1988," Coleman quipped.

When the prosecution launched their case-in-chief, they first called Martin Bashir to the stand. A TV journalist from Britain who'd been at the BBC, who'd been working in the business for twenty years, told the jury that prior to the Jackson documentary, he'd done a film about "Satanic Lovers," and had produced a one-hour film about a serial killer. Those were Bashir's claims to fame before 1995, when he snagged an interview with Princess Diana. Bashir had produced an hour-plus documentary about Diana that aired on ITV, England's largest commercial network.

When Bashir first entered the courtroom, Katherine stood up and walked out. She couldn't stand to be in the same room with a man who had so unabashedly deceived her son. Though Katherine would return to sit through part of the TV documentary—it was evident that she was disgusted by its content, and was enraged by yet another "media trap" that her son had fallen into.

Bashir told the jury that his documentary, *Living with Michael Jackson*, produced by Granada Productions, had first aired in February 2003. And, as the documentary was offered into evidence, the judge admonished the jury that the DVD was not being offered for the truth. The judge explained that the DVD would have passages within it that would be identified as "truth," warning the jury panel to regard the rest of the program as hearsay.

Then, as the first exhibit began to play on the giant courtroom screen, the jury and the courtroom observers were transported to a world where they were reminded of Michael's larger-than-life image. As they sat wide-eyed, staring at Jackson's lavish place called Neverland, they were captivated by the icon that was Michael Jackson. Everyone in the courtroom was bouncing, listening to his tunes, which Bashir had used conspicuously in the background. As Michael's music filled the courtroom, it made people groove and sway. Some of the jurors were tapping their hands to the beat of the music, and even Michael was unable to stop himself from bobbing his head with the rhythm.

It was like watching a full-blown movie, seeing the Bashir piece.

And at first, it almost seemed like fun.

The jury watched as Michael talked to Bashir about his amusement park and how he loved going on rides. They noticed an intimacy about the interview, an intimacy about Michael that most people had never seen before. Michael was baring his soul. He was being candid about why he liked children's rides and games. As he and Bashir walked around the spectacular amusement park area, Michael confided that he found the Ferris wheel soothing. He told Bashir that he'd go on the rides at night, oftentimes by himself.

In court, Martin Bashir, who held his head down when he first sat on the stand, was unwilling to face Michael Jackson from the witness stand. During the viewing of the documentary, for practical purposes, Bashir was allowed to sit with the rest of courtroom crowd, and he seemed to sneer at rest of the media. If nothing else, Bashir seemed to exude a superior attitude.

There was something smug about him.

He was shrewd, and he was proud of himself.

As courtroom observers watched the DVD, it was clear that Mr. Bashir's British accent, his sweet voice hiding his cunning ways, absolutely fascinated Michael Jackson. Everyone watched as Bashir seduced the superstar. The British journalist was being so complimentary, acting so enthralled with Jackson's great talent. For Bashir, it was as easy as taking candy from a baby. With each compliment and promise, the journalist was able to get the King of Pop to open up about everything in his world. Somehow Bashir had won so much trust—that *nothing* about Jackson was deemed off-limits.

In the end, Bashir had used Michael Jackson to pull off a great media stunt.

Now, as the documentary played, as jurors sat looking at Neverland with amazement, they watched Michael happily take Bashir on a drive through the twenty-seven-hundred-acre property known as Neverland. Jackson was acting like a kid, his voice full of excitement as the two of them spent time riding on go-carts. And Bashir played along, pretending to be happy to ride around like a child.

Bashir raced Jackson, driving along the Neverland Valley racetrack, and it was all good fun—or so it seemed. Then suddenly, Bashir used his go-cart to cut in front of Jackson, and the jury watched Michael yell, "He's cheating, hey, he's cheating!"

How true those words would ring.

Bashir wanted to be everywhere that Michael was—and he was granted full access to Michael's private life. But as it turned out, Bashir used that access to make a mockery of Michael. He traded on Michael's goodwill, and, having sold his documentary to the ABC network in the United States, Bashir landed himself a new career and a substantial salary at the ABC television offices in New York. Because of the Jackson documentary, Bashir had become one of the prime time correspondents for *ABC News*, a colleague of Barbara Walters.

As the DVD continued to play for the jurors, Martin Bashir, who was a central character in the piece, had a strange look on his face, sitting among the courtroom audience, watching people as they judged his clever handiwork. What jurors would notice as they studied Bashir's interview, watching the journalist act like he was in complete awe of the pop star, was Bashir's bait-and-switch routine. In hindsight, Bashir was such an absolute traitor. It wasn't long into the documentary before jurors would hear Bashir's voice go from sweet to menacing.

As Bashir smiled and joked with Jackson, his voice-over comments began to suggest there was something very wrong with Jackson's life—with Jackson's obsession with his face, with Jackson's relationship with children.

"How do you write a song?" Bashir asked. "Teach me!" Bashir pleaded, begging Jackson to show him how to dance, how to sing.

Michael, who seemed self-conscious, said he was shy. He said he was "embarrassed" and didn't want to get up and dance in front of the camera. However, coaxed by Bashir's feigned schoolboy curiosity, Jackson agreed to do the Moonwalk.

As Michael slid across the wood floor, Bashir made a feeble attempt to follow him. It was an ugly game Bashir was playing. He was sucking up beyond words, anxious to make the entertainer comfortable and happy. As courtroom observers watched, it was clear that Michael liked having the attention, that he liked being treated like a "special entity." Bashir seemed to know how to work on Michael's weakness, and the journalist praised him to the high heavens.

"Slide back on your heel, not on your toe," Michael said.

But it was obvious that Bashir couldn't dance at all. Bashir was just looking for interesting footage, and his cameras would shift from Michael in the dance studio to a painting that hung overhead. It was a painting of Michael as an angelic figure surrounded by cherubs of all creeds and colors. The focus on the painting, as Michael spoke about his songwriting, about how the music "comes when it wants to," was Bashir's attempt to make Michael look self-obsessed.

When jurors began to see footage of Jackson's Neverland home, decorated with castles and toy rooms and life-sized mannequins everywhere, a few of them looked stunned to see the childish sensibility that overshadowed the lavishness of Michael's ornate home. Nonetheless, they rocked to the beat as Jackson 5 clips were heard, and again, Michael grooved and swayed when some of his hit songs were played through the courtroom speakers.

Michael talked about Neverland, saying, "I'm Peter Pan in my heart." He explained that he identified with Peter Pan because Peter Pan represented "everything that children, magic, and wonderment are about." Michael made a rare exception for Bashir, showing him his "giving tree," the spot where he climbed to be alone and write his music. Michael listed a number of songs he'd written there, "Black and White" and "Heal the World" among them.

"Come on! Aren't you coming?" Michael asked Bashir. "This is a big secret. I've never showed anybody my giving tree. Don't you want to climb it?"

But Bashir didn't want to climb trees. He seemed to have other things he planned to climb: corporate ladders and roads to fame. For Bashir, this was a money tree. It offered a close-up view of something never seen about Michael Jackson——ever.

"You don't climb trees?" Michael asked, bewildered.

"No, I do not," Bashir said.

"You're missing out!" Michael told him as he handed over his umbrella and quickly climbed up the branches.

Bashir wanted to know how climbing trees could possibly be Michael's favorite thing to do. He wondered if Michael didn't prefer making love or performing. Michael seemed puzzled that Bashir would question his moment of happiness and said that while nothing could compare to performing, climbing trees and water balloon fights were his favorite pastimes.

Bashir didn't stay on the subject of pastimes for long. He wanted to get past Michael's genius, to get past Michael's musical gift. He wanted to talk about Michael's personal private world, and he didn't waste much time before he arrived on a subject that would make Michael cry.

The courtroom crowd sat silent as Jackson was prompted to talk about missing his childhood. As he was asked questions about being disciplined by his father, as he was asked to detail the whippings he and his brothers got as children, Michael's body was rocking and shaking. According to Michael, if they weren't performing up to Joe's standards, he and his brothers would get hit.

For Michael's family, the documentary had to be very painful to watch. As the documentary became even more personal, Michael became visibly upset sitting behind the defense table, and Katherine and Jackie were also shaken. To Bashir, Michael confided that Joe had treated all of his boys with strict discipline, that he had hit them with a belt, that he would hit his brothers with ironing cords, with anything he could grab.

"I remember hearing my mother scream, 'Joe, you're gonna kill him! You're gonna kill him!'" Michael admitted. "He couldn't catch me half the time, but when he would catch me, it was bad. We were terrified of him. Terrified. I don't think he realized, to this day, how scared we were."

Michael confided that he was so afraid of his father, that sometimes he'd faint, and his bodyguards would have to hold him up. He mentioned that he himself would never lay a finger on his own children. It was clear that the memories from thirty years prior were very vivid for Michael.

"He didn't allow us to call him Daddy," Michael whispered. "He'd say, 'I'm Joseph to you. I'm not Daddy.' So I do the opposite. I don't let my children call me Michael. My children call me Daddy."

Courtroom observers watched as Bashir followed Michael around the world, joining Michael on shopping sprees in Las Vegas, joining Michael in his lavish hotel suites, where the two would talk about private, intimate subjects. As he spoke about his first crush, Tatum O'Neal, Michael had a very bashful attitude toward sex. Michael admitted that in his early years, he couldn't bring himself to "do it" with Tatum. He apologized for revealing that truth, and told Bashir that back when he was young, he was "too shy" to take his clothes off.

Later, when they approached a Las Vegas mall for a shopping extravaganza, Bashir wanted to know if Jackson ever bought any jewelry.

"I buy jewelry for my mom, for Liz Taylor, and for the girl I like at the moment," Jackson said.

"Do you have one now?" Bashir asked.

"No."

In the Vegas mall, Michael couldn't wait to get upstairs to his favorite store. He wanted to show Bashir all the beautiful, ornate pieces of art and furniture he'd recently purchased. Jackson pointed to a dozen giant urns, then he focused on a couple of large marble pieces, priced at $275,000 each. As Michael went through the store, Bashir pointed out that 80 percent of the place had been bought by the pop star. Bashir questioned the volume of his spending, and Jackson, like a child playing a game, pointed to the store manager and said, "But he's going to give us a bargain. Celebrities like bargains too!"

As the documentary evolved, what was becoming obvious was that the bargain Michael had made with Martin Bashir, was a complete and utter mistake. Bashir was getting everything for free—from Michael's open sadness about being made fun of as a pimple-faced kid, to unprecedented visits with Michael's three children. And in return, Michael had become Bashir's vehicle, an unwitting victim in a house of cards that was about to fall down around him.

"Do you try to give your kids a normal life?" Bashir wanted to know.

"Yes," Michael said.

"You send them to school?"

"No. I saw what happened to me," Michael said. "Jealousy. Teachers would treat them different."

"Do you think they can have a normal life?" Bashir asked.

"No."

Bashir pressured Michael into talking about his children's mothers, wanting to know if the kids missed their moms, wanting to know who the mom of his infant son was. Michael said he had a "contractual agreement" not to talk about Prince Michael II's biological mom. He promised Bashir that his kids were happy, that they were well taken care of.

"Women are everywhere in my house," Michael said. "They're with women all day long."

As fate would have it, Bashir joined Jackson in Berlin just in time for the infamous episode involving Michael's infant, Prince Michael II, in what became known as "the baby dangling" incident. Martin Bashir joined Michael shortly after the scene occurred, thus he had inside access to Michael's newest scandal, which Michael didn't see as a scandal at all. With Bashir's cameras rolling, Michael's fans were still outside the hotel, screaming for him to come back out to his balcony, and the pop star wanted to appease them.

Jackson threw a pillow down to the fans, which he signed *With Love*. Fans down below blew kisses to Michael, they were screaming to see more of him. Some held banners that said: "Fuck the press, Michael, you're the best."

When Bashir asked what the signs meant, Jackson told him: "Look what they did to poor Lady Diana. It was sick. She was hunted by these people. I hate the tabloids. It's ignorance. They should all be burned."

Bashir mentioned that a storm was brewing about infant Prince Michael II, whom Jackson called "Blanket." Bashir wanted Jackson to explain why he would hang his baby out a window, telling Jackson that the media was pouncing on him. He was hoping to get the star agitated.

"We were waving to thousands of fans down below," Michael told him. "I wasn't trying to kill my child. Why would I throw a baby over a balcony? I was holding the baby with strong arms. Why would I want to hurt the baby? That's ignorance. They wanted to see the baby, and I showed them."

From Michael's perspective, he had done nothing wrong. For many courtroom observers, watching the scene from Michael's point of view, watching Michael dote on his infant—rocking "Blanket" on his knee, feeding him a bottle, trying to calm his baby who clearly didn't like Bashir's cameras—the whole thing seemed quite innocent. In fact, it seemed Michael was not so crazy after all.

It was clear that the Berlin balcony scene happened because Michael had wanted to please his fans. There were thousands of people outside in a frenzy, hovering below his balcony, begging for Michael to show them his new infant son. When Michael went outside to the balcony, he quickly lifted up his infant so that fans could catch a glimpse.

For Jackson fans in the courtroom, it was disturbing to sit and watch Jackson's innocent gesture in Berlin, as compared to the American media footage, which ran so many times over. The media showed the Jackson clip in a way that made him look crazy, always with nasty comments and rumors flying about Jackson having his children taken away from him. The media couldn't get enough of Jackson's "baby dangling," and they harped on his irresponsibility as a parent.

No wonder Jackson hated the media.

It was ironic that he would admit that to Bashir.

As the Bashir documentary continued to play, the piece became more antagonistic toward Jackson, and some courtroom observers believed that Bashir was out to humiliate Jackson at every opportunity. When Jackson went on a trip to the zoo with his kids, Bashir made Jackson look like an unreasonable person for wanting to accompany his kids out in public, where they would be subjected to paparazzi. Bashir was suggesting that, had Michael stayed out of the picture, his children, Prince and Paris, would have never been subject to such a feeding frenzy, pointing out that Prince almost got trampled by paparazzi. Michael said that he didn't trust anyone else to take his kids outside. He said he was overprotective of them because he loved them more than life.

Toward the end of the footage, when Bashir turned the attention back to Neverland, everyone watched Jackson spend the day at Neverland with a group of disadvantaged children. The kids were happily touring Neverland Ranch on Jackson's full-sized train, and Michael acted like a kid, eating ice cones with them, just having a ball watching inner-city children with sparkles in their eyes.

Then, out of left field, Bashir suddenly made reference to the "millions" Jackson once paid to a kid who had slept over—ten years prior. As Bashir's sinister voice-over filled the courtroom, the documentary switched to a scene involving Michael and the Arvizo kids—Gavin, Star, and Davellin—which would change the tone of the room completely.

Michael was shown with twelve-year-old Gavin, as Gavin rested his head on Michael's shoulder, and the two of them held hands. Michael talked about how great it was that Gavin no longer had cancer. Michael said the doctors had pronounced that Gavin was going to die, and Jackson was so pleased to see Gavin healthy and happy. Jackson insisted that he got his inspiration from children, telling Bashir, "I see God in the face of every child."

That comment would later be fodder for satire and further condemnation of Jackson by mainstream media, who were able to use it for laughs and giggles.

But in the courtroom, none of the footage seemed funny, and the DA was quite focused on having the jury concentrate on Jackson's comment about Gavin and his brother sleeping in his bedroom with him. In the documentary, Jackson said having kids sleep over wasn't sexual. He insisted that sharing his bed was a loving thing to do. Michael explained that he hosted the Arvizo boys, along with his good friend Frank Casio, for the night, clarifying that he and Casio actually slept on the floor so that Gavin and his brother could sleep in the bed.

When the scene played throughout the courtroom, it seemed like it ran in slow motion, and many heads were shaking from side to side, wondering why the pop star chose to share his bedroom with young boys.

Looking over at the people sitting in the jury box, it appeared there was a tremendous disapproval about the strange behavior of Michael Joe Jackson. With Sneddon putting a twisted spin on it, no one could understand why Jackson had children in his bedroom. The DA felt very, very proud of himself, especially since the jury looked completely thrown out of their element.

"Wanna Be Startin' Something"

When the documentary was over, with Tom Sneddon having no further questions for the British journalist, it was Tom Mesereau's turn to cross-examine Bashir, and the defense attorney seemed ready to duel.

"Mr. Bashir, in order to produce the show we just watched, you had to speak to Mr. Jackson, true?" Mesereau asked, his tone somewhat friendly.

"Correct," Bashir said.

"Mr. Bashir, you had Michael Jackson sign an agreement without a lawyer present, is that true?"

"Mr. Jackson signed two agreements, in which he asked for no conditions whatsoever, and agreed that I was free to make the film with him," Bashir said.

As Tom Mesereau began his litany of questions, it was obvious that he'd done his homework. Mesereau wanted to know why Bashir had been reported in England for "unfair" journalistic practices on three separate occasions.

"Mr. Bashir, have you been sanctioned by the Broadcasting Complaints Commission?" Mesereau asked.

"The answer to that question is, three complaints were made against me," Bashir testified. "Two of the key complaints were entirely rejected, and they were to do with balance and fairness. One of the three was upheld. Just so I can explain so people will understand?"

"Certainly."

"The British Standards Commission is not a legal body," Bashir told jurors, "and it has no particular merit in a legal setting."

"Nevertheless, a complaint against you as a journalist was upheld, true?"

"As I said, sir, three complaints were made. The two key complaints were entirely rejected. One complaint was upheld of the three," Bashir testified.

To Mesereau, Bashir admitted that he'd been accused of "unfairness" and of "breaching an agreement." Bashir testified that, while these two complaints were "rejected," the third complaint against him was cause for him to be sanctioned. The complaint alleged that Bashir was unbalanced in his reportage, that he was "not representing the entirety" of the subject—the same allegation Michael Jackson would later make against Bashir.

As Mesereau asked questions about the journalist's problematic background, it was obvious that Bashir had not expected anyone to have known unflattering details about his past. Bashir tried to shrug it off, but courtroom observers could see that the mention of his "unfair" journalistic practices made Bashir highly uncomfortable.

Tom Mesereau asked questions about Bashir's representations to Jackson, about Bashir's many promises to Jackson, which were used to lure Jackson into full and unfettered cooperation with the Bashir project. Though Mesereau found himself being blocked by Bashir's high-powered attorney, Theodore Boutrous, a man who represented the ABC network, Mesereau continued his line of questions. Often, the objections were sustained on the grounds that Bashir was protected by the California Shield Law, which states that reporters cannot be forced to testify about things they learn while working on a story.

Bashir's lawyer, Theodore Boutrous, was seen as a "fixture" in high-profile cases, and media observers were not surprised to see him appear on behalf of Martin Bashir and ABC News. ABC was not only Bashir's current employer, the ABC network had aired the Bashir documentary just days after it ran in England, and now Boutrous was in court to protect Martin Bashir and ABC news. Boutrous was a heavyweight—and he was at the Jackson trial, not only to represent ABC News, but also to represent the interests of NBC Universal, CBS Broadcasting, FOX News, and Cable News Network, among others.

Throughout Bashir's testimony, Boutrous interrupted the proceedings, objecting on the grounds that Mesereau's questions violated the California Shield Law and Bashir's First Amendment rights. Mesereau was well aware that Martin Bashir had not wanted to testify in the case against Jackson, he was aware that Bashir did not want to be cross-examined because just weeks prior to the trial, Bashir filed a motion asking Judge Melville to deny the DA's request to have him testify. But Bashir's motion was rejected.

Of course, Bashir didn't want to be subject to questioning. Instead, Bashir wanted the ABC Network to verify his documentary, and then let the documentary speak for itself. Bashir was hoping to avoid facing Michael Jackson altogether. However, Judge Melville required that Martin Bashir show up in court. So there he was, keeping his head turned away from Jackson, being shielded by his ABC lawyer, refusing to answer most questions posed by Mesereau on the grounds that they violated his rights as a journalist.

"Mr. Bashir, in the show you prepared, which we've just seen, Mr. Jackson made statements to the effect that nothing sexual happened in his bed, correct?" Mesereau asked.

"Correct," Bashir testified.

"To obtain that interview you had with Mr. Jackson when he made that statement, you told him he was underappreciated, true?"

That particular question, like many questions before it, was objected to by the ABC lawyer under the Shield Law, but Judge Melville overruled the objection, asking Bashir to respond. The jury was stunned to see that Mr. Bashir refused to answer, telling the court, "I'm standing on the broadcast privilege and the Shield Law, Your Honor."

"Mr. Bashir, you wrote to Mr. Jackson's assistant and said you would very much like to feature Michael with a large group of children, around fifty, welcoming them and sharing with them his extraordinary home so that, for one day, their lives can be enriched, right?" Mesereau asked.

"Objection," Boutrous argued.

"Mr. Bashir, did you request that Michael Jackson bring Macaulay Culkin so you could film him at Neverland?"

"Objection, Shield Law," Boutrous said.

"In the process of putting this film together, Mr. Bashir, did you write to Michael Jackson's assistant and say that you wanted to film the beautiful landscape, encouraging all of us to become as little children again?"

"Objection, Shield Law, First Amendment," Boutrous repeated.

As irritating as it was, virtually every question that Mesereau asked was objected to by Boutrous, and the objection was sustained. On the few occasions when Mesereau framed a question in such a way that it was not objectionable, Martin Bashir made no attempts to answer.

Bashir refused to respond, and he let the jury know that he had the right to do that as a journalist. As the non-testimony continued to frustrate the defense team, everyone in the courtroom became miffed, including Michael, who was watching Bashir slither his way out of having to answer for anything.

"Mr. Bashir, in the show about Michael Jackson, Mr. Jackson says that nothing sexual went on in his bedroom. To obtain that statement, you told Mr. Jackson that your romantic development was partially shaped by his records, true?"

"Objection, Your Honor," Boutrous said. "Same grounds, First Amendment, Shield Law."

"Do you wish to answer that question?" Judge Melville asked.

"No, Your Honor," Bashir said.

And so it went.

Martin Bashir, who had a blank expression as he continually declined to answer questions—had taken every opportunity to publicly hide. For the jury, the amount of objections and Bashir's refusal to answer, was making heads spin. It was becoming difficult for anyone without a legal background to keep up with the technical mumbo-jumbo.

The jury of twelve ordinary citizens seemed baffled.

"Mr. Bashir, on your show, Mr. Jackson says that nothing sexual ever went on in his bedroom. To obtain that statement from him, you told him that you believe in his vision of an International Children's Holiday, correct?"

"Same objections, Your Honor," Boutrous asserted.

"Overruled," Melville said. "Do you wish to answer that question?"

"I don't, Your Honor," Bashir told the court.

But Mesereau wouldn't let up. He repeated his questions to Martin Bashir, phrasing them with as many specifics as possible, and the jury watched as Bashir refused to testify about anything.

"Mr. Bashir, did you, in the process of making contact with Mr. Jackson so you could make this film, misrepresent that you were putting together a trip to Africa for Mr. Jackson to visit sick children?" Mesereau asked.

"Objection," Boutrous said.

"Mr. Bashir, you complimented Michael Jackson for what he does for disadvantaged children from the ghetto, true?"

"Objection, Shield Law, First Amendment."

"Mr. Bashir, you interviewed Mr. Jackson and repeatedly asked him questions about his desire for an international children's holiday, correct?"

"Same objection."

"Mr. Bashir, in order to obtain the statement from Mr. Jackson that nothing sexual goes on in his bedroom with children," Mesereau continued, "you told him that you were going to arrange a meeting with Kofi Annan, the secretary general of the United Nations, and would plan a trip to Africa with Mr. Jackson and Kofi Annan to help African children with AIDS, true?"

"Same objections, Your Honor," Boutrous argued.

It was painfully clear that, although certain objections were overruled, Bashir was not going to testify about his promises to Jackson, or the techniques he used in order to get the superstar to cooperate in the making of a British film without pay. Tom Mesereau finally decided to ask Bashir, point-blank, if he was going to answer any questions about how he managed to get "face-to-face" time with Michael Jackson, about Bashir's alleged promises to Michael Jackson, and again, the TV journalist looked over to his ABC attorney for a cue.

At that point, the high-powered attorney, Theodore Boutrous, interrupted the proceedings, telling the court that Bashir was not going to give Mesereau a response. Bashir had rights as a journalist.

Tom Mesereau tried every possible angle he could. The defense attorney used every vein in his body to find a way to get Bashir to tell the jury something, any kind of truth. But in the end, the witness had to be excused, subject to a possible recall.

During an afternoon break in the day's session, when questioned by media about how he was feeling, Michael said softly, "I'm angry." It would be one of the last times he would address any member of media during the trial.

Though Bashir was never recalled, Mesereau had sent the message to the jury: Bashir misrepresented himself to get the interview with Michael Jackson. It wasn't necessary for Martin Bashir to testify about the specifics. Through Mesereau's highly crafted questions, the jury learned that Bashir had done everything to win Jackson over. Bashir capitalized on his "friendship" with Princess Diana. He flattered Jackson for his parenting skills. Bashir played up his love for Jackson's music, naming tunes and joking with the pop star. And more than anything, Bashir complimented Jackson for all the charity work, for all the time and money Jackson donated to help children throughout the world.

Of all the inconsistencies Mesereau mentioned, the one tangible thing that would become most vital to the defense was the outtake footage of the Bashir documentary, which would later be entered into evidence as part of their case-in-chief.

During Bashir's taping of his documentary, Michael Jackson had asked his own personal videographer to roll tape the entire time. The never-before-seen footage existed, and since the judge allowed the Bashir documentary into evidence, the outtake footage would also be allowed in.

Because Michael had supplied the entirety of the Bashir footage to the defense, the jury would eventually see the raw footage of Jackson, the "uncut" version of what Jackson had really told Bashir. Jackson's defense team would later prove just how vulnerable and gullible Michael Jackson had been throughout the months of taping with Martin Bashir.

The unused Bashir footage would show jurors the "out of context" aspects of Bashir's infamous documentary. Michael's extremely candid and off-camera persona—would offer a powerful insight to the jury. Based on the two and a half hours of Jackson speaking straight from his heart, people were able to make their own decisions about the mentality of the King of Pop. Certain folks on the jury later confided that they listened to the voice of Jackson himself, in order to help them answer their own questions about why the pop star preferred the company of children.

Following Bashir, Assistant DA Gordon Auchincloss called Ann Marie Kite, a public relations woman who worked with the Jackson "crisis management" team in the days following the Bashir documentary. Ms. Kite was there to support the DA's charge that Michael Jackson and his associates had conspired to keep the Arvizo family under tight control at Neverland, alleging that the Arvizos were being held captive by Jackson and his "people." According to Gordon Auchincloss, the Arvizos were held against their will and were pushed into making a rebuttal video that would shed a positive light on Michael's relationship with Gavin.

The witness, Ann Kite, was a pretty blonde, a sweet-talking lady who said she was hired by Jackson's team on February 9, 2003. Her stated goal was "to resuscitate" Jackson's career after the airing of *Living with Michael Jackson*. Of course, the fact that Ms. Kite had zero high-profile PR experience, seemed a bit unusual. As she tried to explain the situation, the jury learned that Ms. Kite had been terminated from her "Jackson PR" job within six days.

Throughout Kite's testimony, it became evident that in the wake of Bashir, Michael Jackson wasn't at all involved with handling any public relations problem. That's not what Michael did, and it seemed the pop star wasn't nearly as worried about a public relations nightmare—as perhaps, he should have been. Instead of feeling he'd done something wrong, Michael was letting everyone else handle what *they* thought was a crisis. So Ann Kite, the one-time girlfriend of one of Michael's attorneys, found herself in a very high-profile circumstance—and she was in way over her head.

The jury learned that Ann Kite was hired when her ex-boyfriend, David LeGrand, asked her to help with Michael's "image management." Ms. Kite testified that she was looking to combat all of the negative press launched by Bashir, by creating positive PR for Jackson. Kite claimed she was reporting directly to Jackson's team—Ronald Konitzer, Marc Shaffel, and Mark Geragos—who were allegedly making decisions about Jackson's next PR moves. She told the jury that she and her former boyfriend, LeGrand, both lived in Las

Vegas, and admitted that LeGrand had gotten her paid a $10,000 advance on what was to be a one-month $20,000 contract.

Ann Kite testified that she wanted to formulate a "clear plan of attack" against all the negative press, that she wanted to put a halt to the "downward spiral" that the Bashir documentary might produce. Kite said she was concerned about documents that had been released on the Internet, which added further damage to Michael's image. Apparently, the Court TV site, thesmokinggun.com, had posted documents pertaining to the Jordie Chandler settlement, detailing the explicit allegations about sexual molestation made by the 1993 accuser.

Ann Kite told the court that she was trying to fight media who were attacking Jackson personally, and explained there was so much negative press, she felt the media had gone overboard. Kite recalled that even pediatricians were weighing in on TV—concerned about what type of baby formula Michael was seen feeding his infant—questioning Michael's abilities as a father.

Ms. Kite felt that Michael should be proactive in the PR matter. She felt Jackson should "come out to the world" by making a public statement himself. Apparently, Michael Jackson had no intention of doing that, and instead, had enlisted Fire Mountain Corporation, along with producer Marc Shaffel, to develop a rebuttal film about him that was slated to air on FOX.

According to Ms. Kite, FOX network had agreed to give Marc Shaffel a "degree of creative control" in making the film. She testified that FOX outbid ABC for the rights to air the production, *The Michael Jackson Interview: The Footage You Were Never Meant to See*. It would include rebuttal statements from people like Debbie Rowe, the Arvizo family, and the original statements made to Bashir by Michael Jackson himself.

But Ann Kite felt that a rebuttal video—which would not air for weeks or months—was not enough to combat the seventy two hours of adverse publicity the Bashir film had already generated. She knew that Jackson was going to face another barrage of negative publicity, and told Jackson's advisors that the problem needed to be addressed immediately.

Ann Kite said that she began her mission to "save" Michael on Valentine's Day, February 14, 2003. Prior to that date, she testified that she'd seen a statement from Bell Yard in England, something regarding Janet Arvizo, which was going to be released to the media at some future date.

As Assistant DA Auchincloss worked his way through the questioning, the jury understood that Ann Kite was testifying in furtherance of the conspiracy charge against Michael Jackson, and Ms. Kite was asked about a call she received from Marc Shaffel on February 13, 2003. Kite told jurors that Marc Shaffel was "extremely agitated" when he called to report that Janet Arvizo had taken her kids and had left Neverland Ranch, and recalled that sometime later, Shaffel called her back to report that the situation had been "contained." Shaffel allegedly told Kite that, within twelve hours, the Arvizo family had been brought back to Neverland.

Ann Kite told the Assistant DA that when Shaffel used the word "contained," it made her feel very uncomfortable. Ms. Kite seemed a bit air-headed as she failed to recall certain names and documents pertaining to her testimony, but her statement, nevertheless, did seem to help establish the reason for the conspiracy charge against Jackson.

Ms. Kite testified that when she spoke to David LeGrand, she confirmed that Janet Arvizo had left Neverland Ranch, but then had returned back to Neverland from Los Angeles. Judging her tone of voice, it seemed that Ms. Kite was worried about what was happening with the Arvizos.

"Don't make me believe that these people were hunted down like dogs and brought back to the ranch," Kite later asked LeGrand.

"I can't discuss this right now," LeGrand allegedly told her.

In another conversation with LeGrand, Kite testified that LeGrand made mention of the team's plans to destroy the name of the Arvizo mom: "He said that they no longer had to worry about [Janet Arvizo] because they had her on tape, and they were going to make her look like a crack whore."

Ms. Kite further testified that after her chat with LeGrand, she also spoke to Ronald Konitzer, who was the man "in charge" of the damage-control team for Jackson. When she asked Konitzer about the Arvizo family, he told her that "the situation has been taken care of."

Apparently, Konitzer's answer made her feel even more uneasy.

Kite testified that she had made an arrangement to go on the TV show *Access Hollywood*, prepared to make a pro-Jackson statement on Valentine's Day. Kite told the court that she was actually wired and made-up, sitting on the set with Pat O'Brien, when suddenly Mark Geragos placed a call to the Hollywood set, and insisted that the interview be held off.

Ann Kite said that, while still on the set of *Access Hollywood*, she got on the phone with Geragos, and was told to stay in LA overnight, to come visit the Geragos & Geragos offices the next morning. When Kite arrived there, Attorney Mark Geragos allegedly asked her to sign a confidentiality agreement, which she refused to do. She told the court, "I believe it was designed to shut me up."

Kite testified that she was later terminated by e-mail, without cause.

On cross-examination, Mesereau quickly established that Ann Kite's public relations agreement was not with Michael Jackson, that she'd never met with or spoken to Michael Jackson, nor had she spoken to the Arvizo family, for that matter. Ms. Kite hadn't been to Neverland, and had only worked with "Michael's team" for less than a week. Furthermore, the jury learned that Ann Kite had *one* other client in the time period that she worked for Jackson's team, and that was her own company.

Kite described her work as the president of Webcasters Alliance, her company that was working on getting legislation passed that would allow webcasters to play music on the Internet. Other than working for her own company, Ms. Kite didn't seem to have much else going on in her professional life. She was certainly not versed in the ways of celebrities, nor did she seem to be savvy about the music industry. As Mesereau questioned her, the jury discovered that Ms. Kite was a very strange choice to represent the King of Pop in a "public relations crisis." It became clear that Ann Kite had never represented any celebrity as a PR person, whatsoever, which made people on the jury wonder just how much Jackson knew—about any of his "handlers."

"I'm asking you to answer a question," Mesereau said. "You really weren't very experienced in handling media crisis management for celebrities before you joined this team, right?"

"I believed I was," Kite testified.

"Because you represented one?"

"Because I've seen a lot."

"I'm not asking what you've seen," Mesereau said. "I'm asking you what you've done, okay?"

"Yes, I have represented one person that was a celebrity, sir."

"Okay, his name was Sylver?" Mesereau wanted to confirm.

"Marshal Sylver, yes. S-Y-L-V-E-R," Kite answered.

"To your knowledge, is he on television a lot?"

"He had been at the time. I don't believe he is anymore."

"He had been on television in what capacity?"

"He had produced infomercials."

When it came to being a public relations wiz, when it came to being an expert about anything do to with Michael Jackson, Ms. Kite was neither. To courtroom observers, the idea that this woman was handling Jackson's "crisis management," even for a minute, was mind-boggling.

Then as Mesereau brought up the subject of Ann Kite's police report, which included a narrative summary of what she'd told Santa Barbara police, even more mind-blowing things began popping up about the people who were "handling" Michael Jackson in his time of crisis. In her police report, Ann Kite told the Santa

Barbara sheriffs that Mark Geragos "had the final say" on everything to do with Michael, which, as his initial criminal attorney, was the one thing that made sense.

But as Ann Kite was being grilled by Mesereau, the rest of her testimony began backfiring for the prosecution. For one thing, she testified that she told police that she "believed," based on what David LeGrand had told her, that Ronald Konitzer "had power of attorney over Michael Jackson" and had used that power of attorney to "embezzle $980,000" from Jackson.

"When you had your interview with Santa Barbara sheriffs, you were asked by Detective Zelis, if you knew if Michael Jackson was aware of what the team was doing. Do you remember that?" Mesereau asked.

"Yes, sir, I do," Kite said.

"And you told Detective Zelis, you had no idea whether Michael Jackson knew what his team was doing, is that correct?"

"That's correct. Because I never spoke with Mr. Jackson."

Kite's testimony was eye-opening, particularly on cross-examination, during which time, the unknown PR woman showed jurors that Michael Jackson seemed to have no clue about the people who were "in charge" of his future well-being. At one point, Kite told the jury that she had become so concerned about what was going on around Michael, that she felt compelled to call his brother Jermaine. Kite testified that, following her meeting with Jermaine at his Encino home, the power of attorney was revoked from Ronald Konitzer.

Ann Kite told the jury that she actually asked David LeGrand to investigate Mr. Konitzer and Mr. Shaffel because she "couldn't allow Mr. Jackson's reputation to fall into total ruin in the press." She alleged that Mr. Shaffel told her that he was concerned that Gavin Arvizo's mother was going to sell her story to the British tabloids. When it came to Michael Jackson, Kite implied that she wasn't sure where anyone's allegiance was.

It seemed Ms. Kite distrusted almost everyone involved in "Michael's team." However, it was her ex-boyfriend, David LeGrand, who wound up getting fired from the "damage-control team" early on.

Marc Shaffel and Ron Konitzer, along with three other men—Deiter Weisner, Frank Casio, and Vinnie Amen—were the five individuals who had been named by the prosecution as Michael Jackson's "unindicted coconspirators." Mysteriously, none of the five men had been charged.

At least, not at the time of the criminal trial.

"Rock With You"

With the trial in full gear, the TV chatter surrounding it added a surreal dimension, not only on cable news, but on entertainment shows around the world.

E! News wanted to take their viewers inside the courtroom, and the cable network, known for puff pieces, known for promoting Paris Hilton and Nicole Ritchie and other "living dolls," was presenting a serious reenactment of the trial.

Hosted by James Curtis, the *E! News* presentation of the Michael Jackson trial was expected to be a hit. A mock trial had aired successfully during the O. J. Simpson civil trial, and now *E!* expected to capitalize once again, using the Jackson *buzz* to bring an audience of Jackson-starved fans who had no way of knowing what was actually going on inside the courtroom.

The idea sounded great, but in reality, it was a disaster.

Their first mistake was hiring an actor who once parodied the King of Pop in *Scary Movie 3.* It wasn't the actor's fault. There was just no way for anyone to credibly reenact the real Michael Jackson. The idea that *E!* thought Jackson fans would buy into this was bizarre. Jackson fans wanted Michael, not some skinny actor wearing costumes and layers of face makeup.

As for the media, most people present at the trial absolutely refused to watch the *E!* reenactment show. As it was, media people were overwhelmed with the tight schedule, consumed with the constant battle between Michael, the media, and his fans. The media concerned themselves with the titillating details about Michael. The idea of reliving what was really happening, by watching second-rate actors, seemed ludicrous.

Ed Moss, the guy who played Michael Jackson, had a difficult job. With his wire-rimmed glasses and all the makeup in the world, he tried to act pensive and majestic, occasionally whispering to an "attorney," sometimes making a gesture to a "witness." But Ed Moss didn't even come close to representing the pop icon. His failed efforts made the show seem even more surreal.

To be fair, the *E!* show was a tall order for all of these actors, who found themselves in the awkward position of having to act out a daily version of the trial based on trial transcripts, who relied on paid journalists to fill in details about what was happening *live*. The actor playing Judge Melville appeared to be more stiff than Melville ever was in person, and the guy playing Tom Sneddon, frankly, didn't capture the DA's anger. Sneddon had a sense of righteous indignation that was pervasive throughout the trial, but none of that translated to the *E!* production. As for Tom Mesereau, the actor who portrayed him, wasn't acting confident. The guy had none of the presence of Tom Mesereau, who, in real life, was so sure of himself, he dwarfed the rest of the defense team—Susan Yu, Robert Sanger, and Brian Oxman.

In the actual trial, it was Mesereau who handled the majority of the witnesses for the defense, whereas, for the prosecution, the witnesses were split up between three men: Tom Sneddon, Assistant DA Gordon Auchincloss, and Assistant DA Ron Zonen, who probably was the best among the prosecutors in the case. In the court of law, all three prosecutors seemed to display superior attitudes, but that important detail wasn't revealed in the TV reenactment.

The idea that *E! News* wanted to present a case that was believable, that they thought they could hire a list of B-actors to pull off the machinations of these strong personalities in a criminal trial, was a statement about art imitating life that was mystifying. It was incredible that the *E!* executives believed that a criminal proceeding would serve as good fodder for entertainment. Not only were the B-actors bad at portraying Michael Jackson and the teams of attorneys, they were having a hard time imitating the personalities of stars like Macaulay Culkin, George Lopez, Chris Tucker, and Jay Leno.

It was a side-circus, yet the *E!* network ran the show for months.

At the same time that *E! News* was getting off to a rocky start with their version of the "Jackson Trial," *Tonight Show* host Jay Leno was making a public effort to have the right to discuss the case on late-night TV. At that time, Mr. Leno, who had been subpoenaed to testify in the trial, was subject to Judge Melville's gag order—which prevented any potential witness from talking about Michael Jackson.

For years, Jay Leno regularly joked about Jackson's affinity for children and little boys. Now, the entertainer had filed a motion, requesting he be given an exemption from the gag order. Leno asked that he be limited, solely, to not being able to reveal anything that he had firsthand knowledge about regarding the case.

"As part of his role on *The Tonight Show*, Mr. Leno comments and engages guests on noteworthy and contemporaneous issues of public interest," the motion said. "Until Mr. Jackson served Mr. Leno with a subpoena, nobody could even argue that Mr. Leno was limited in any way from commenting on, and discussing at will, issues related to the case."

The motion, filed by Theodore Boutrous, hoped to clear up the question as to whether or not Jay Leno could make nightly "Jackson" jokes during the trial. Attorney Boutrous, acting on behalf of NBC, wanted to remove the threat of a court sanction. Mr. Boutrous didn't want the gag order to be interpreted in such a way as to limit Mr. Leno's ability to speak publicly about Michael Jackson.

While waiting for Judge Melville's ruling, as a way to get around the court sanctions, Jay Leno decided to bring other people on stage to make fun of the daily happenings surrounding the criminal trial. It was easy enough to have "unknowns" come forward to deliver lines that poked fun at Jackson's misfortune, and people seemed eager to help Leno out.

People had no problem doing that.

People loved making jokes about Michael's plight.

As it happened, Judge Melville ruled that Jay Leno could indeed make public jokes about the trial, and he limited the gag order to Leno's personal knowledge about certain facts that the comedian would eventually testify about. For Jay Leno, once the gag order was lifted, all bets were off. The late-night star held back no punches. Poking fun was his job, as a comedian, but it seemed unkind, really, that Leno would make more jokes about Jackson during the trial than he ever had before. Mr. Leno, without care, was adding fuel to the court of public opinion— a court that was already on fire about Michael's strange lifestyle.

"Michael Jackson's lawyer said that he will not play the race card—mainly because he can't figure out what race Michael is," Leno said, opening his monologue to a gaggle of laughter.

As the *Tonight Show* went back to its old tricks, the list of Jay Leno's jokes about Michael Jackson became even longer. Everything the media was reporting became daily fodder for Leno's team of producers. But no matter how much the trial seemed like a joke, the life and reputation of Michael Jackson was really on the line. The prosecutorial team was not laughing about seeing Michael Jackson put behind bars. They wanted the entertainer to serve hard prison time.

On day three, Michael—dressed in a dark suit accented by an embroidered white vest, and an expensive bauble hanging from his neck—looked crisp. Testi-

mony was now well underway, with Ann Kite being followed by one of the deputies who videotaped the raid on Neverland Valley Ranch.

In the morning session that day, Michael carried a small gift-wrapped box,
tied with a simple red ribbon. When he exited the courtroom during the first
break, gift in hand, Michael stayed close to Katherine. As everyone watched him,
people couldn't help think that Michael, when it all boiled down, was still a
mama's boy. He loved Katherine, and he wanted her to be proud of him.

Michael and Katherine were silent as they walked away from the flashing camera bulbs, the TV cameras, and the crowds of fans in the hallway. As usual,
Michael took the elevator to a secret room upstairs. Of course, no one in the
media was permitted to ask exactly where Michael and his family went during
breaks. Outside the court of law, Michael Jackson was off-limits. During breaks
and recesses, courthouse deputies guarded Jackson like he was the president of
the United Sates. And perhaps they had to, because behind the scenes, there were
fears about bomb threats—members of law enforcement were acutely aware of
countless things that could go wrong.

Because of the tight security, the situation for people in the courthouse every
day was not pleasant. The media was relegated to an area dubbed "the green
monster," a fenced-off space where pundits spoke to cameras, where people did
not have the ability to move freely. In a strange way, this imposed "lock up" was
a reflection of Michael's life. Michael's celebrity made him, and everyone around
him, a prisoner. His great fame cost him freedom, and the ordinary people who
surrounded him were feeling the same pinch.

Sometimes Michael would pop downstairs a few minutes early, looking to give
a smile or wave to the fans who had won lottery seats in the public area. But
oftentimes, fans were unnecessarily yelled at or shoved out of Jackson's way. In
general, the fans, as well as the media, were treated harshly by courthouse deputies. It seemed that the power of authority had gone to people's heads. The pack
of deputies and law officials were often trying to outdo each other. Some were
taking their roles far too seriously, intoxicated by their power.

Just like the pop star, everyone in his presence was being watched like a hawk.
The public scrutiny became a regular part of being near Michael Jackson. Every
movement was being monitored, and everyone knew that one move out of place,
would cost dearly. From day one of the trial, certain fans were permanently
banned from the courtroom for walking the wrong way. On a regular basis, there
were media members who were kicked out if they inadvertently brought a cell
phone or Internet device into the courtroom.

There was a constant push-and-pull between the fans, the media, and the courtroom officials, who seemed to take extreme pleasure in slapping down media peacocks. Media folks were not allowed to have water, not allowed to chew gum, not allowed to even whisper, as the trial was in process. Most media members wanted to be rescued from the scene; they wanted their privacy back. Ironically, media people didn't enjoy the feeling of being scrutinized for every little move they made. They wished they could find an exit, an escape from the constant eyeballing.

As media watched Michael handle all the adult egos with an undeniable charm, it became obvious, so crystal clear, as to why Jackson needed to create a life that was free of adult constraints. Given the constant scrutiny, the ever-present expectations from adults, it seemed understandable that Michael had taken such great pains to build a self-contained world at his home. Neverland was his getaway from the TV cameras, the flashbulbs, the gossip columns, the gawkers, the whole universe of adults who placed him in a fishbowl from the time he first became star.

In court that afternoon, Deputy Sheriff Albert Lafferty took the stand to detail his involvement with the raid that took place at Neverland Ranch on November 18, 2003. As the deputy testified, confirming that he videotaped Neverland in its entirety, courtroom observers were told they were going to be given an insider's view of Michael's home. The way Michael lived, his most private rooms, and all of his personal possessions were going to be on display. As a DVD was inserted, an image of Neverland popped up on the big screen in the courtroom. For the first time ever, the jury, the judge, and the entire media world were given the chance to examine Michael's private life. They gawked at his art pieces, they made notes about his rooms of toys, his stacks of junk—piled up in his private baths and his bedroom suite. What a nightmare for Jackson. No one on earth would want the public to see every inch of their closets, their cubby holes, their bathroom drawers.

Albert Lafferty testified that he was part of the forensics unit in the criminal investigation division of the Santa Barbara County Sheriff's office, saying it was his job to document crime scenes, to collect and preserve evidence. Of the seventy law enforcement members who raided Neverland in November 2003, Albert Lafferty was assigned to shoot video footage and take photographs of the main residence. Lafferty explained that he captured all photo evidence before any police search was conducted, and testified that he documented the "scene" before anything was disturbed by law enforcement. Lafferty told the jury that he processed the Jackson footage, and placed it into evidence.

For the jury, Lafferty helped the Santa Barbara DA identify the various build-ings that were displayed on the maps of Neverland. Pointing to a large aerial view of Neverland, Lafferty used a red laser to highlight Figueroa Mountain Road, fol-lowing the road from the town of Los Olivos to the gates of Neverland Valley Ranch. The deputy pointed out the locations of the main house, the arcade, the train station, the amusement park, and the zoo.

As Lafferty's red laser moved beyond the gates, the deputy showed jurors the private road that swirled around Neverland which led to another gate, this one being an ornate Disney-like gate that opened automatically, with a control booth operated by life-sized mannequin security figures. Music was piped out through speakers, and a "Neverland" that people had never seen a glimpse of—was shown to the jury, inch by inch.

As he pointed to the first close-up exhibit, Lafferty showed the jury the path down Michael's elaborate driveway. He explained that jurors were looking at the main house, and then the guest units, where people like Elizabeth Taylor and Marlon Brando had been regulars. Lafferty showed the panel Michael's amuse-ment park rides, and then moved on to the train station, with its larger-than-life clock, the centerpiece of Neverland that most people recognized from worldwide news footage.

As everyone viewed the aerial footage, the level of Michael's wealth was aston-ishing. Neverland was not just a ranch or a place of amusement. It was an estate, sitting on twenty-seven hundred acres, complete with its own security patrol, its own fire department, and beautiful Tudor-style buildings that housed a separate arcade, a movie theater, a garage filled with Rolls-Royces and a Bentley, as well as a main house, complete with chefs, butlers, and catering and cleaning staff.

The amount of power and money it had taken to establish this place was keenly evident. The fact that Michael Jackson was clearly the wealthiest inhabit-ant of the Los Olivos area was a fact to be pondered. People had to wonder why the Santa Barbara DA used more law enforcement to raid Neverland than was ever used to catch any serial killer in the history of the United States.

When Tom Mesereau would later question why the police force would need as many as seventy people to do an inventory of Neverland, he would point out that, at the time of the raid, Michael was not even on the premises. That Michael's ranch needed to be raided by a small army of law enforcement, seemed excessive.

As the Neverland footage continued to roll, Lafferty told jurors that law enforcement had arrived at 9:07 the morning of November 18, that they had started taking videotape of the interior of the residence at approximately 9:55 AM, and the search of Neverland did not end until late in the night. Lafferty said that at 8:40 PM, the search of the main residence had been completed, except for the master bedroom. He told jurors that at approximately 10:38 PM, the video documentation of Michael's bedroom began. It was a two-level bedroom suite, and it took Lafferty almost twenty minutes to get video footage of just that area alone.

Before he left the stand, Lafferty testified that the last thing he did at the residence was to go back into Michael's formal dining room, where the official search warrant was laid out. Lafferty videotaped the search warrant, showing that it had been left for Michael Jackson at his residence. That night, when he returned to the Santa Barbara sheriff's station, Lafferty placed the video and film footage in a locker in the forensics unit property area.

Entered into evidence, People's exhibit 336, was a twelve-minute DVD that documented Michael's private Neverland.

The video started off in the main foyer, where a statue of a butler greeted guests. But then the camera quickly turned left, leading jurors down a hallway toward Michael's bedroom suite. Michael's bedroom door, though it had key code alarms, had already been unlocked by law enforcement.

The video showed the master bedroom's first level, with its fireplace and giant sitting room, complete with a grand piano. It breezed past the master suite's lower bathroom area and proceeded up the stairs to show Michael's king-sized bed, covered with a glittery blue comforter that made it twinkle. A strange painting of Michael in a version of "The Last Supper" hung directly over the bed. It was hard to determine all the figures in the painting, but, like Jesus, Michael was depicted in the center of twelve men. Rather than seeing apostles, jurors strained their eyes to decipher those depicted at Michael's left: Abe Lincoln, JFK, Thomas Edison, and Albert Einstein. The video footage was too fuzzy to allow jurors to see who was seated to Michael's right, though one of the figures looked like Little Richard.

It was bizarre.

And then "The Last Supper" image disappeared.

As the jury watched the DVD presentation, taking notes without turning their heads away from the screen, the DVD footage moved quickly. Fascinated by the images of Michael's private sanctuary, people in the courtroom could not believe their eyes.

In the grand foyer, where things were organized and formal, people gawked at cherubs, big marble statues that led through the entryway to the house. Life-sized nude figurines of cherubs standing on ornate parquet floors were overshadowed by expensive wall hangings, by paintings of Michael surrounded by children from every nation under the sun. Because the camera moved so quickly, the white marble statues seemed to stand out. The cherub figures looked brighter than snow.

Courtroom observers were impressed by the majesty of the entrance hall, but then the footage moved to a more cozy place, the kitchen area, showing a giant hearth and two food preparation islands. As the camera rolled, numerous kitchen staff stood frozen. They were dressed in black and white formal "kitchen help" attire, and they seemed startled by the presence of law enforcement in the house.

The footage then moved to show Michael's huge living room area, where at least three chandeliers hung. Among the couches and coffee tables, there were so many giant urns and unusual art pieces, it was difficult to single anything out. However, along one wall, the formal living room housed a model of a lavish miniature castle, which had two life-sized figurines guarding it. The castle seemed to be a custom-made copy of an ancient place, complete with a moat and serfs. It took up almost a quarter of the living room space. On the other side of the room, surrounding a couch facing a gigantic fireplace, there was a rack of expensive statues and glass objects, too numerous to count.

Sculptures and figurines filled the living room, as well as expensive oil paintings of Michael, some of them representing Jackson as a king, others of Jackson as an angel. There was so much artwork in the room, it looked like a gallery warehouse. It was impossible to imagine anyone sitting there, among all these ornate objects, and actually being able to kick back and relax. The living room was not a place, from the look of it, where Michael lived. It was a place where Michael displayed part of his vast collection of art.

As the footage moved from the hallway and led into the bedroom area, there were statues of a different kind—mannequins of little kids hiding in every corner—and the jury saw an entire bedroom devoted to dolls. Another bedroom was filled with life-sized toys, complete with *Star Wars* characters and every popular superhero—from Spiderman to Batman to Superman. The bedrooms of Prince and Paris were passed by quickly, and the video focused on the hallway leading directly into Michael's bedroom, which was so cluttered, it was hard to decipher what was there. Among Christmas decorations, books, paintings, and antiques, there were cardboard cutouts that resembled—it seemed like—Hulk Hogan, and perhaps a gremlin. Then, just inside the entrance of the bedroom, in the sitting room area, there was a huge gold throne, which held a mannequin of a kid doing a handstand.

For Michael, kids were king. That was the thread, in every fiber of his home.

Displayed in a glass case, on the first floor of the master suite, were figures of the Seven Dwarfs and other expensive Disney collectibles. In an alcove filled with puppets, there was a stork carrying a baby "package" and a hoard of stuffed animals. All around the bedroom there were cartoon characters represented—from Mickey Mouse to Fantasia to the Ninja Turtles. Life-sized action figures and cardboard cutouts of personal heroes included people like Michael Jordan and Bruce Lee. Peter Pan was depicted everywhere—and was prominently featured in a mural on the wall.

Photos of children were in frames all over the tables. Images of children were displayed all along the fireplace mantle and along the bedroom walls—anywhere Michael could find room. The clutter made the place feel busy, but it was shocking to see that Jackson felt the need to surround himself with so much "stuff."

Apparently, Michael relied on "objects" as company.

On one wall, a menagerie of jeweled items were on display. The American Flag, a ruby-red apple, a great big heart—all sorts of miniature jeweled figurines. Prominent among them: Peter Pan and Tinkerbell.

But the DVD moved quickly, and the jeweled items became a blur.

In their place, jurors began to see giant cardboard images of famous sports heroes. The jury could see numerous statues made out of papier-mâché, but as the footage moved faster, the lifelike mannequins of characters from sports, of characters from films, and the life-sized images of knights in shining armor, all meshed together.

In Michael's downstairs closet, everything was extremely neat and organized. His clothes were color coded—a series of black pants, a series of white shirts, a series of red shirts—his closet looked like a very expensive boutique. That was until the camera shifted its angle up above the clothing, where Michael's shelf space was chock-full of children's memorabilia and unopened toys.

Upstairs in the bedroom suite, around the perimeters of Michael's bed, there were multiple Spiderman figures, black felt hats, tennis rackets, unopened toys, stacks of books and CDs, four different TVs, speakers with a sound system that looked like it was hooked up to an elaborate flat screen computer, as well as a baby's crib—the place was absolutely crammed. Next to Michael's twinkle-bed, there was so much to look at, it was hard to distinguish all of the cartoon character figures. Still in their boxes were Daffy Duck, Captain Hook, and Alice in Wonderland, and mixed in with other toys and games, there were stacks of presents that were left half-wrapped.

It was the biggest kid's room in the world.

Among the photos of Peter Pan, Shirley Temple, and Tinkerbell, there were posters of the *Wizard of Oz*, the Three Stooges, *Pinocchio*, Charlie Chaplin, *Star*

Wars, Bambi, Indiana Jones, *Roger Rabbit, Singin' in the Rain,* and of course, a life-sized poster of Macaulay Culkin in *Home Alone.*

Between all the piles of videotapes and DVDs, strewn among cardboard cutouts of kids, stuffed animals, mannequins, boom boxes, artwork, Gameboys, and reading lamps—there was not one photo of Michael. Instead, above it all, displayed prominently on top of a dresser near Michael's bed—was a photo of Marilyn Monroe. And next to Marilyn was a book about Pope John Paul II.

No one in the courtroom knew what to make of it.

"Stop! The Love You Save May Be Your Own"

The eighteen-year-old sister of Gavin Arvizo, Davellin, was reserved and soft-spoken when it was her turn to take the witness stand. As she adjusted the microphone, the young lady seemed nervous. She refused to look in Michael's direction, other than to identify him as the defendant in the case, whom she hadn't seen in two years.

Davellin was asked to go back to a time in 1999, when she was accepted as a student at Hollywood High School in Los Angeles, being bused there from her family's one-room studio apartment on the other side of town. Davellin said she was a "magnet student," detailing her good grades and interest in the performing arts, explaining that she was given special entry into a school that was far from her home in East LA.

Tom Sneddon asked Davellin to describe the size of her family residence on Soto street, a place that was so small, the young lady was able to point to the railing of the jury box and then point over to the court clerk, indicating that all *five* of her family members lived in space that was, perhaps, less than five hundred square feet.

Davellin talked about how she and her brothers were introduced to Jamie Masada, the owner of a legendary club, the Laugh Factory, located on the Sunset Strip. She explained that she and her brothers were part of a "comedy camp" for inner-city kids, and told the jury that in the summer of 1999, they'd been taught comedy techniques from stars such as Paul Rodriguez, Shawn Wayans, and

George Lopez. The kids had fun, using their poverty to gain laughs in the skits they performed, and the comedians they worked with absolutely adored them.

It was sometime in the year 2000 when the Arvizo family learned that Gavin, at age ten, had been diagnosed with a life-threatening, mysterious type of cancer. At that time, their mom, Janet, presented a wish list on Gavin's behalf to Jamie Masada, who wanted to do anything in his power to help save the cute little boy. Gavin's dying wish was to meet Chris Tucker, Adam Sandler, and Michael Jackson. Through Masada's show business connections, Gavin and his family became friendly with both Chris Tucker and Michael Jackson, each of whom reached out to Gavin in 2000, as the boy suffered with severe bouts of nausea and lifelessness, being treated with adult forms of chemotherapy.

Once he was well enough to leave the hospital bed, Gavin stayed at the home of his grandparents in El Monte, and celebrities held fund-raisers so that Gavin's room could be outfitted with high-standard equipment for air and quality control. While the boy battled with cancer, Gavin had a fair share of celebrity visitors, not all of whom were household names, but who, nonetheless, donated money and toys and gifts to the boy. Davellin testified that there were "big name" celebrity visits at times, and that Gavin had his picture taken with legends, among them, Kobe Bryant. As a photo of Kobe and Gavin was shown to the jury, Davellin said the basketball superstar had given her brother a special jersey to keep.

Davellin told the jury that Michael Jackson had initially called her brother while he was at the hospital, and had later made calls to Gavin at his grandparents' home. All throughout this period, Michael was calling to give Gavin the hope to grow strong, telling Gavin to "eat up all the cancer cells like Packman." Michael was trying to teach Gavin a visualization technique, suggesting that the boy visualize himself using healthy cells to eat up unhealthy cells. Jackson wanted the boy to get well, and invited Gavin to make his way to Neverland.

The Arvizo family's first trip to see Michael was an all-expense paid trip, the beginning of many extravagant luxuries that Michael was always happy to give. A stretch limo arrived at their East LA studio apartment to transport the Arvizo clan up to the ranch, where they were greeted in the main residence by kitchen staff, and then by Michael, who was eating a sandwich and being extremely humble. The Arvizos were each assigned guest units, three in all, and after they got settled in, Davellin and her brothers were driven around on golf carts, taking a quick tour of the arcade, the zoo, and the movie theater.

On their initial visit there, Davellin testified, her parents got into an argument that became violent. Apparently, David Arvizo was jealous that Janet was enjoying herself with Michael, and in his rage, he threw a soda can at her and stormed out of the guest unit, leaving her mother in tears. When asked if she'd seen her mother being hit by David on other occasions, Davellin said, "Yes." She told the jury that her mom had been hit so often, on so many occasions, there were "too many to count." She also testified that her father had hit her and her brothers "lots."

When the DA asked Davellin to recount her first visit to Neverland, she talked about the whole family having dinner with Michael in his formal dining room, recalling that, while at the table, Gavin asked his parents if he and Star could stay with Michael in the main house. She told jurors that Gavin asked to stay in Michael's bedroom, which the Arvizo parents had no objection to.

The next time she and her brothers would visit Neverland, Davellin said, was on a trip with Chris Tucker, who accompanied the Arvizo family there on two occasions: one, when Michael wasn't present, and the other, when Bashir filmed his infamous documentary. In between those visits, Davellin testified that her brothers had gone to Neverland on numerous trips in the company of their dad, but she had not been present.

Sometime during that same year, by the end of 2000, the Arvizo parents had separated. According to Davellin, the Arvizo family suffered once David was gone, and their mother, Janet, had to struggle even harder to get Gavin to his doctor appointments. Because Gavin was not over his cancer, because Janet no longer had access to David's automobile, the family approached Michael for help. Davellin told jurors that Michael Jackson had given her mom a car to use—a Ford Bronco.

As Sneddon questioned the young, dark-haired girl, most of her testimony related to the allegations that Michael Jackson and his five associates had conspired to abduct, falsely imprison, and extort the Arvizo family in February and March of 2003. Davellin testified about a "conspiracy" that started just after the Bashir documentary aired in England, at which time she, her brothers, and her mom were flown to see Michael on a jet chartered by Chris Tucker.

Davellin stated that during her family's stay with Michael at Miami's Turnberry Isle Resort, the family was prevented from watching the U.S. airing of the Bashir documentary on ABC television. She testified that she and her family, though they had their own hotel room, felt that they were captive, unable to leave Michael's hotel suite. She said she witnessed her brother being taken into rooms to talk with Jackson and his associates "privately," and said that on three occasions, her brother was acting differently, explaining that Gavin became "very hyper, running around, very talkative, and playful."

Davellin told jurors that on their trip back from Miami to Neverland, she saw Michael and Gavin whispering to each other, passing a Diet Coke can back and forth. She could not state what was in the can, but led jurors to believe that Michael was trying to ingratiate himself with Gavin, her implication being that Jackson was plying her brother with wine. As for other observations, Davellin testified that, while they were on the plane ride from Miami back to Santa Barbara, Michael handed Gavin a $75,000 watch as a gift, as well as a rhinestone-studded jacket.

Once they returned to Neverland, Davellin told jurors, with Chris Tucker no longer around, she and her family felt uncomfortable being around Jackson's associates, who seemed to be "monitoring" the family and were claiming that the Arvizos were possibly subject to death threats. Jackson's associates were frightening her, Davellin asserted, at the same time that public relations efforts were in the works. Apparently, Jackson's associates were concerned with a PR campaign that was being launched, which was meant to thwart the Bashir documentary.

Upon their arrival back to Neverland, Davellin testified, she and her family were "given a list of nice things to say" for a rebuttal video about Michael Jackson. Tom Sneddon questioned the young lady for hours, during which time Davellin repeatedly claimed that she had felt she and her family were being held captive at Neverland. Davellin testified that the Arvizo family had left the premises under strange circumstances.

"We were scared by the whole situation," Davellin explained. "The whole situation, the whole secrecy. The—just real aggressive. I was just scared. I didn't understand what was going on and why it was like this."

Before her testimony ended, Davellin alleged that she had never tasted alcohol until she was handed something alcoholic to drink by Michael himself. The young woman also spoke about her mom's involvement with a new boyfriend, Major Jay Jackson, with whom she and her family stayed in the aftermath of the Bashir documentary. Davellin recalled, in detail, an interview that took place at Jay Jackson's apartment in Los Angeles. It was an interview conducted by Brad Miller, a private eye working on behalf of famed attorney Mark Geragos, who still represented Michael Jackson at the time.

The interview was audiotaped by Miller and would later be entered into evidence. In it, the Arvizo family—Gavin, Star, Davellin, and Janet—gave a glowing review of Michael Jackson, telling the private investigator that Michael had been "like a father" to them, that Jackson was a man who was unselfish and kind, who had exhibited "unconditional love."

EXHIBIT 5000-A in the case of *The People of the State of California v. Michael Joe Jackson* was a transcript of the interview given to Brad Miller. That exhibit would show that on February 16, 2003, the Arvizo family had expressed sentiments about Michael Jackson that didn't seem to match anything that Davellin had testified about.

On the tape, it was clear that the Arvizo family, Janet and her children, each participated in the interview willingly. They had given permission to have it audiotaped, and were very chipper and upbeat as they spoke. At that time, Davellin was age sixteen, Gavin was age thirteen, and Star was age twelve. Brad Miller started with Janet, asking her how the family came to meet Michael Jackson, and Janet was anxious to talk about the year of chemotherapy and radiation that Gavin received, which had somehow saved his life.

As Janet spoke of Gavin's extensive cancer treatment at Kaiser Permanente Hospital on Sunset Boulevard, she explained that a team of twelve doctors was unable to state what type of cancer Gavin suffered from. It was still a mystery that her son was alive and cancer-free.

For the record, Janet stated that Gavin lost his kidney to cancer, his left adrenal gland, the tip of his pancreas, his spleen, and multiple lymph nodes. She told Miller that doctors also extracted a sixteen-pound tumor from Gavin, and that the stage-four cancer had gotten into Gavin's lungs as well. Gavin had undergone multiple blood transfusions, both white and red blood cell transfusions, sometimes simultaneously.

When the private investigator asked Gavin about his friendship with Michael, the boy said, "Michael told me to hurry up and finish your chemotherapy and come to Neverland." On tape, Gavin recalled being in the hospital, always thinking of going to Neverland, of seeing Michael Jackson in person. "That would always make me happy," Gavin said, "'cause Michael would always put a smile on my face."

Brad Miller wanted to know if Michael had ever gone to the hospital to visit Gavin, and Gavin said that Michael was always traveling, stating that rather than visit, Michael would call and sometimes talk for hours on the phone, speaking from remote places all around the world. Gavin felt like Michael was a great friend, and told Miller, "I would be able to call him at any time and talk to him."

As for Janet, she insisted that the role Michael played was to be "a father figure" to Gavin, as well as to Star and Davellin. She said that Michael "knew that all three of them needed him," especially since their real dad, David Arvizo, had treated the family poorly. Janet claimed that David's role was to "make sure that he appeared to be a good father" but insisted that David had, in fact, caused harm to her and her children for years.

Janet wanted the PI to know that she and David were legally separated, pending divorce, and stated that David was arrested for domestic violence in October of 2001. Janet claimed that David Arvizo pleaded guilty to domestic violence charges, and said that, after an investigation was conducted, "the investigators saw that there were *more* crimes here that David had done, not just on me, but on my three children."

Janet claimed that there were nine criminal charges that David Arvizo faced, including "child endangerment" and "terrorist threats." She alleged that all three of her children had been beaten by David, at which point Gavin jumped in, claiming that his dad beat him, even throughout his cancer treatment, even after surgery. Star Arvizo told Miller that David had kicked him in the head. On tape, Davellin alleged that David once broke her tailbone.

It was sad. As the Arvizo kids made their allegations, they talked about David throwing them up against walls, pulling out clumps of their mother's hair—there was so much domestic violence. Janet told Miller that she had been granted a five-year restraining order to keep David away from the children and their dog, "Rocky," whom Janet claimed had been physically abused by David as well. Janet said that anything she and her children loved—David Arvizo took away.

David Arvizo, a warehouse worker for Vons supermarkets, a Safeway Company, was born September 20, 1966. Janet had been married to him for seventeen years, and said that for most of that time, she prayed to "be delivered from this evil." Janet told the private investigator that when Michael Jackson came along, Michael was such "a kind, gentle, and loving person," that she felt that he too, "had to be delivered from David."

Janet said that her soon-to-be ex-husband had met Michael numerous times, and was involved in their initial trips to Neverland. According to Janet, early on, when things were going well in their marriage, David had witnessed a "beautiful story about Michael and Gavin" being filmed on the grounds of Neverland.

The film Janet was referring to was a short clip of Michael taking Gavin on a walking tour around Neverland. The jury later watched the clip and saw Gavin's small, frail body, so weak that his brother, Star, who wheeled Gavin in a wheelchair, seemed ready to cry. In the background, as a camera followed the three of them—Michael, Gavin, and Star—Michael holding his umbrella to shield himself from the sun, his song "I'll Be There" was playing in the background.

"If you should ever find someone new ... I hope that he'll be good to you ... 'cause if he isn't ... I'll be the-eere."

It was touching, watching the three of them move quietly over small bridges, near beautiful ponds, under giant oak trees, with Michael's angelic voice piercing the heart of anyone who listened.

"I'll be the-eere ..."

"I'll be the-eere ..."

"Just call my name ... and I'll be there."

As the clip was played for the jury, all eyes were glued to the image of Michael with this frail, young child in the wheelchair. Many people watching were teary-eyed, and courtroom observers could feel a lump in their throats.

But Gavin's happiness at Neverland was not quite as simple, not as easy, as Michael's heart-wrenching song made it seem. Janet would tell Brad Miller that David Arvizo had his own plans about who would be friends with Michael at Neverland. She claimed that David no longer allowed her to visit Neverland because he was afraid that Janet was going to "tell Michael everything about what the children were undergoing." Janet said she was afraid of David and his "demonic ways," and wished that Michael could protect her from him.

Janet described a particular visit to Neverland when she and Michael were dancing, having fun, and David later flew into such a rage, he beat her up so badly that Michael never saw her again during the rest of that trip. She described Michael as "a family man," as someone who would protect her and her kids. Each of her children told Brad Miller that they considered Michael to be "like a father." They said Michael had given them safety, had given them love, and had tried to make them "as happy as possible" because he didn't want Gavin's cancer to come back.

On the tape, Gavin told Brad Miller that he'd been to Neverland with David "more than ten times" and explained that on each visit, during which time Gavin still had cancer, they would stay overnight. Sometimes, Gavin would stay in a guest unit with his father, but he said that he felt safe with Michael and preferred to stay in the main house, in Michael's room. On more than one occasion, Gavin told Miller, he and his brother would sleep in Michael's bed. Sometimes Michael would sleep on the floor, but sometimes they all slept together—Michael, Gavin, and Star.

Gavin insisted that Michael had never acted inappropriately with him, and repeatedly said that he thought of Michael "like a father." According to Gavin, Michael wanted to make sure that the cancer would go away and stay gone. The boy said that Michael loved him so much. Gavin told the private investigator that Michael did everything he could to keep him from feeling unhappy. Michael didn't want Gavin to be stressed out about the cancer.

All three children told Brad Miller that Michael had been nothing but "good" and "nice" to them. As for Janet, she insisted that she was very "sensitive to any little thing" that went on with Gavin. She told Miller that she was very protective over her children, and had absolutely no misgivings whatsoever about them spending time with Michael.

As Janet spoke her mind, she assured Miller that she and her kids had known nothing but neglect and rejection until Michael came along. "We've been rejected, neglected, spit on, fried, tried, burned, abused, the doors shut on our face, opportunities lost," Janet insisted. "And Michael took us from way behind in the line, and pulled us up to the front of the line, and said, 'You matter to me. You may not matter to many people, but you matter to me.'"

Janet spoke about the media pounding down her doors from the moment the Bashir documentary aired, referencing the calls she'd received from newspapers around the world, from television networks around the world. "You name it, everyone has called."

Janet told the private investigator that she and her children had no stories to sell to the media, that whatever the media was trying to buy just didn't exist. The relationship between Michael Jackson and her children was pure and innocent. Janet said that Michael had prayed along with her and her kids, that Michael had talked to them about God. Janet Arvizo was annoyed that somehow, after the Bashir documentary, everything was being twisted by the media people who were bombarding her apartment, bombarding her parents' home in El Monte, offering cars, offering money, desperate to get a sound bite or a photo of anyone in the family.

Janet couldn't understand how reporters could be so callous. She resented all the calls being made to her cousins and distant relatives. She hated the attempts on the part of the media to "get the story" by any means possible.

Gavin, for his part, was very unhappy about being made fun of at school and in his neighborhood. Gavin told Miller that after the Bashir documentary aired, he was hurt by the public allegations and all the commotion that was made over a comment about him sharing a bed with Michael Jackson. Gavin said he was angry about the looming allegations, and even more outraged about the rumors that were flying, which were a pack of lies.

"They called me a homosexual," Gavin said. "They say that I'm lying and I haven't even gone through cancer. Come on. I suffered through that whole year going through adult doses. Chemotherapy is toxic. It hurts. I was throwing up so much, I was throwing up acid, I was throwing up blood. And reporters and all these people just say that it never happened."

For Gavin, the backlash from the Bashir documentary was more than upsetting. It was frustrating and spiteful. Gavin said he felt sorry that the media had done this to him, and felt sorry that they had done this to Michael. Janet felt equally upset, especially because her parents were being hounded in their own front yard every day.

"My parents are trustworthy. They are strong on their virtues," Janet told Miller. "They see how important and what a beautiful impact Michael has had on me and Gavin and Star and Davellin, and there's no, no amount of money that could make them sell [a story] because what's more important in this whole life is love. Everything begins with love, everything is colored by love, and everything ends with love."

These were the words from Janet and from the mouths of her babes on Sunday night, February 16, 2003. And it was that same night, before the audio recording ended, that the Arvizo children swore, under penalty of perjury, under the laws of the State of California, that everything they had stated during their interview about Michael Jackson was true.

"Do You Remember the Time?"

At the end of the court day, Thursday, March 4, when Michael was asked about Davellin Arvizo's testimony, he told the media he found it "frustrating." Actually, that comment from Jackson would be his last, at least when it came to the media throng, because his attorney would not permit any further comments. Mesereau loathed the media who were present, and felt that the media was there to capitalize on sensational accounts of Michael Jackson's folly. Of course, not even Mesereau could have predicted the worldwide sensation Jackson would generate on the day he went into court wearing his pajamas.

"Pajama Day" happened in the days following Davellin and Star's testimony, just as Gavin Arvizo took the stand. Leading up to Gavin's appearance, Davellin and Star had told the jury that they lied on previous occasions, both siblings testifying that they were forced to compliment Michael Jackson. When Star Arvizo gave his own account about Michael's alleged sexual acts, Star's testimony would later be contradicted by Gavin, who recalled a different version of the "incidents." Between the admitted lies and the contradictory testimony, the Arvizos seemed to have the jury confused.

As Michael listened to accusations being hurled around the courtroom by the Arvizo siblings, the superstar looked like he was getting sick to his stomach. Watching these kids twist the facts around, hearing them try to convince the jury that Michael hadn't helped them, that they were his victims, was making Michael increasingly ill.

On the morning of Gavin's testimony, rather than head straight to court, Michael went to see a doctor at a nearby hospital. In chambers, Mesereau went to talk to Judge Melville to ask that Jackson be afforded some special consideration, but Melville didn't want to hear it. Melville required that everyone appear in court precisely at 8:30 AM—and Jackson was no exception.

That morning, the judge ordered Michael Jackson to appear in court within one hour, and threatened to have the superstar arrested and thrown in jail if Jackson did not comply. Following Judge Melville's command, Jackson and his entourage drove at high speeds, and Jackson arrived to the court wearing a jacket over a pair of pajama bottoms, looking dazed and tired as he emerged from his SUV. For Jackson, it wasn't a publicity stunt. For Jackson, it wasn't an act of disrespect.

Some people were convinced that this was Jackson's attempt to gain sympathy from the jury. But insiders knew that the jury wasn't brought into the courtroom until after Michael was seated behind the defense table. The jury could only see Jackson from the waist up, so they didn't know Michael was wearing pajama bottoms at all.

Still, it was the perfect type of weird thing that occurred in Michael's life, one that allowed the media to continue calling Jackson a freak. The image of Jackson in pajamas would be splashed on the front page of the *New York Times* and other major newspapers around the world. In America, Michael going to court in his pajama bottoms was a top news story, and the "wacko" image filled TV screens for days. For the media, it became an excuse to talk about Michael's instability. For a while, the media became so obsessed with pajamas, people forgot that a criminal trial was in progress.

The most interesting thing about Star Arvizo's testimony was his reaction to Mesereau during cross-examination, which had members of the jury scratching their heads. Star told the jury about a deposition that he'd given some years prior, confirming that the Arvizo family filed a civil suit against the JC Penney Corporation. For the jury, Star confirmed that he had previously lied, but when Mesereau asked him to recall an alleged molestation that Star witnessed in a JC Penney parking lot in 1998, Star said he couldn't remember much about the event.

With Star claiming to have witnessed multiple acts of molestation at Neverland, Mesereau kept asking about what type of molestation allegedly happened to his mom, Janet, in a JC Penney parking lot. Tom Mesereau was referring back to Star's JC Penney deposition, but Star was stalling. Ultimately, the jury discovered that an "incident" occurred in 1998, after Gavin Arvizo had taken an item of clothing from a JC Penney store, supposedly to "trick" his father into buying it. They learned that because of Gavin's theft, JC Penney guards followed the Arvizos out to the parking lot, where Star claimed he witnessed JC Penney guards assaulting and inappropriately touching his mother.

Under oath, Star wanted to clarify that his brother would never steal anything, asserting that Gavin wanted to be a comedian and a priest. Fourteen-year-old Star testified that he never used the F-word, but insisted that he heard cursing in the parking lot as JC Penney guards approached them. According to Star's sworn testimony, the JC Penney guards allegedly beat up Janet Arvizo, and also touched her private parts.

To courtroom observers, it seemed that Star admitted too readily that he had previously lied under oath. Star admitted that he'd given false statements about his parents never fighting. Star admitted that he lied about his father never having hit him. Star was trapped by his own deposition and could only say, "It happened a long time ago."

As Mesereau switched the subject to Michael Jackson, Star was already on the defensive, visibly angry that the defense attorney had nailed him.

The day before, under direct examination by Tom Sneddon, Star claimed he had seen his brother being molested by Michael on two specific occasions. Star also claimed that Michael had shared porn magazines with him and his brother, had given wine to both of them, and had simulated having sex with a mannequin in front of them.

However, under cross-examination about the alleged incidents, Star admitted that he had not said anything about the porn, the alcohol, or the molestation to police—not until after he and his family had gone to see Attorney Larry Feldman, the man who handled the famous settlement case for Jordie Chandler and his family.

On the stand, Star testified that it was *Larry Feldman* who suggested that the Arvizo family go see a counselor about the alleged molestation incidents. Star testified that it was sometime in March of 2003, just after Michael Jackson broke off contact with the Arvizo boys, that the Arvizo family was referred to psychologist Stanley Katz. For the jury, Mesereau established that it was only after Star and Gavin voiced their accusations to Feldman and Katz—the same team who had been enlisted by Jordie Chandler and his family—that the Arvizo family decided to go to the police.

As he grilled Star on the stand, Mesereau brought out a number of eye-popping facts. When the testimony became graphic, it was painful to hear the allegations, especially since the boy's testimony wasn't completely adding up. As Star spoke, he seemed cavalier. However, the more detailed the testimony became, the more everyone in the courtroom became part of a collective cringe.

"You told Stanley Katz that Michael Jackson had his left hand on Gavin's crotch, right?" Mesereau asked.

"Yes," Star testified.

"You never told him that Michael Jackson was masturbating Gavin?"

"He wasn't masturbating, he was just feeling," Star said.

"He was just feeling him?"

"Yes."

"Do you remember yesterday you told the jury he was masturbating him?" Mesereau asked.

"No, I said Michael was feeling my brother while he was masturbating."

"Okay. Did you ever tell the jury yesterday that Michael was masturbating your brother?

"No."

"Did you ever tell that to anybody?"

"No," Star insisted.

But Star had implied that he witnessed Jackson masturbating his brother. That was Star's direct testimony the day prior. Now, in front of Mesereau, the judge, and the jury, Star seemed to be backpedaling. The boy seemed to be making things up as he went along.

"Do you remember when you described for Stanley Katz a second time that you went up the stairs and observed Michael touching your brother?"

"Yes."

"Did you tell Stanley Katz that Michael Jackson had his hand on your brother's crotch?"

"Yes."

"That's not really what you told him at all, is it?" Mesereau quipped.

"What are you talking about?" Star said, flustered.

"Well, you told Stanley Katz that Michael Jackson was rubbing his penis against Gavin's buttocks, didn't you?"

"No."

"Would it refresh your recollection if I showed you his grand jury testimony?"

Mesereau pulled out Stanley Katz's grand jury testimony, but Star didn't want to see it. Star denied ever telling Katz anything about Gavin's buttocks, and Mesereau quickly moved to another subject.

"You tried to tell Stanley Katz that you smelled marijuana, didn't you?"

"No," Star testified.

"Would it refresh your recollection if I showed you that page of his testimony?"

"No."

"Okay. Now, are you saying that you never told Michael Jackson you wanted to be an actor?"

"No."

"Never told him that at all?" Mesereau asked again.

"No."

Though Star denied that he ever wanted to be an entertainer, the boy had been in dance school, he'd been in comedy school, and Star had even been the host of a video that was made at Neverland. The jury later viewed the video and saw Star pretending to be a Neverland tour guide, presenting an ad campaign for the Disney-like place. In the video, Star seemed overly zealous, anxious to be on camera. The boy was auditioning, beaming as the centerpiece in a tour of Neverland. It was obvious that Star hoped that this would be his "big break" in show business.

But Star told jurors that he didn't care about making the Neverland video. Star acted like he was doing Jackson a favor by hosting a video tour of Neverland. As Mesereau moved to another topic, the defense attorney wanted Star to explain how he and his brother, Gavin, had gained knowledge of all the alarm codes at Neverland. When Star testified that he and his brother had gotten into Michael's main house "hundreds of times," jurors looked surprised. They learned that the Arvizo family was given the house alarm code *after* their trip to see Michael in Miami. Star testified that, once he knew the code to the main house, he had access to every room in the place, including Michael's bedroom.

At one point, Mesereau asked Star to recall an occasion where he and his brother were caught drinking wine in Michael's wine cellar without Michael being present. Star denied this ever happened, but admitted that he and Gavin knew where the wine cellar key was located. Star denied that he and his brother had ever been caught drinking alone on any occasion. However, Neverland staff members would later testify that they saw Star drink liquor, which the boy had added to his milkshake. On other occasions, Neverland staff had witnessed Star Arvizo drinking alcohol—with Jackson nowhere in sight.

Star wanted to appear innocent. But, observing Star on the stand, he was clearly a boy with an attitude, a boy with a chip on his shoulder. As jurors remained glued to Star's testimony, people on the panel were becoming suspicious.

Star denied ever having done anything wrong at Neverland; he denied having rummaged through Michael's closets and drawers. However, he did admit that he and Gavin were once caught sleeping in Michael's room, when Michael was not on the property.

When Mesereau brought out a briefcase filled with "girly magazines," which Star had identified as the magazines that Michael showed him and his brother, the defense attorney questioned Star about a particular magazine, *Barely Legal*, and Star testified that this was the exact magazine Michael had shown them. Star was positive that he'd handled that magazine, until Mesereau pointed out the date on it was August 2003, months after the Arvizos had left Neverland for good.

Another thing Mesereau brought up was that Star had the weird nickname "Blowhole," which was carved into the cover of the Neverland Valley Ranch guest book. As Mesereau questioned the boy about it, Star admitted he had made that name up for himself, saying that he "got stuck with that name."

For courtroom observers, it was unsettling to note that Star Arvizo admitted to carving up Jackson's leather-bound guest book, Michael's personal keepsake, which was filled with "thank you" notes from celebrities such as Marlon Brando and Jessica Simpson.

The more he testified, the more Star Arvizo had people wondering how anyone could be so brazen, could deface another's property and think nothing of it.

Later, when Star was shown a card that he had written to Michael for Father's Day, in which he referred to Michael as his "super, super best, best friend," the card was signed by "Blowhole Star Arvizo." The card emphatically stated, "Michael, we love you unconditionally, to infinity and beyond forever. Thank you, Michael, for being our family."

Mesereau introduced a number of cards and notes written to Michael by the Arvizos, all of which seemed diametrically opposed to the characterization that Star Arvizo had given the jury about Michael Jackson. In one card, Star wrote, "When we get our hearts broken into tiny little pieces, we always still love, need, and care about you with every tiny little piece of our heart, because you heal us in a very special way."

Star told the jury that he had written that card to Michael when he was age ten, claiming that he didn't mean what he'd written, asserting that he "copied" the words from a card that his grandmother bought in a supermarket. All through his testimony, Star was trying to get around the fact that he and his siblings had been referring to Michael Jackson as "family." Star denied that Michael had acted "like a father" toward them. Star downplayed Michael's charitable role as much as possible.

Though Star refused to admit that he considered Michael a father figure, Star had said otherwise on two tapes, one recorded by Brad Miller on February 16, and another, the rebuttal video, taped by the Arvizos on February 20, 2003.

The Arvizo rebuttal tape would be played over and over again during the trial, and would come back to haunt the accuser and his family, who maintained that none of their comments on the rebuttal tape were true. Star and his family would tell jurors that they never meant to praise Jackson in any way, shape, or form. But in the end, the Arvizos' testimony lacked credibility.

It all seemed so disingenuous, especially when every Arvizo who testified—Davellin, Star, Gavin, and Janet—claimed that they never spoke to each other about the Michael Jackson case whatsoever. Moreover, as each of the Arvizos insisted that the rebuttal tape was a pack of lies, Janet Arvizo went one step further and denied that Michael had done anything to help her son. When it was her turn to testify, Janet told the jury that she and her kids were "reading from a script," and was adamant that none of their praise for Michael was heartfelt.

But if the Arvizos didn't love Michael, they certainly didn't come across that way on the rebuttal tape. Not at all. In that rebuttal tape, the Arvizo kids seemed like they were a part of Michael's inner circle. Well mannered and nicely dressed, all three kids were clearly following their mom's lead. The Arvizos, in unison, were singing Michael's praises to every rooftop. Star Arvizo, along with his mother, brother, and sister, looked into the camera and talked about Jackson being "like family" to them. Each one of them stated that they were grateful that Jackson had taken an interest in them, and said the superstar had helped them when no one else seemed to care.

"Askin' Him to Change His Ways"

With every word of Star's testimony under scrutiny, with the "Neverland Channel" demo tape starring Star Arvizo still fresh in jurors' minds, courtroom observers were struck by Star's glee as he led a group of kids through rides, games, and popcorn fights. The person in the video was entirely different from the young man who sat before the jury. Michael Jackson, watching Star say that he didn't care about narrating the video, claiming that he was "kind of tired" when he taped the "demo" piece, sat extremely still behind the defense table as the young man testified. Michael never moved a muscle. He sat frozen in his seat, watching Star reveal opinions that, frankly, were just not believable.

When another DVD was played that showed Gavin looking sickly, people saw a vision of Michael Jackson that was contrary to any of the dazzling images that Michael was synonymous with. The jury watched Michael walking very slowly with the dying boy, leading Gavin toward a fountain near a pond. It was darling, watching Michael and Gavin walking together, holding each other's back in a very gentle embrace. In a voice-over, Star made the comment, "I feel really bad about my brother. All they know about his cancer is it's aggressive and everything."

In the background of the DVD, Michael was heard singing the words, "Smile, though your heart is breaking … smile, though your heart is aching." It was Michael's attempt to light up Gavin's life, and Gavin was being brave, trying to hide traces of sadness. But it was heavy, that little video clip. The jury saw that Michael was trying so hard to lift Gavin's spirits, but little Gavin was so sickly, the superstar could hardly get a smile out of him.

Tom Mesereau asked Star if Michael spent a lot of time trying to help cure Gavin, if Michael tried to help rid Gavin of his cancer, at which point Star became hostile on the stand. Star didn't recall Michael telling Gavin to use a visualization technique, to suggest that Gavin try to "eat up all the bad cancer cells." If anything, Star seemed angered by Mesereau's questions, because he wanted the jury to believe that Michael had little to do with Gavin's eventual recovery.

When Mesereau introduced the Avrizos' "rebuttal video," Exhibit 340, it started off with the Arvizos getting seated and situated in a grouping of four—Janet and Gavin in the first row, Davellin and Star seated directly behind them, on a small platform. As Janet and her kids whispered to each other, their comments were audible. Clearly they didn't realize that they were being taped the entire time, that the outtake footage of the rebuttal video—and all of it—would be used in court.

An unidentified man called for quiet on the set, and Hamid Moslehi, Jackson's videographer, let the Arvizos know that he wanted them to feel comfortable. He assured them that if there were any questions they didn't want to answer, if there was anything the Arvizos didn't want to discuss, they could speak up, and the matter would be dropped.

As the tape started off, Janet Arvizo seemed to be orchestrating her children, telling them to sit up straight, giving them commands as she prepared to talk about Gavin's cancer. To the camera, Janet explained that "this beautiful relationship [between Michael and her son] was born from something that was very traumatic that flourished into something wonderful."

Gavin detailed the exact moment when he got the first call from Michael, and expressed his shock and thrill when he heard Michael's voice on his grandmother's telephone. Gavin said he and Michael talked for a while about his cancer and confessed that when Michael first mentioned coming to visit Neverland Ranch, he had not heard of Neverland before. Gavin thought Michael was talking about a dude ranch with "horses and stuff."

The boy explained how exciting it was to pack his overnight bag, to get into a limo with his family, to take a two-and-a-half-hour drive to one of the most beautiful places he'd ever seen. Gavin described Michael as "cool." He said that when the family first arrived there, Michael was eating something, that Michael came over and gave everyone a hug and then "left real quick because he had to go do something."

Gavin recalled that first afternoon, when he and Michael "started hanging out together," and said that he asked Michael if he could stay in Michael's room. He said his brother, Star, wanted to stay with Michael too. The idea that Gavin preferred to stay with Michael in the main house, rather than stay in a guest unit with his parents, was evident from the tone of his voice.

"If it's okay with your parents, it's okay with me," Michael told him.

Gavin said he was really happy to hear his parents give their approval. Gavin talked about being in Michael's room, about Michael pulling out a lot of blankets, telling him and Star to sleep on the bed, Michael offering to sleep on the floor. Gavin said that he and Michael went back and forth about it, that Michael finally said, "Okay, if you love me, go sleep on the bed."

Gavin said it was fun sleeping on Michael's big king-sized bed and said that Michael, along with his friend Frank, packed up a bunch of soft blankets and slept on the floor that night, the night of Gavin's very first visit to Neverland.

Gavin's impression of Michael was that he was a "kind, loving, and humble man." He said that "when you talk to him for awhile, it feels like you've known him for a long time." Gavin asserted that he "took to Michael" really quickly and claimed he could feel Michael's "goodness and happiness."

Janet's first impression of Michael was similar. She was thrilled to meet the superstar, and to see her son's face light up the way it did—just took her breath away. Janet said that Michael was an answer to her prayers. Janet swore that the doctors had said there was no way to cure Gavin, that all the treatments were experimental, that the doctors were saying that Gavin's cancer was violent and aggressive. Janet described Michael as "a much necessary love in a very traumatic time in our life."

"You bring him to me, and we will coat him with love," Michael once told Janet. When the doctors were saying there was no chance for Gavin to live, Janet told the camera, "Michael would say, 'I will not have that.' When the doctors said there was no hope, Michael said there was hope.

"By God's grace, God works through people," Janet explained, "and God elected to work in Michael to breathe life into Gavin and to my two other children and me."

Janet went on to describe the fatherly acts that Michael "took upon himself." She said that Gavin needed so many blood transfusions, because he had a rare blood type, O negative. She explained that Michael took an "active fatherly duty" to make sure that Gavin had enough blood, even hosting a fund-raiser so Gavin would have no worries about future blood transfusions.

Janet said that as Michael began helping Gavin more actively, the relationship between Michael and her family started growing. Michael was taking the kids "under his wing," Janet told the camera, and she was elated because with Michael around, "they lacked no father."

The jury watched as Star told the videographer that his first impression of Michael was that he was like a father. "Actually, he seemed more fatherly than my biological father," Star said.

"He gave my brother the extra little spark he needed in his mind," Davellin chimed in. "Because my brother was to the point where he couldn't move, he couldn't even talk. He gave my brother so much."

Janet confided that it was Gavin who asked if he could refer to Michael as "Daddy," and Michael said "of course." Janet said that, for her three children, every door in Neverland was open, and insisted that Michael considered them family. According to the Arvizo kids, Michael acted like a father, sometimes giving them advice, sometimes helping them with homework.

"What I love about Michael is how his interaction is as a father with my children," Janet said. "He gives them direction. He has an awesome sense of humor. He helps them believe that dreams come true for a faithful heart."

The videographer asked Gavin to explain what a "normal day" with Michael was like. Gavin said that he and his siblings would go in the house, find Michael, and greet him. Michael would tell the kids where he was going to be, perhaps in his studio, and then tell the kids "go have fun." The three of them would go play on the rides and watch movies and have fun all day, then later hang out with Michael. Whenever Michael had free time, they would wrestle together, they'd go on rides with Michael, or watch movies together—and they'd always laugh and make jokes.

"He shows them the basic foundation of what life is, and that's a loving family," Janet interjected. "Michael is filled with a lot of loving thoughts. All he wants them to be—is a lady and two gentlemen. And he's assisting me in fulfilling a father figure role they've never had."

"My responsibility as a mother is to make sure that my children are in safety, in a nonharmful environment," Janet continued. "When my children are around Michael, that's what he provides. He spreads his wings and makes sure that the most important thing is that my children are safe and happy. It's a happiness they've never had in their life."

The exact words the Arvizos used to describe Michael were: honest, very trustworthy, humble, loving, caring, funny, unselfish, and attentive. Each of the kids referred to him as "my father," and Janet said how grateful she was to have Michael take her "three little munchkins as his kids."

Gavin spoke of the faith Michael gave him—of the faith Michael kept telling him to have, of Michael providing him with the faith to look forward to the future. Gavin said he never forgot Michael's words, asserting that, early on, he depended on those words of faith to get him through many rounds of chemotherapy.

When the interview turned to the subject of the Bashir documentary, the Arvizo family became agitated. They each expressed disgust with the way Martin Bashir twisted Gavin's relationship with Michael into something that might seem dirty and wrong. In particular, they were angry that Bashir had made Gavin and Michael's relationship seem sinister. They resented the sexual innuendos, and felt that the media was out for Michael's blood, that the media was dragging them through a scandal that had no merit.

For the record, Janet defended her position as a mom, stating that whenever she had been at Neverland with her family, she had "full access to go anywhere in the house."

"They [the media] were the ones with the dirty minds," Davellin said.

"They're the ones that stirred all this up," Gavin said. "They're the ones that have problems themselves."

"It disturbs me terribly, anyone who is thinking wrong, who is making innuendos," Janet said. "Gavin, out of all three, has had the most traumatic endurance, and Michael was giving him support. They were both on camera [in the Bashir documentary] and holding hands was a natural thing. Tell me, you fathers out there, or the ones that wish they could be a father, or the ones that were once a child. Didn't you want your father to hold your hand? Especially through the most troubling times? Especially when you knew and were given no chance to live?"

Janet looked into the camera and said that the doctors had told her to "plan for a funeral." She said the doctors told her that if the cancer didn't kill Gavin, the chemotherapy would. When Janet complained to Michael that her son was "not going to make it," Michael would tell her not to listen to that. Michael insisted that Gavin would live. Years later, Gavin would be told by doctors that there was no scientific explanation for him to be alive, that his cancer cure was a "miracle."

As she continued to praise Michael, Janet called Michael a "very fit parent" who took every opportunity to give expressions of love and affection to his own children, as well as her three rascals. She said that Michael was very proud of Gavin "as a little warrior" in his fight against cancer.

"Because Michael believed, we all believed," Janet said. "When Michael makes expressions of love towards my children—for someone to taint that and make it a disturbing turmoil and spin it out of control, I could only say to reach inside their heart and pull out an innocent love, 'cause that's what Michael and Gavin have."

"They don't understand Michael," Gavin concluded. "The reason they have a misconception and don't understand is—they could understand him—but they don't know Michael. They say all these things and they don't even know Michael. The misconception is that they could take a word, like any word I say, and they could change it up and say all these bad things about it. It's their own misconception, they make it a misconception."

Before the rebuttal video ended, Janet admitted that all three of her kids had a "humongous wish to be in movies." She indicated that her children expressed their showbiz dreams to Michael, who allegedly once told Gavin, "Okay, okay, you're all better now, and you're going to be in movies."

"If You Wanna Make the World a Better Place—Take a Look at Yourself and Make a Change"

When fifteen-year-old Gavin took the stand, he looked clean-cut, wearing a blue button-down shirt with dark dress pants. Gavin talked about the one-room bachelor apartment that he and his family had lived in on Soto Street, testifying that the whole family slept in one bed together. Gavin explained that after he got cancer, he moved into his grandparents' home to live in a sterile room, and during that time, his mom and dad "would fight every day" over bills and other "control" issues. Gavin said he witnessed physical violence between his father and mother. He then talked about his introduction to the Laugh Factory, where he received coaching from comedian George Lopez.

Once he became sick with cancer, Gavin testified, he made a request to meet Jay Leno. Gavin thought Leno was a "really nice comedian," and said that Leno was someone he always wanted to meet. Through Jamie Masada, Gavin was given Leno's phone number, but according to Gavin, he only spoke to an answering machine, where he left numerous messages for Leno, without ever talking to the entertainer.

Of all the celebrities Gavin met during his fight with cancer, including Chris Tucker and Kobe Bryant, he said Michael Jackson was his favorite. Gavin testified that other celebrities had held "benefit" performances at the Laugh Factory in order to help pay for his cancer treatments, and testified that, once Michael Jackson started calling the hospital, more than twenty phone conversations transpired between him and Michael—before he actually met the superstar. When the Arvizo family first went up to Neverland, Gavin said he thought Michael was the "coolest guy ever." Within hours of their first in-person encounter, Gavin felt like Michael was his "best friend in the world." Gavin spoke in a soft voice, looking away from Michael Jackson. As members of the jury took vigilant notes, they were watching Jackson's cold stare. The superstar seemed utterly disgusted with the boy.

Gavin said that on his first visit to Neverland, he took a "driving test" with Michael in a golf cart. Michael wanted to be sure that Gavin was able to drive around the property on his own. He wanted to be sure that Gavin was strong enough to handle going on rides. When Gavin proved that he was feeling okay, that he could handle driving the golf cart, Michael let him go off with his siblings for a day of fun.

Contrary to what he'd said in the rebuttal video, Gavin claimed that the subject of sleeping in Michael's room was not his idea. He testified that it was Michael who had suggested it, claiming that Michael suggested that Gavin ask his parents about it at dinner that first night.

Later that night, up in Jackson's bedroom, Gavin said he and his brother watched episodes of *The Simpsons* and were introduced to porn sites by Michael's close friend Frank Casio. Gavin described looking at "female adult materials" with Michael and Frank on the Internet—photos of topless women whom Michael allegedly made fun of and said, "Got milk?"

Gavin testified that he'd visited Neverland Ranch a total of seven times during his battle with cancer, stating that he was accompanied there by his mother only once—on his first trip to the property. The boy confirmed that he made a short video with Michael, where he was in a wheelchair being led around by Star. Of the seven occasions that Gavin visited the ranch in that given time period, he testified that he only spent time with Michael on two occasions.

Throughout the rest of his visits to Neverland, Michael was either not on the property or was not available. Gavin seemed angry about a time when he "bumped into" Michael at Neverland after having been told that Michael was not on the grounds. The boy testified that "Michael played it off" like it was no big deal. But it was obvious that Gavin was hurt about not having the chance to spend more time with Michael, that he felt betrayed by Michael's evasive behavior.

When Tom Sneddon asked Gavin about the Bashir documentary, the boy recalled being driven up to the ranch by Chris Tucker—accompanied by his brother and sister. Gavin claimed that Michael had contacted him by phone, that Michael wanted him to come to the ranch to meet Mr. Bashir, and Gavin agreed, though he said he wasn't sure what the "meeting" was about. Gavin testified that when he arrived at Neverland, Michael talked to him about another young man, a burn victim named David, whose father had poured gasoline all over his body. To Gavin, Jackson explained that Mr. Bashir was doing a documentary about some of the kids whom Michael had helped. In his testimony, Gavin claimed that Michael made it seem like this would be Gavin's opportunity to "act" and "audition" for the camera, emphasizing that Michael personally requested that Gavin tape an interview with Bashir.

As Gavin answered questions, he seemed to be telling the jury that his Bashir interview wasn't genuine, that Michael had coached him, that Michael had asked him to call him "Daddy" or "Dad." Gavin intimated that Michael had asked him to portray a certain image for the camera, that Michael wanted Gavin to give the impression that the two of them were like "family." Gavin testified that Jackson wanted Bashir to know how much he helped him, and claimed that Michael told him to say "he pretty much cured me of cancer."

Gavin trashed the Bashir documentary, particularly the scene where Gavin had praised Michael and had spoken highly of Michael's care and concern as a father figure in his life. On the witness stand, Gavin denied almost everything he told Bashir. Gavin told the jury that Michael "was hardly even there" during his cancer treatments, that it was Chris Tucker and George Lopez who visited him in the hospital. Gavin was hard-pressed to admit his admiration for Michael, and though he couldn't completely deny the nice things he'd said about Michael in the Bashir interview, Gavin no longer wanted to credit Michael with healing him.

On the stand, Gavin seemed to be annoyed with Michael, explaining that just hours after the Bashir footage was taped, Michael had left Neverland, and seemed to vanish into thin air. Gavin testified that he and his siblings stayed in a guest unit for one night, but they never saw Michael Jackson again on that particular visit, nor did Gavin hear from Michael again—until after the Bashir documentary aired, several months later.

"A Bizarre Day in the Jackson Case"
"Jackson Avoids Arrest During Drama-Filled Day"

It was the next morning, March 10, 2005, when Michael Jackson had not shown up to court on time. Inside the court, Mesereau explained to the judge that Jackson was receiving medical treatment at a nearby hospital. Everyone could see that Judge Melville was visibly upset, and the judge ordered Mesereau to produce Michael Jackson by 9:30 AM—or have Jackson face arrest and forfeiture of his $3 million bail. Outside, the media was all aflutter, watching Tom Mesereau talking on his cell phone in the parking lot, looking concerned and anxious over his client's whereabouts.

As the media continued to gather outside under their tents, placing wagers about whether Jackson would make it to court in time, news producers were tracking Jackson's motorcade via helicopter updates. Reporters in helicopters supplied news teams on the ground with a minute-by-minute account of Jackson's motorcade, which was spotted about forty-five minutes away from the courthouse and was traveling at speeds exceeding ninety miles an hour.

Everyone wondered if Melville would actually throw Michael in jail for being late, and people were placing imaginary bets on the outcome of the morning, wondering if Melville would revoke Jackson's bail if the superstar didn't manage to make it through traffic. As Michael and his motorcade were fighting to beat the clock, fans were clinging to the courthouse fences, hoping to overhear details about Michael's progress. Many fans were tuning into the news by using their car radios. The buzz was tremendous. People were on their cell phones, people were text messaging—it was clear that everyone was nervous.

And then—out of a cloud of cheers—Michael's car appeared about five minutes after the deadline. Fans were going nuts as Michael walked slowly from his vehicle. Wearing blue pajama bottoms, slippers, a white T-shirt, and a dark blue blazer, everyone was gawking a the concocted outfit. People in the media were dumbfounded, unable to make sense out of it. For fans, there was jubilation that Michael had managed to make it to court on time. For the media, there was a mix of reactions, primarily geared at tearing Michael down.

"Oh my God, he's wearing pajamas!" people were whispering. Cell phones and BlackBerrys were buzzing, and live reports were being broadcast about Michael looking "groggy" as he made his way into Judge Melville's court. As observers watched Michael take his seat behind the defense table, people couldn't stop making comments about Michael's "crazy pajamas." Some media folks talked about his hair being out of place, and concluded that Michael was wearing a wig that hadn't been combed. Others asserted that Michael was "overmedicated" and noted that his steps were sluggish. Everyone had remarks they whispered under their breath—and all were in agreement that Michael's appearance was not going to be appreciated by the judge.

Regardless of what anyone thought of Michael's bizarre appearance, the courtroom buzz quickly ended as Judge Melville entered the room. When the jury filed in, they were politely told by Melville, "I'm sorry for the delay. Mr. Jackson had a medical problem this morning, and it was necessary for me to order his appearance."

With those words, Gavin Arvizo was brought into court via a special entrance, and that morning, Thursday, March 10, the boy's graphic allegations against Michael Jackson would describe two acts of specific molestation.

Everyone in the court wondered why Gavin's account of these alleged acts differed greatly from the account that Star had already given about the same two incidents. But people were giving the witness the benefit of the doubt.

Regarding the alleged molestations, no exact time or date was given by Gavin, but the boy testified that the alleged acts occurred in the weeks following his family's trip to Miami, just after the airing of the Bashir documentary. To courtroom observers, the time line seemed weird, especially when evidence was presented that showed the list of media who were hounding Neverland Ranch in the aftermath of the Bashir piece. Apparently, "Jackson's people" were being bombarded for days, and the phones at Neverland rang off the hook.

The messages left for Michael Jackson, specifically on February 6, 2003, came from *Entertainment Tonight*, *Extra*, *Good Morning America*, Jack Sussman, the top executive at CBS, *Larry King Live*, Connie Chung at CNN, SkyNews London, Bell Yard in London, and Barbara Walters on behalf of *20/20* for ABC. And that was only the first round of messages.

Inside sources would confide that for days, the whole world was calling, trying desperately to gain an interview with Michael about the mysterious boy, the cancer victim with whom Michael had held hands, with whom Michael had admitted to sharing his bed. Though Michael told Bashir that their relationship was innocent, that he and Gavin and other children slept in his bed together, the media didn't believe Michael when he said that "sharing your bed" was a loving act. The media wanted more. They wanted dirt.

In front of the jury, Gavin claimed that Jackson molested him in the wake of a brewing scandal, with the media world calling, with authorities beginning investigations—but his manner and tone just didn't seem right. Gavin would give specific testimony about the two alleged acts. He would talk about being masturbated by Jackson. But there was something about his calm demeanor that seemed staged. Gavin's recollection appeared to be questionable.

Gavin told the jury that Michael had reached into his pajamas, that Michael had said that masturbation was natural—but those were the same words that had been used in the Jordie Chandler suit. Because Gavin admitted that he and his family had gone to see Jordie's lawyer before ever going to the police, people in the courtroom were trying the read between the lines. At first, Gavin's testimony seemed to have a ring of truth, but then, so much of what he said seemed scripted, perhaps by his mother, and Gavin's recollection of events was later contradicted by other witnesses. The boy testified that he was given wine to drink on the private plane ride back from Miami, that he and his family were taken back to Neverland in a white SUV limo with Michael. Gavin explained that when they arrived there, after driving around in the golf carts for awhile, later that night, Star and Gavin slept in Michael's bed with him—but still—nothing sexual happened. Gavin recalled that on that night, he and his brother, along with Frank and Aldo Casio, and Michael, made crank "phony" phone calls and goofed around for hours.

Gavin asserted that, upon his return to Neverland from Miami, he was drinking alcohol "every night," and described the secret wine cellar that Michael had in his arcade, hidden behind a jukebox that opened up onto a small staircase. Gavin testified that he'd been given wine by Michael at that location and said that he and Michael went down to the wine cellar by themselves on five occasions— bringing alcohol upstairs so that he and his brother could drink with Michael "in his office and in his room."

For the record, Gavin admitted that he and his brother had gone down to the wine cellar on at least one occasion—without Michael present.

As he spoke to the jury, Gavin swore that he told Michael it was bad for him to drink alcohol. Gavin claimed that he told Michael that he only had one kidney, but Michael said it was "okay," that "nothing was going to happen." Gavin testified that Michael provided him with Bacardi, Jim Beam, vodka, and wine, which Michael called, "Jesus Juice" because "Jesus drank it."

Gavin told jurors that the first time he tasted vodka was in the secret wine cellar, when Michael handed him a big glass, which he thought was water. He claimed he "chucked down" the whole glass all at once, and "it started burning." A few seconds later, Gavin testified, the whole room was spinning, so he put his head down on a couch. The boy claimed that he "passed out" from drinking once or twice and that he felt nauseated a lot at Neverland, though he never vomited or complained to his mother.

Gavin would later admit that, in the weeks following their trip to Miami, his mom, Janet, along with his sister Davellin, and brother Star, were staying at Neverland the entire time that Gavin was a guest there. Tom Sneddon asked when Gavin began calling Michael, "Daddy," Gavin said it was a few weeks after they returned from Miami that Michael started calling him "son," that he would call him "Dad."

Then Sneddon showed Gavin a note, allegedly handwritten to him by Michael:

"I want you to have a good time in Florida. I'm very happy to be your DADDY. Blanket, Prince, and Paris are your brothers and sisters. But you really have to be honest in your heart that I am your DAD and will take good care of you." DAD

As Sneddon continued his line of questioning, Gavin Arvizo admitted that at the time of the rebuttal video, February 20, 2003, "nothing bad happened" when he stayed with Michael Jackson in his bedroom. Gavin further testified that on the same day that the family taped their rebuttal video, they had also been interviewed by three social workers who worked for the Department of Children and Family Services in Los Angeles.

That interview, Gavin said, was conducted at the home of Major Jay Jackson, his mom's new boyfriend. When the three LA social workers asked the Arvizo family a series of questions about Michael Jackson—once again, Gavin would insist that "nothing bad happened" with Michael in his bedroom.

As Gavin spoke to the members of the jury, Michael sat stone-faced.

At times, the superstar would shake his head in disbelief, especially as Tom Sneddon continued to prod the boy for answers. Gavin was able to recall things he had told the grand jury and mentioned that Michael had once walked into the master bedroom naked, telling the Arvizo boys that being nude was "natural." Contrary to his brother's testimony, Gavin said that Michael was not in an aroused state when he happened to walk by the mirror in the nude. The jury seemed a bit perplexed to hear that Gavin's version of events didn't mesh with his brother's testimony.

Many things that Gavin swore to were in direct contrast to the testimony of his siblings. But as the jury watched Gavin weave his story, there was only one thing they wanted to focus on: the specific claims about molestation.

Though it was difficult for people in the court to hear Gavin talk about it, the young boy didn't seem uncomfortable. Gavin spoke in "matter-of-fact" terms. There were no tears from the boy. There was little emotion, really, whatsoever.

"So you were in the room a while, and the defendant started talking to you about masturbation?" Sneddon wanted to know.

"Yes," Gavin said.

"What did he say to you?"

"He told me that if men don't masturbate, they can get to a level where they might rape a girl, or they might be, like, kind of unstable. So he was telling me that guys have to masturbate," Gavin explained.

"What else did he say to you?"

"He told me a story of how he saw a boy one time—he was looking over a balcony or something—and he saw a boy who didn't masturbate and he had sex with a dog."

"Did he say anything else to you during this conversation?"

"He told me that males have to masturbate."

"All right. Now, when he said that, what, if anything, did he do or say after that?" Sneddon asked.

"He said that if I masturbated, and I told him that I didn't," Gavin answered. "And then he said that if I didn't know how, he would do it for me."

"And what did you say?"

"And I said that I really didn't want to."

"All right. And then what happened?"

Gavin testified that Michael went under the covers, put his hand in the boy's pajamas, and started masturbating him. He told the jury that he didn't really look at Michael while this was happening, but claimed that he could feel Michael moving himself, though he never saw Michael moving. When Star had given his account of the event, claiming that he had witnessed the molestation from Michael's staircase, Star said he saw Michael reaching into Gavin's "underwears." The two accounts didn't match at all—Gavin was telling the jury that this act happened while he and Michael were alone "under the covers," yet Star claimed that he'd seen the actual act, watching from Michael's bedroom staircase, just a few feet away from the bed—after having tripped an alarm that made a doorbell sound when Star first entered Michael's bedroom suite.

"Do you know approximately how long Mr. Jackson masturbated you?"

"Maybe five minutes, I guess."

"Do you know what an ejaculation is?"

"Yes," Gavin said.

"And did you have an ejaculation?"

"Yes."

Gavin testified that he felt embarrassed about it, but Michael told him it was "natural." The boy said he felt weird about the incident, but then fell asleep a few minutes later. The next time Michael touched him, Gavin claimed, was a few nights later. They had just come back from the arcade, they were sitting on the bed watching TV, and then, "He did it again."

"Now, tell us what happened," Sneddon asked.

"The same thing happened again," Gavin said. "He said that he wanted to teach me. And we were laying there, and he started doing it to me. And then he kind of grabbed my hand in a way to try to do it to him. And I kind of pulled my hand away, because I didn't want to do it."

"How long do you think it lasted the second time?" Sneddon asked.

"The same time," Gavin said.

"Did you ejaculate the second time?"

"I think I did."

When Gavin told the jury that there was no other occasion where Mr. Jackson had done anything inappropriate to him, Tom Sneddon had nothing further. The boy was now Mesereau's witness, and as he did with every person who took the stand, the defense attorney spoke the words:

"My name is Tom Mesereau, and I speak for Mr. Jackson, okay?"

Gavin said okay.

"I'm on his side, all right?" Mesereau wanted Gavin to be sure.

"All right," Gavin answered.

As Mesereau reassured Gavin that he was not on the government's side, that he was on the side of Michael Jackson, the defense attorney made it very clear to Gavin that he wanted the young man to speak up if there was anything about a question that he didn't understand.

"Now, you've told the jury that it was not until after your interview with three social workers that any inappropriate touching happened, right?" Mesereau asked.

"Hmmmmm?"

"Did you tell the jury that it was not until after your interview with three social workers in Los Angeles that Mr. Jackson inappropriately touched you?"

"It was after," Gavin said.

"It was after, right?"

"Yes."

"Now, in that interview, you told the three social workers that Mr. Jackson was a good guy, right?" Mesereau asked.

"Yes."

To Mesereau, Gavin admitted that he'd told the social workers that Michael was "a father figure." As Mesereau seemed to spin Gavin around on the stand, it wouldn't be long before Mesereau established that the alleged molestation incidents didn't occur until after the Arvizo family visited a civil attorney, about a week before the Arvizos left Neverland Ranch for the last time.

Tom Mesereau decided not to treat Gavin Arvizo as a child. He took his chances, and sunk his teeth into the witness, using a staccato-style of questioning, quick and to the point. The gamble paid off, it seemed, because the jury came to see another side of Gavin Arvizo, one that wasn't so sympathetic. The charming side of the boy—which was apparent in the rebuttal tape and in the Bashir documentary—had suddenly disappeared. With Mesereau at the helm, Gavin Arvizo quickly became testy and argumentative.

"So what you're telling the jury is that after you were interviewed by three social workers investigating Michael Jackson, and after all the commotion that followed the Bashir documentary, somehow, Mr. Jackson starts to improperly touch you, correct?" Mesereau wanted to know.

"No, it was more toward the end," Gavin said. "Toward when we were about to leave, after we'd been drinking alcohol and all that stuff. It was maybe a week before we left Neverland for good," Gavin said.

At times, during his many days of testimony, Gavin would look over at Michael and flash the superstar disapproving looks. Occasionally, the boy would mumble under his breath, especially when Tom Mesereau would insinuate that Gavin Arvizo and his siblings were liars, coached by their mother. Mesereau would systematically bring up the JC Penney case, reminding jurors that the Arvizo kids had lied in the past—and had gained a financial civil settlement out of the JC Penney Corporation.

The implication was the Arvizos would say anything to get money.

About the conspiracy theory, about the Arvizos being held against their will at Neverland—Mesereau would argue that this was nonsense. The defense attorney was able to prove that the Arvizos left Neverland—then returned—on as many as three occasions. During that time, while the Arvizos claimed they were being held "captive," Janet and her children were treated to hotel-style living at Neverland. In addition, Janet and her kids were being escorted to local towns by Michael's drivers, they were going to see dentists and were purchasing toys—all at Michael's expense. Mesereau produced a list of financial transactions showing that Neverland Valley Entertainment had paid "several thousand dollars" for cosmetics, clothing, beauty treatments, meals, and lodging.

"We proved that these children were taught to lie under oath, that was one of our arguments to the jury," Mesereau later confided. "The Arvizo kids learned to work with lawyers at an early age. We were using the JC Penney case as an example of that. We hoped to show the jury that these children were taught to exaggerate, to make things up, to support their mother and father's allegations, whether they were true or not, at an early age."

The information about Janet Arvizo's previous allegations, about her family's claims that Janet had been assaulted and sexually molested by JC Penney guards, would be more than devastating for the Arvizos. As Gavin was asked basic questions about the case—about the Arvizos receiving a $152,000 settlement from the JC Penney Corporation—the boy seemed unable to dig himself out of a hole.

"We felt the Arvizos' claims were outrageous," Mesereau continued. "We proved that the mother alleged that JC Penney guards had done belly flops on top of her in the parking lot. When the incident happened in the parking lot of JC Penney, the Arvizo parents were arrested. Looking at Janet's intake forms on the day she was arrested, she indicated that she didn't need any medical attention. Janet claimed she didn't have any medical problems. When we looked at the booking photos, Janet Arvizo didn't have a hair out of place. We think that evidence was devastating."

Ron Zonen would introduce photos of Janet Arvizo's alleged bruises, asserting that Janet Arvizo had been badly beaten. But Mesereau would later prove that Janet was not beaten on the day of her arrest. The attorney thought that perhaps the photos were fake, or perhaps they were taken some time after her arrest and release. In the face of police booking information—none of the Arvizos could provide testimony that explained the evidence Mesereau presented, which indicated that Janet had been beaten up *days after* the JC Penney incident. Mesereau's research would show that some time after the fact, Janet Arvizo brought photos of herself "full of bruises," handing them over to an attorney in order to file a civil suit against JC Penney. To her civil attorney, Janet claimed that the bruises had shown up days later, even though on the day of her arrest at JC Penney, Janet had filled out a police booking form stating that she needed "no medical treatment." To fortify her case, Janet used Gavin and Star Arvizo, both of whom swore that they witnessed a brutal sexual and physical assault of their mother on the cement ground of a parking lot.

"You went to two lawyers and a psychologist, whom Larry Feldman referred you to, before you went to any police officer, right?" Mesereau asked, returning back to the subject of Jackson.

"Yes," Gavin admitted.

"Now, these weren't the first attorneys you've ever talked to, correct?"

"I've talked to other attorneys before."

"You had an attorney representing you in the JC Penney case, correct?"

"I think so, I'm pretty sure."

"You testified under oath in that case, correct?"

"Yes," Gavin said.

"Did you tell the truth under oath in that case?"

"Of course."

"Didn't tell one solitary lie?"

"No."

"You said that security guards had body slammed your mother in the parking lot?" Mesereau snapped.

But Sneddon objected to the question, and Mesereau had to move on.

(above) A vehicle drives by the train station at Neverland as police begin their search of Jackson's estate. (State's exhibit)

(below) Aerial view of the Neverland grounds, detailing where Jackson spent most of his time on the twenty-seven-hundred-acre. (State's exhibit)

(above) The front door entrance to the main house at Neverland. (State's exhibit)

(below) A partial view of Jackson's living room, cluttered with toys and books. A law enforcement agent studies Peter Pan depicted on a mural. (State's exhibit)

(above) A partial view of Jackson's living room, with Michael prominently depicted as an angelic figure. (State's exhibit)

(below) Law enforcement agents are baffled by the mannequins that fill Jackson's home. A painting of Jackson being crowned in the forefront. (State's exhibit)

(above) Another view of Jackson's bedroom suite, law enforcement pointing to an adult magazine mixed in with all the clutter. (State's exhibit)

(below) The "toy room" in Jackson's house, featuring Superman, Batman, and R2-D2, located next to the "doll room" on the upper level of the home. (State's exhibit)

(above) Michael Jackson's bedroom, upstairs, with a strange painting of "The Last Supper" depicting Jackson in the center, flanked by Abe Lincoln, JFK, Thomas Edison, and Albert Einstein to his right. The images to his left are not clear, though one appears to be the entertainer Little Richard. (State's exhibit)

(below) A side view of Jackson's bedroom, the upstairs suite, showing the collection of toys and unopened games that Michael kept by his side. (State's exhibit)

(above) A law enforcement agent inspects Jackson's master bathroom in the 1993 raid on Neverland. (State's exhibit)

(below) Law enforcement takes inventory of the types of games that fill Jackson's arcade. (State's exhibit)

(above) View of Jackson's arcade from another angle. (State's exhibit)

(below) Jackson's personal movie theater included a separate bedroom where anyone could watch a film through a glass wall. (State's exhibit)

(above) Jackson's garage was filled with Rolls-Royces. One Rolls-Royce was used to drive the accuser and his family from Neverland to LA. (State's exhibit)

(below) Outside the Jackson's garage, there were golf carts that looked like mini cars. The accuser later crashed one of these carts, even though he had passed a driving test. (State's exhibit)

(above) Michael Jackson, in his recording studio, seems more concerned about his music than anything else. (State's exhibit)

(below) Jackson, under his trademark umbrella, personally escorts accuser Gavin Arvizo (in wheelchair) and his brother, Star Arvizo, around Neverland. (State's exhibit)

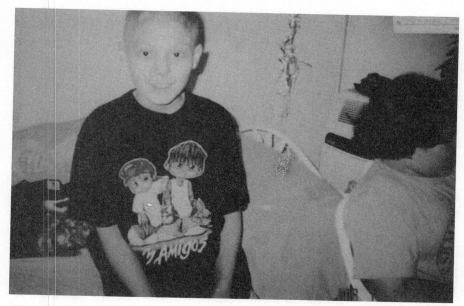

(above) Accuser Gavin Arvizo met Michael Jackson while he was being treated for an unknown cancer. Seated in his grandparents' "germ-free" bedroom, the boy lost his hair when he underwent chemotherapy. (State's exhibit)

(below) The accuser (center) with his brother (left) and his sister (far right) enjoys a party at Neverland. All three are escorted to Neverland by *Rush Hour* star Chris Tucker. Michael Jackson was not on the property that day. (State's exhibit)

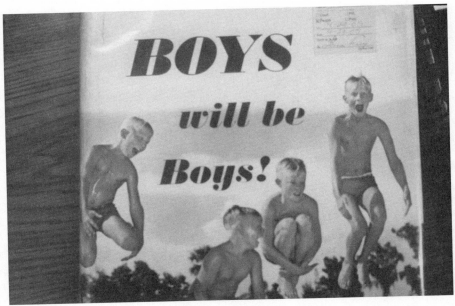

(above) *Boys will be Boys* was one of the books prosecutors used to try to affirm their sexual allegations against Jackson. (State's exhibit)

(below) Law enforcement displays the two bottles of open alcohol that were found in Jackson's bedroom suite in the 2003 raid. (State's exhibit)

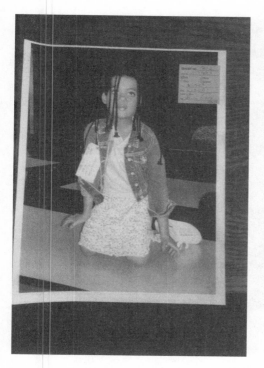

(left) The accuser and his brother claimed that Jackson simulated having sex with the mannequin depicted here. Jackson's defense team would deny that allegation and would point out that this mannequin was a replica of one of Michael's cousins. (State's exhibit)

(below) Jackson and Jordie Chandler wear matching hats, as they sit with a group in Las Vegas. Jordie Chandler, who received a large settlement from Jackson, did not cooperate with prosecutors. (State's exhibit)

(above) *Home Alone* star Macaulay Culkin was part of Jackson's "Apple Head" club. Culkin would later testify on behalf of the defense. (State's exhibit)

(below) Accuser, Gavin Arvizo, writes a note to Jackson, signing it, "your son, Gavin." (State's exhibit)

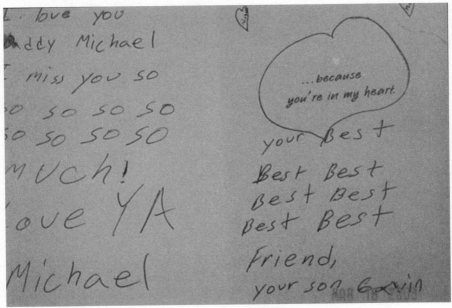

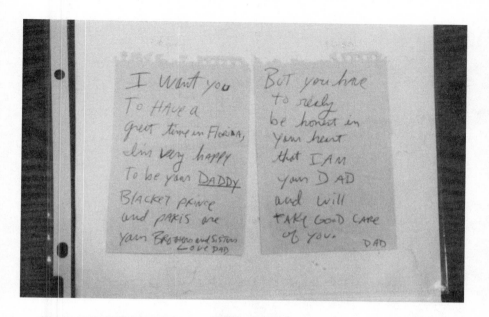

(above) Michael Jackson writes a note to Gavin, saying that he will take good care of him, signing it, "DAD." (State's exhibit)

(left) Frank Casio (left) was the person Michael Jackson trusted most, especially when it came to issues involving the accuser and his family. (State's exhibit)

(left) Aldo Casio, Frank's younger brother, was a regular in Jackson's life, spending a lot of time with the accuser and his family. (State's exhibit)

(right) Marie-Nicole Casio, Frank's younger sister, was with the accuser and his family on the private plane flight from Miami to Santa Barbara. Marie Nicole was a fixture in Michael's bedroom suite, and was also like "family" to Michael Jackson. (State's exhibit)

(above) Janet "Jackson" Arvizo, the accuser's mom, was a disaster for the prosecution. (State's exhibit)

(below) David Arvizo, the accuser's dad, drove his kids to Neverland on numerous occasions. Though he did not appear in court, the testimony against him was damning. (State's exhibit)

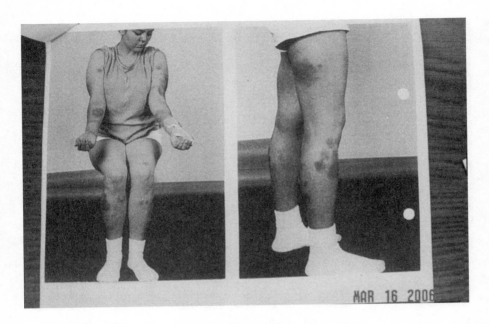

MAR 16 2006

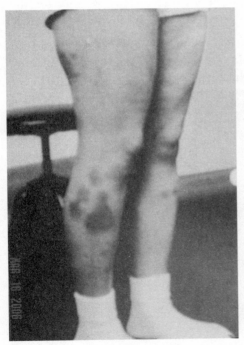

(above) The bruises on Janet Arvizo, who filed a previous sexual abuse and assault case against JC Penney guards. Though she had no bruises visible to police on the day of the alleged attack, some time later, Mrs. Arvizo would take these mysterious snapshots to a civil attorney. (State's exhibit)

(left) Close-up of Janet Arvizo's bruises, allegedly the result of an attack by JC Penney guards. Both of her sons (Gavin and Star) would give sworn testimony stating that they witnessed the attack. The JC Penney Corporation would later settle with Mrs. Arvizo and her children by paying Janet Arvizo $152,000. (State's exhibit)

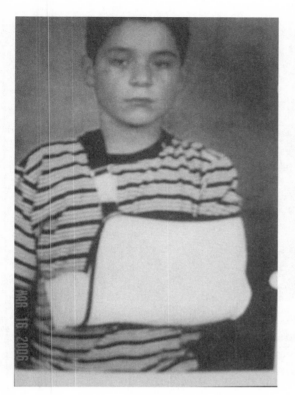

(left) Accuser Gavin Arvizo gave a sworn statement in the JC Penney civil case, offering this photo as "proof" that he too, was beaten up by JC Penney guards. The defense would assert that, like his mother, Gavin's bruises did not materialize until many days after the alleged attack. (State's exhibit)

(below) The leather-bound cover of the Neverland Valley guest book defaced by the accuser's brother, Star Arvizo. (State's exhibit)

(above) Outside the Santa Maria courthouse, former O. J. Simpson prosecutor, Marcia Clark, happily provides coverage of the trial for the popular show *Entertainment Tonight*. (Author's photo)

(below) Michael Jackson supporters were adamant that the King of Pop was the victim of a conspiracy.

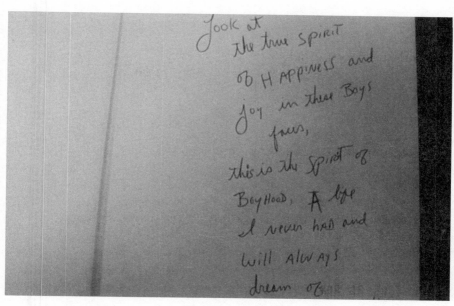

(above) Michael Jackson's inscription on a book about boys was largely ignored by mainstream media. (State's exhibit)

"Who's Bad?"

The trial entered its third week of testimony with Gavin Arvizo still on the stand, but the media was distracted as Pope John Paul II was released from the hospital, having undergone surgery to ease his breathing. In Rome, Pope John Paul II was making international news, where a gray Mercedes minivan that carried the eighty-four-year-old pontiff to the Vatican had Santa Maria news teams scurrying to make plans to fly to Vatican City.

As Pope John Paul II waved and blessed the thousands of cheering Romans and tourists in St. Peter's Square, news teams learned that the pope was not cured. News media became so concerned about the pope, they ignored details about Jackson's accuser, who was now under heavy attack by Mesereau. Rather than pay close attention to Gavin's testimony, news teams were worried that they might have to pull the plug on the Jackson coverage altogether. There were rumors that the pope would not recover.

Michael Jackson, who had come back into the courtroom looking strong, wore a bold red jacket on the day his accuser was under fire. With Mesereau ready to impeach Gavin Arvizo, the pop star looked rather confident, yet at the same time, Michael was in a pensive mood. Michael was reflective, and seemed saddened that his attempt to help the Arvizo clan had backfired so drastically.

As Mesereau began firing questions, Gavin admitted that he'd met with the dean of his Los Angeles middle school, Jeffrey Alpert, just days after the Bashir documentary aired. The dean, Mr. Alpert, called Gavin in to ask him a direct question about the allegations regarding Michael Jackson. From the witness stand, Gavin looked down at the floor and admitted that he'd told his middle school dean that nothing sexual had happened between himself and Michael.

Mesereau went through a laundry list of Gavin's disciplinary problems at his high school. Referring to detailed school records, Mesereau told the jury that Gavin Arvizo had been disruptive in many classes, had been asked to write another student an apology note, had been accused of singing in the classroom, had been accused of talking and disrupting testing, and had been accused of being defiant and disrespectful to a list of teachers. Gavin Arvizo was the subject of numerous memos commenting on his bad behavior and his refusal to do homework, and Gavin's rude behavior seemed to translate, at times, to his manner in the court.

"Do you remember having discussions with Mr. Davy [the school vice principal] about your disciplinary problems?" Mesereau asked.

"Yes," Gavin said.

"And please tell the jury what those discussions were all about."

"I don't really remember too good."

Mesereau showed Gavin a copy of his school records, from which dates and memos were extracted.

"Did you ever have a discussion with Mr. Davy about your disciplinary problems with other teachers?"

"Yes."

"Please tell the jury what went on in that discussion."

"I don't really remember too good. I mean, he would tell me to get better, and stuff like that."

"Do you know someone named Bender?"

"Yes, yes. Miss Bender."

"You entered Miss Bender's class in world history and geography in 2002, right?"

"Uh-huh," Gavin nodded yes.

"Okay. And she complained that you were defiant on a regular basis and disrespectful to her, correct?"

"Yes, I believe so."

"She also said that you appeared to have good acting skills, right?"

"I don't know if she said that."

"Would it refresh your recollection if I show you her memo to Mr. Davy?"

Gavin claimed his memory couldn't be refreshed. He denied having "good acting skills" even though he admitted that he was studying drama with an acting teacher, Mr. Martinez, another teacher who'd written Gavin up as a disciplinary problem.

As for Michael, who sat quietly for much of Gavin's testimony, there were times when he would whisper to his defense team, especially when Gavin's answers were contradictory and antagonistic. Gavin was trying to deny that he had written many cards and letters referring to Jackson as "Daddy Michael," but Mesereau had the actual cards and letters, which were entered into evidence.

"Have you had a chance to look at that document?" Mesereau wondered.

"Yes," Gavin said.

"And you wanted to go to New York and be with Mr. Jackson in a recording studio, right?"

"I guess. [Long pause.] I mean, yeah."

"And that didn't happen, right?"

"No."

"You never traveled with Mr. Jackson to New York?"

"I never traveled with Mr. Jackson."

"You called him the nicest, most loving person in the world, right?"

"Yes."

"You said, 'I love you, Daddy Michael,' right?"

"Yes."

"You said, 'Thank you, Daddy Michael, for being my best, best friend, for ever and ever,' right?"

"Yes."

"Okay. You sent a lot of cards that were signed, 'Your son, Gavin,' true?"

"Yes."

"Do you recall saying the words to Mr. Jackson, 'Come back, I miss you, I love you'?"

"I mean, I probably did, but I don't remember sending a letter."

Rolling his eyes at times, Michael sat quietly as Gavin testified. In the days that Gavin was under cross-examination, Tom Mesereau was able to point out inconsistencies about two critical things: the amount of alcohol that Jackson allegedly gave the boy and the dates that the alleged molestations occurred. Most revealing, as well, was the moment when Gavin admitted that he'd told Santa Barbara detectives that his *grandmother* was the person who told him that men masturbate "so they do not rape women."

Over the span of a few days, Gavin Arvizo offered the jury multiple sides to his personality. Although he sometimes seemed like a kid, courtroom observers noted that the fifteen-year-old boy had a demeanor that reached far beyond his young age. The list of key elements that Gavin Arvizo's testimony brought forward were as follows:

* In the first few weeks after they left Neverland, Gavin and his family had been to see not one, but *two* civil lawyers, perhaps hoping for a settlement from Michael.

* Gavin, until the age of eighteen, would be entitled to sue Michael Jackson in a civil court, should a criminal conviction occur in the molestation case.

* Gavin studied at an acting school, and was coached by veteran actress Vernee Watson, a star on the hit show, *The Fresh Prince of Bel-Air*.

* Gavin was designated a "disciplinary problem" when he attended John Burroughs middle school. He disrespected teachers and authority figures, and was often sent to detention.

* Gavin told Chris Tucker, star of *Rush Hour*, that he and his family were being hounded by the media, that he wanted to see Michael in Miami. Gavin wanted to help Michael hold a press conference to denounce the Bashir documentary, to report that nothing sexual had ever happened in Jackson's bed.

* Gavin and his siblings were rarely left alone with Michael. Oftentimes, Michael's friend Frank Casio and his two young siblings, Aldo Casio and Marie Nicole Casio, were there with Michael as well. The Casio kids were with the Arvizos in Miami. The Casio kids were on the return flight to Neverland from Miami. The Casio kids were "regulars" in Michael's bedroom suite.

* Gavin admitted that he liked being at Neverland and said that he never felt fearful there. Gavin claimed it was his mom, Janet, who felt "afraid" to be at Neverland, who expressed "worry" about being held captive.

* From Neverland, Gavin went with Michael on a trip to Toys "R" Us in Santa Maria, and Michael picked up some local fans along the way, buying toys and gifts for everyone. During that trip, Gavin never complained to anyone about being held "captive."

* From Neverland, Gavin was driven in a Rolls-Royce to nearby Solvang, where he had his braces removed at Michael's expense, because "the wires were all broken." Again, during that trip, Gavin was accompanied by his mother and siblings, and never complained of being held captive.

* While at Neverland, in the weeks following the Miami trip, Gavin's brother, Star, was acting in a manner that was out of control. Evidence showed that Star not only defaced the leather cover of the Neverland Valley Ranch guest book, he reportedly defaced other Neverland property as well.

* At some point after the Miami trip, Gavin and his siblings were "being watched" by Michael's associates at hotel in Calabasas for a reason unknown to them. They later filmed the rebuttal video in a location in Calabasas, very near to their hotel.

* During the Arvizos' three-day stay at the hotel, the Arvizos were bought luggage and clothing, allegedly for a trip to Brazil that Michael's associates were planning. However, Gavin "couldn't recall" going out to buy suitcases.

* Michael's associates accompanied Janet Arvizo and her children when they obtained passport photos and visas for an alleged Brazilian vacation. When Janet allegedly learned that Michael was not accompanying the Arvizos on the trip, Janet changed her mind about going, and the trip never materialized.

* After Gavin's mother decided not to take the trip to Brazil, she returned to Neverland, where she determined that she and her children were in danger. Telling her children she was being threatened, Janet refused to stay at Neverland any longer. At Janet's request, she and her kids were brought home to stay with her parents in El Monte.

* After "escaping" from Neverland on two occasions, Janet and her three children returned to the fantastic ranch, even though Janet claimed they "were being watched" and "threatened" by Jackson's associates. Throughout their various stays at Neverland, the Arvizos were pampered. Evidence would show that the kids had the run of the property, that the Arvizo boys were ordering Jackson's staff around. The Arvizos claimed to be prisoners, yet they were living the life of luxury, a life they had never known.

* In the weeks following the Miami trip, Gavin learned about Michael's vitiligo skin disease. However, Gavin never spoke of seeing Michael's skin disease. Gavin never mentioned seeing any parts of Michael's body up close. Instead, he testified that Michael had explained to him that the disease was changing the color of his skin, and talked about Michael using makeup on his face, perhaps to cover blotches.

"Okay, Gavin, I just have one last question to ask you," Sneddon said, ending his redirect examination. "Yesterday, in response to Mr. Mesereau's questions, you told him that Mr. Jackson was like a father figure to you. Is that correct?"

"Michael Jackson?"

"Yeah."

"Yes," Gavin said.

"And you thought that he was one of the coolest guys in the world, correct?" Sneddon asked.

"Yes."

"And you admired him?"

"Well, I only admire God," Gavin said. "But he was a pretty cool guy."

"How do you feel about Mr. Jackson now, in light of what he did to you?"

"I don't really like him anymore. I don't think he's really that deserving of the respect that I was giving him as the coolest guy in the world."

With that, the prosecutor had no further questions for Gavin Arvizo.

DA Sneddon seemed pleased with the way the testimony had gone.

It was disconcerting to notice that Gavin didn't seem embarrassed or disgusted by his testimony in the least. While he was on the stand, Gavin looked over at Michael a few times, who was no longer giving credence to anything the boy was saying.

In the end, Gavin's direct testimony seemed anticlimactic. Gavin Arvizo seemed a bit more animated as he spoke of alleged sex acts, but Michael displayed no further emotion about any of the boy's accusations.

"Now, you complained to the Santa Barbara sheriffs that, 'After I was done with my cancer stuff,' you never saw Michael again, right?" Mesereau asked.

"No. Not until the Martin Bashir thing," Gavin told him.

"Okay. And you wanted to see him after you were in remission, right?"

"Yes."

"You felt he had abandoned you, right?"

"Yes."

"And you felt he had abandoned your family, right?"

"Yes."

"You came up with acts of molestation after you realized that Michael Jackson was fading out of your life," Mesereau argued.

But Gavin quickly denied that accusation.

Watching Gavin leave the courtroom, never to see Michael Jackson again, it was interesting to watch Gavin's expression as the boy realized that he wouldn't ever be a part of Michael's "family" ever again.

Somewhere in his heart, the boy seemed dismayed. Gavin had insisted that he was "healed by God" and not by Michael Jackson. Yet Gavin seemed inexplicably drawn to the star power and magnetic presence of Michael.

"Got to Be There"

Prosecutors showed jurors adult magazines and other adult materials seized from Neverland in an attempt to bolster their allegations that Jackson was obsessed with sex. The DA would accuse Jackson of showing these materials to the Arvizo boys in an attempt to arouse them. Sheriffs from Santa Barbara testified that they sorted through stacks of photography and art books, all kinds of magazines, and movie memorabilia, everything that was strewn throughout Michael's master suite, bathroom, and office area. Some of the adult magazines they found were in two locked briefcases, stashed under Michael's bed. Other such material was found in Michael's bathroom, near the Jacuzzi tub, and the list went on. Apparently, Michael had a taste for porn.

Detective Paul Zelis testified that he found an adult magazine in Jackson's nightstand. He showed a picture of a nude girl, mingled in with photos of two babies in diapers, a toddler in a bathtub, and a puppy. The way it was presented, the combination made Michael look twisted. But as more "adult" evidence was brought before the jury, as people sat there looking at sexy female images, folks felt the images made Michael look more like a normal guy. The fact that Michael liked to look at pictures of nude girls, was news to many courtroom observers.

As for fingerprint evidence, prosecutors alleged that at least one adult magazine featured the fingerprints of both Michael and Gavin. But Detective Zelis later admitted that the batch of magazines seized from Neverland had not been checked for prints until they were presented at a grand jury hearing in March of 2004—during which time Gavin testified. Jackson's legal team was effectively able to argue that Gavin's prints could have gotten on the adult magazine during the grand jury proceedings, especially since Zelis was unsure whether or not Gavin had handled the magazines during his grand jury testimony.

Paul Zelis, under cross examination by defense counsel Robert Sanger, was forced to admit that Gavin had given police differing accounts of when the alleged molestation had occurred. To Detective Zelis, Gavin originally claimed that the molestation occurred *before* he made the rebuttal video on February 20, 2003. Sometime later, Gavin would tell police that the molestation happened *after* the rebuttal video.

Other strong testimony came from Santa Barbara Investigator Steve Robel, who told the jury that Gavin cried tears when he first spoke about the acts of molestation. Robel was a lead investigator in the case, and he explained that Gavin's demeanor changed when he talked about the molestation, telling jurors that the boy "grew very quiet," and later, "got a little choked up."

The interview Gavin Arvizo had done with police was taped, and before the trial ended, it was entered into evidence. It was a dramatic confession, meant to be the nail that would drive Michael to the cross. In it, Gavin explained to Robel and Zelis that he "knew right from wrong." Though Gavin seemed a bit cagey, afraid to talk about anything that was considered wrong, he finally came up with a few examples:

Not listening to your mom—that was wrong.

Killing someone—that was wrong too.

Gavin told police about the long conversations he and Michael had when he was still bedridden. The boy said they talked mostly about video games, favorite TV shows, and celebrities. He described his time at Neverland, saying he and his brother went on a "kitchen raid" every night, preferring to stay with Michael in the main house rather than sleep in their assigned guest units.

Gavin was clearly uncomfortable as he sat with the police, who called him "buddy" and asked him leading questions. Robel and Zelis tried to loosen Gavin up with talk of birthdays and sports and school grades, and Gavin, who was age thirteen at the time, eventually talked about is friendship with Michael, explaining to police that sometimes Michael had disappointed him. Gavin seemed upset, reporting that Michael had given his family a white GMC truck, but later, when the truck broke down, Michael had taken it away.

Gavin was slightly hesitant, but he detailed the molestation, though the boy told police that he "wasn't sure" what an ejaculation was. Gavin said that he never saw Michael's private parts, but recalled that Michael had walked by him one time, naked, as Michael passed through his room.

In the taped interview, Gavin told police that the molestation happened four to five times, which was an inconsistency that the defense team later pounced on. Under cross-examination, Steve Robel would testify that Gavin "couldn't articulate exactly what occurred," stating only that Gavin "was specific about two events that he recalled."

The atmosphere of the courtroom got more down-to-earth when one of Michael's former housekeepers, Kiki Fournier, who worked at Neverland from 1991 through 2003, reluctantly took the stand to testify. As she looked over at the superstar, Michael refused to acknowledge her. With the weight of world hanging on her shoulders, Kiki looked timid. She responded to her first questions with quick, short answers. She seemed scared, she could barely be heard, and the housekeeper was asked to get closer to the microphone. Kiki was clearly nervous about her testimony and was not happy to divulge secrets about Michael.

Miss Fournier told jurors that she had worked for Michael "off and on" for twelve years, explaining that she'd taken a few years off when she had a child and left Neverland on good terms in the fall of 2003. Her job entailed taking care of Michael's guests, cleaning guest units, catching up on laundry, sometimes serving food, and doing basic household chores.

At the start of her testimony, Kiki told Assistant DA Gordon Auchincloss that she didn't want anything to do with the case. From the stand, Kiki made it clear that she wasn't happy being in the middle of these accusations, that she didn't like being in the spotlight. She didn't like being the center of attention. Kiki Fournier was a hard-working mom, a woman with an honest face, who told the jury that she liked her privacy.

Kiki was asked to talk about Michael's demands on her, about her job security, about whether or not Michael had ever threatened to fire her. Kiki told jurors that, for the most part, Michael would give direct orders, and she was happy to serve him. She said she'd never been fired, and talked about the pecking order at Neverland. Her immediate bosses were Joe Marcus, the ranch manager, Jesus Salas, the house manager, and Violet Silva, the head of security. Kiki said she had never seen Michael fire staff. She explained that, if things weren't as he wanted them to be, Michael would have his wishes "communicated" to someone on his staff.

Kiki spoke about Frank Casio, Michael's longtime friend who also worked for Michael as an "assistant" of some kind. Kiki wasn't sure exactly what Frank's title was. She just knew that Frank had been a fixture around Neverland for about ten years and had claimed to work for Michael. Kiki had little to say about Michael's "associates," specifically those people around him during the spring and summer of 2003. Aside from Frank, she would see "businessmen" with Michael "quite a bit," but she wasn't sure what their job titles were.

The four associates Kiki answered questions about were Dieter Weisner, Ronald Konitzer, Vincent Amen, and Marc Shaffel, all of whom were named as unindicted coconspirators in the case.

Kiki recalled that these men were all at Neverland in the summer of 2003, and she testified about preparing for a big birthday party that was being thrown for Michael, with Marc Shaffel coordinating the event. Kiki didn't have much to say about Michael's party, other than by Jackson's standards, it was, perhaps, a simple event. There was nothing special that Kiki could recall about Michael's birthday celebration: no special performances, no special guests. Kiki testified that Michael had a DJ, a giant cake, some artwork on display in tents, and about a thousand guests.

For Kiki, the event meant extra work and extra cleaning. From her perspective, things weren't quite as much fun at Neverland. There was always a lot of work to do and particular needs to be met. Kiki told the jury that she worked mostly night shifts and explained that the ranch manager, Joe Marcus, was in charge of all the staff at Neverland. Kiki said she took her directions from Jesus Salas, the person who Michael Jackson "gave directions" to around the house, and described Michael as a "detail-oriented" person who liked to have his service "the way he wanted it." The housekeeper said the employees at Neverland worked especially hard at their jobs whenever Michael was on the property.

Under direct examination by Gordon Auchincloss, who was arrogant with most witnesses but seemed to be soft-spoken with Kiki Fournier, the housekeeper began to describe the types of guests she'd seen at Neverland over the years. She told jurors that children were overnight guests at Michael's home "a lot" and testified that thousands of children visited Neverland during her tenure there, some with their parents, and some without. With the prodding of the assistant DA, the housekeeper described Neverland as an environment that was permissive, as an environment that allowed children to misbehave, especially if their parents weren't with them.

As she detailed the goings-on at Neverland, Kiki said kids would eat candy, ride amusement rides, watch videos, play video games, and stay up as late as they wanted. Kiki explained that there weren't really any rules at Neverland, telling the prosecutor that there wasn't really any discipline to speak of. For courtroom listeners, the impression being given was that Michael didn't want to reprimand children.

The prosecutor was drawing a portrait that made Michael seem like a destructive, thoughtless adult. And it was working, for the most part, until Kiki began to add her own commentary about Michael getting upset if kids "got too rowdy" at the dinner table. Kiki told jurors there were certain times that Michael would tell kids to behave. For instance, he didn't allow food fights at dinner, and he didn't allow candy-throwing fights in the theater, little things like that.

In general, Kiki admitted, Michael seemed to give kids a lot of latitude at Neverland. She described the kids at Neverland as having a "free hand" to do whatever they pleased. More frequently than not, Kiki thought the kids who stayed at Neverland were rowdy and "rambunctious." Kiki testified that the kids who stayed overnight would often be assigned guest units, but, being given the run of the whole property, they would usually prefer to sleep with Michael in his master suite.

Kiki described her interactions with the children who were Michael's preferred guests at Neverland, but she seemed reluctant to testify, keeping her eyes averted from the superstar. When asked if she ever noticed "a change" in the children who interacted with Michael, Kiki admitted that, in her opinion, kids did seem to change around Michael.

"The more free reign they got," Kiki told the jury, "they became very very wild, and in some ways, destructive." The housekeeper explained that this type of behavioral change was not unusual, and it was something she noticed with Gavin and Star Arvizo, whom she'd come to know when they were guests of Mr. Jackson in the spring of 2003. Kiki testified that when the Arvizos first arrived to Neverland, Gavin and his brother were "very polite," but said that after a time, Gavin and his brother were less well behaved.

When Kiki was asked whether or not Michael "singled out" certain guests to focus on, the housekeeper detailed a list of boys that included Gavin Arvizo, Brett Barnes, Aldo Casio, Wade Robson, Jimmy Safechuck, Jordie Chandler, and Macaulay Culkin. The housekeeper told the jury that the list of boys whom Michael befriended, with whom he formed a "special bond," were all of a certain age—somewhere between ten and fifteen.

Kiki Fournier testified that she observed Michael drinking alcohol during the time period of 2002 to 2003, stating that his beverages of choice were wine, and sometimes vodka. Though she couldn't say that she'd ever seen Michael serving alcohol to a minor, the housekeeper told jurors that she witnessed kids around Michael who appeared to be intoxicated. Kiki recalled a dinner in September of 2003, where Michael was at the table with four or five children, three of whom she "believed" were intoxicated.

Of course, Kiki couldn't be sure that the kids were drinking alcohol. She assured courtroom observers that she had not served alcohol to any of the kids herself. Kiki wanted the jury to know that she was not in charge of keeping tabs on the kids, that she wasn't watching them, nor had she seen them consume alcohol. As Kiki qualified her response, Mesereau objected to the testimony on the grounds of speculation, and the judge agreed.

Judge Melville admonished the jury to disregard the testimony about children being intoxicated at Michael's dinner table, because for one thing, the incident Kiki was recounting had occurred after the Arvizos had been gone from Neverland for months. But more importantly, as Kiki sat there in front of the jury being asked to recall any other incidents where children seemed to be drinking alcohol with Michael Jackson, Kiki could not recall one specific incident where she could say, with certainty, that kids spending time around Michael were actually intoxicated.

Kids became wild, they became overactive. They might have sometimes appeared to be intoxicated. But Kiki could not offer any proof. The housekeeper could *not* substantiate the prosecutor's allegations.

On cross-examination, Mesereau asked Kiki about a frequent young female guest of Michael's, Marie Nicole Casio, Frank Casio's little sister, who spent a great deal of time at Neverland. The jury learned that Marie Nicole Casio was someone who spent much of her time in Michael's bedroom. Marie Nicole was almost always there with her brothers, Aldo and Frank, and she was staying at Neverland during the same period of time that the Arvizo kids were there.

Though Marie Nicole Casio was someone whom prosecutors conveniently forgot to mention, Kiki described the Casio family—Frank, Marie Nicole, and Aldo—as "regular guests" of Michael. This was a family who had spent a lot of time at Neverland, who spent Christmas with Michael, who were "very close" to Michael throughout the years. As Kiki recollected, Michael spent more time with the Casio family than he did with the Arvizo family—that was something she had noticed during the time of the Arvizos' visit.

As for other kids, Kiki talked about the busloads of children who visited Neverland during her twelve years there, describing thousands of children who arrived to Neverland from the inner city, all of whom came to spend a day of sheer fun and amusement, usually with only a few adults escorting large groups. Kiki said it wasn't her job to supervise these kids—her job was to clean and serve.

As it was with every child who visited Neverland, Kiki confided that the inner-city kids would get wild and rambunctious, especially when they'd see the elephants come walking through the property and when they'd be let loose on the amusement rides. Kiki told the jury that most children would "go wild" on the rides and would throw candy and act up in typical kid fashion.

Kiki also testified that, most often, the large groups of kids who visited Neverland didn't get the chance to meet Michael. Sometimes Michael was available to play with the kids, but because Michael allowed kids to visit his home throughout the year, his being out of town or his being unavailable would prevent "in-person" contact.

As for the superstar's relationships with his associates, Kiki admitted that she wasn't really sure what positions Ronald Konitzer and Deiter Weisner actually held, nor was she certain about what Frank Casio or Marc Shaffel were doing with Michael Jackson. Kiki was in the dark about Michael's associates. She was under the impression that they worked for Michael, but she couldn't be certain. Kiki could only describe them as "businessmen."

She thought that these men might be "promoters" of some sort, but clearly, she didn't have any firsthand knowledge about what these men had to do with Michael's work. The only thing Kiki could remember was that Dieter had a three-foot-tall porcelain doll made to look like Michael Jackson.

Kiki recalled that the doll had broken, and she offered to fix it, but Dieter explained that she didn't need to glue it back together because "there was many, many more where that came from." Kiki had the impression that Deiter was in the "Michael Jackson doll" manufacturing business, though she wasn't sure where this business was located, nor did she know whether Michael was even aware that this business existed.

With the exception of Frank Casio, whom she thought was "trying to get into the music business," Kiki described the men who were around Michael—Deiter Weisner, Ronald Konitzer, and Marc Shaffel—as men who seemed to "appear and disappear" without ever saying much. She had no knowledge of partnerships or actual business ventures these men had with Michael. In her view, these men all had high opinions of themselves for just "hanging around" with Michael. In particular, she thought that Marc Shaffel was "an opportunist."

"He [Shaffel] was one of the many opportunists that you bumped into while working at Neverland, right?" Mesereau asked.

"Yes," Kiki said.

"Now, if Deiter was telling things to Michael, you don't know what they were, right?"

"No."

Kiki didn't know about anything that was or was not being communicated to Michael by these men. The way Mesereau posed his questions, it seemed likely that men surrounding Michael—his "associates"—were not necessarily acting with Michael's full knowledge or cooperation. Kiki told jurors that, with the exception of Frank, these men would show up once in a while, then disappear, recalling that their visits were "unpredictable."

Though she worked at Neverland for so many years, it seemed Kiki didn't really know that much about Michael Jackson's inner being. Of course, Kiki's job was only to know small details about Michael, like when he would be using the movie theater or when he needed a floor waxed. She was in awe of the superstar, but even after spending all those years around him, Kiki was unable to tap into Michael's creative side. Kiki would observe him all the time, but she never got to know Michael. In terms of what made him tick, all she could say was that she knew Michael liked to be alone with his creative thoughts.

Over the years, Kiki had seen Michael go into his dance studio and work on choreography and music. Kiki had seen the superstar walking around the property alone, walking by himself in the dark on many nights, going up into his special tree. But Michael remained, forever, an enigma.

As she testified, the jury learned that Michael was not in control of the details of day-to-day life at Neverland. Michael traveled a lot and would sometimes be gone for months at a time. What became clear was that Michael had set up Neverland to be run by various longtime employees. He had fifty to sixty people working at his home at any given time, employees with tasks spelled out—the zookeeper, the security patrol, the fire department, the house staff, the chefs—the list was long. They each reported to the ranch manager and had little contact with Michael himself.

Kiki told the jury that even if there was a problem or an incident at Neverland, staff members would not go to Michael about it. His longtime assistant, Evvie, his trusted nanny, Grace, and his ranch manager, Joe, were the only people who had immediate access to Michael. Everyone else made reports, which kept Jackson removed from what was actually going on at his home.

As Kiki Fournier was asked a barrage of questions by Tom Mesereau regarding her previous testimony, Kiki confirmed that the superstar had a "family relationship" with the entire Casio group—Frank, Marie Nicole, Aldo, as well as the Casio parents. As for the other young boys whom Kiki had mentioned—Jimmy Safechuck, Jordie Chandler, Wade Robson—the jury discovered that Michael's young friends all visited Neverland with their families.

Mesereau made a point to ask whether Kiki recalled that Jimmy Safechuck had gotten *married* at Neverland, but Kiki didn't seem to know anything about that. The housekeeper did know, however, that Macaulay Culkin's whole family would often come to visit, that other celebrity families would visit as well, including Marlon Brando's family, Tommy Hilfiger's family, and Chris Tucker's family. Kiki couldn't recall all of Michael's celebrity friends, but knew that many famous basketball players visited. In particular, she mentioned seeing Elizabeth Taylor and Chris Rock on the grounds.

Kiki spoke about the various functions that Michael held at Neverland; she often served and cleaned for weddings, birthday parties, and other special events. As the jury listened, they learned the superstar was quite generous with his home, allowing guests to walk freely through the main house to look at his artwork and antiques, allowing people open access to his private world. Even if the party was being held on another part of the grounds, whenever a guest asked to see a tour of the main house, that request was granted. Kiki said she thought Michael was too generous and too nice to his visitors.

Kiki described Michael being like a "big kid" who liked to go on rides and eat lots of candy with the children who visited Neverland. She told the jury that Michael seemed to enjoy playing with kids, that he seemed to enjoy the whole spirit of Neverland. When the subject of alcohol was reintroduced by Tom Mesereau, Kiki said that in all the time she worked at the place, in a span of over twelve years, she'd never seen Michael Jackson hand any type of alcoholic drink to a child. When pressed on the issue, the housekeeper honestly couldn't say that she'd seen the Arvizo kids intoxicated on the property.

As she testified, Kiki described a blood drive that Michael had held for Gavin sometime in 2002, using Neverland to help raise money for the Arvizo family. Kiki told the jury about how happy and surprised she was "to see Gavin coming back to life" in the spring of 2003, after having met such a "frail and weak" boy initially.

Kiki Fournier confirmed that during the time period between February and March of 2003, when the Arvizo clan stayed at Neverland for a number of weeks, Gavin's transformation back to health seemed to be complete. From the look on Kiki's face, it seemed that in the housekeeper's opinion, Gavin's new healthy, bright spirit was nothing short of a miracle.

"Okay, did you ever see the Arvizo family riding around in a limousine?" Mesereau asked.

"I know they were taken in Mr. Jackson's vehicles sometimes," Kiki said.

"Okay. Describe the vehicles, if you would."

"Rolls-Royces. I know that he owns a blue Navigator. So just, different cars."

"Was it your understanding that these kids [Arvizos] would demand that they be taken places in those vehicles?" Mesereau asked.

"I don't know about that."

"Okay. Did you ever see the [Arvizo] mother very much?"

"No. Not that much. She pretty much stayed in her guest unit."

"You ever see her in the theater?"

"Can't remember if I've seen her in the theater or not," Kiki said.

"How about the main house?" Mesereau prodded.

"Yes."

Kiki recalled that Janet Arvizo spent a lot of time in the main house, that she would usually see Janet having dinner in the kitchen area at night, and would also see Janet having breakfast there in the morning.

"Okay. Now, you've indicated that there were times you cooked for the Arvizo family, right?" Mesereau wanted to know.

"Did I cook for them? I don't remember."

"Do you remember Star pulling a knife on you in the kitchen?"

"Yes."

"And when Star pulled a knife on you in the kitchen, were you preparing food?"

"I was doing the dishes," Kiki explained.

"Okay. And he was trying to cook in the kitchen?"

"Yes."

"And that was against the rules?"

"Well, it's just really not wise to have a child in there cooking with everybody," Kiki said. "Because it's kind of, you know. Plus, you've got things that you have to do, so you have to work also."

As the questions became more pointed, Kiki was hemming and hawing, trying to avoid saying anything that might make her look stupid. Kiki was not happy about being asked about Star Arvizo playing games with a knife. She had not wanted to cooperate with the prosecutors, she had not wanted to divulge personal things about herself. Kiki Fournier did not want to tell Mesereau anything more than she had to.

In her direct testimony, Kiki said that she "thought" the Arvizo boys were intoxicated at Neverland, however, on cross-examination, she had to admit that she'd seen the wine cellar door open and unlocked on numerous occasions. With Kiki's vivid description of an open wine cellar door, a door that was located in the arcade, away from most house staff, Mesereau had planted the seed in the minds of the jurors. It was quite possible that the Arvizo boys had helped themselves to Michael's secret stash.

Kiki wished to explain that it was not her job to look after the wine cellar. She wanted the jury to know that her own busy life and hectic schedule kept her from worrying too much about the Arvizo boys. However, the more Kiki protested, the more obvious it became that the Arvizo boys were free to roam throughout Neverland, that they were acting up and were taking advantage of the situation. Kiki made excuses for not paying strict attention to the Arvizo boys. She said she was a part-time college student in the spring of 2003 and explained that she had a lot of work to do at Neverland, that she had specific jobs to do, and was too pre-occupied to worry about the Arvizos' every little move.

With Mesereau's pointed list of questions, Kiki's answers were not only making the Arvizo family look ungrateful, they were also beginning to make the Arvizo family look somewhat conflicted. For instance, Kiki testified that she often saw the Arvizo kids eating dinner at the dining room table with the Casio kids and that sometimes Janet would join the group. However, she pointed out that Michael was most often *not present* for sit-down meals, that he wasn't around the Arvizo kids as much as they might have suggested.

Kiki described a barstool area that Michael had next to the kitchen, where food could be ordered at any time of the day, complete with a chalkboard menu listing daily "specials," and a staff that was prepared to serve anyone's whim. Michael's kitchen was fully open to his guests, twenty-four hours a day. Kiki said people were free to order from a menu that had three meals listed each day, or they could order special requests. Guests were free to help themselves to home-made doughnuts and muffins, and said that Jackson kept large refrigerators stocked with fresh juice, drinks of all kinds, bottled water, and wine. She recalled the Arvizo kids were quick to help themselves to anything they wanted.

"Approximately two weeks before the Arvizos left for good, you noticed that Gavin and Star's room was consistently messy, right?" Mesereau asked.

"Yes."

"And that indicated to you that they were staying in that room, right?"

"I thought they were. But I don't know if they were or not."

"But there was a period when you would often see their room was a mess, right?"

"Yes. I mean, they were sloppy. And towards the end, their room was—things were broken, and it was a mess."

Kiki had to admit that the Arvizo boys' room was such a disaster that she and another housekeeper, Maria, both decided to make a verbal report to the house manager. Kiki told the jury that the Arvizo boys had "trashed it," that their room was "just torn apart."

"Please tell the jury how they trashed it, if you know?" Mesereau asked.

"I can't say for sure what happened, but there [were] things spilled. There [were] glasses broken. The refrigerator was a mess, too. Every unit has its own refrigerator, and it was—it just looked like somebody had gone in there like a tornado—like a whirlwind."

Kiki said that she had not talked to the Arvizo boys about it because it was "not her place" to do that. She said had gone to the house manager, Jesus Salas, and had filed a complaint because the Arvizo boys had left food and garbage all over the room, they had broken things. Apparently, they had moved the furniture around, had spilled drinks everywhere, and had broken some wineglasses.

Before she left the stand, Kiki Fournier was asked by the DA if she felt Star Arvizo was joking around when he pulled the knife on her in the kitchen. Kiki said she felt it was meant to be a joke, but clarified that Star was "trying to assert some sort of authority" with her. She indicated that the Arvizo boys were inappropriate and destructive.

Courtroom observers were stunned when they heard about Star Arvizo pushing Michael's housekeeper around. People were gaining a new perspective about the Arvizos, and with each new witness, Mesereau would bring out more compelling evidence, focusing on the outrageous behavior of these particular houseguests.

Though it wouldn't be reported in the daily newscasts, it seemed Michael Jackson was the last person to know what the Arvizo kids were doing while at Neverland. And as for claims that the Arvizos were being held captive on the property, Kiki Fournier testified that Neverland had no tall fence surrounding any part of the property. The housekeeper laughed at the idea of a conspiracy, telling the jury that anyone could freely walk out of Neverland at any time. There was no actual fence or gate that surrounded Neverland. In her opinion, the idea that the Arvizos could feel imprisoned there was absolutely ridiculous.

"Livin' Off the Wall"

As Pope John Paul II continued to deteriorate, unable to attend the Easter Vigil Mass in Rome, media crews were now beginning to pull out of Santa Maria. Leaving a gaping hole in the front of the courthouse, media members had begun their journey to the Vatican, anxious to capture the thoughts and concerns for Pope John Paul II, whom the eyes of the world were looking toward in prayer.

Back at the Santa Maria courthouse, with less media covering the Jackson trial, prayers by fans became more important to Jackson than ever. Looking at Michael's face as he scanned the crowd, the superstar needed to see solidarity. Jackson had been under attack for so long—it became painfully obvious that he needed people in his corner. The idea that Michael surrounded himself with puppet characters at home, the notion that Michael was unable to relate to "real" people, certainly didn't have any bearing on Michael's mammoth need to feel loved. The pop star reached out to his fans every day—smiling and holding a victory sign toward them.

As the criminal trial progressed, Michael began to suffer a subtle physical meltdown. His fans gave him a sense of hope as he battled through a legal storm. But the remaining media continued to pick Jackson apart, focusing on the possibility that the testimony from past accusers might be allowed into the trial. More than ever, Michael needed to feel the energy of people who cared about him. It seemed that his fans were just as important to him as his family, and both groups were outraged about Michael's public humiliation. His fans, even more than his family, were outraged that Michael was being so harshly judged.

In the midst of the chaos, Michael appeared to become closer to his fans than anyone might have imagined. He certainly was depending on Tom Mesereau and his defense team, but in the end, Michael's strength came from the people who loved him and admired his life's work.

Die-hard fans, people who were camped out at the fences surrounding the courthouse, people who were camped out at the gates of Neverland, had become enormously important to Michael's mental state. They were strangers, really, but to Michael, they were the people who sustained him throughout his life. The stage was all he'd ever really known.

Fans stayed the course with Michael through his worst public ordeal.

Their posters lined the streets, and their boom boxes played Michael's music. Songs from the "HIStory" album, songs from "Thriller," could be heard every day, so even in the midst of all the turmoil, Michael's music prevailed. Many of the fans had been following the story of Michael's alleged molestation charges from the time that the story first broke in 1993 and felt that Michael had been taken advantage of by tabloids, by rumors, by "evil people" who were out for money. Some had cut out news clips of the accusations back in 1993 and brought them to the courthouse to argue about how unfair the media had been to Michael for decades. There were fans who tried to convince the media that Michael was the victim of a conspiracy, that tabloids and money-grubbing people had conspired with Sony to destroy Jackson long before the trial in Santa Maria ever began.

No other entertainer could have drawn people from so many walks of life: every creed, race, and nationality was represented. People of all ages and religious denominations had flown in and had dedicated themselves to Michael. The fans who were there created a synergy that was undeniable. But the media thought that Jackson fans were completely off the wall.

While millions of people around the world wondered if Michael was guilty, his fans in front of the courthouse had anger in their eyes when they heard about the porn that had been introduced by prosecutors to try to smear the pop star. They were giving away T-shirts in support of Michael, commemorating Michael by wearing images of the superstar emblazoned on their backs, chanting out printed messages:

"Hey, hey, we're here to stay. We shall not be moved ... by all this negative media ... Hey, Hey, hypocrisy was never a friend of mine. You commercialized, to victimize, deceiving minds," people chanted. "America is supposed to be ... the land of milk and honey, overflowing in equality. Michael Jackson should be treated with dignity. He's a part of humanity ... Flesh and blood like you and me ... You need to stop being greedy, using Michael as a commodity, trying to sell your philosophy."

As fans became more vocal, deputies who surrounded the courthouse continued to beef up their security measures. Still, their array of weapons and tactics couldn't prevent Michael from having a united group of fans, new people who continued to arrive every week, waving flags from countries all over the world.

Each day, the superstar would emerge from his SUV wearing a sharp suit and tie, sporting an eye-popping vest and matching armband. Without fail, Jackson's presence caused fans to scream with glee. Some of his female fans openly thanked God that they had a chance to see that Michael was really okay. Others appeared intoxicated, just elated by their close proximity to the pop star.

But then, at certain times, fans would notice that Michael's walk lacked energy. There was none of the upbeat skip that people were used to seeing. The few people who won lottery seats to sit inside the courtroom were disturbed to see that Michael was often trembling, holding a tissue to his face—fighting back tears.

Some days, Michael's brothers would help escort him into the courtroom, and there were times when Michael looked like he was about to faint, as if he couldn't stand on his feet. It was hard for the pop star to return to court each day to watch the parade of people who hurled accusations at him.

As the trial proceeded, his brothers Jackie, Tito, Jermaine, Randy, and Marlon were taking turns sitting through the grueling testimony. La Toya and Rebbie would show up in shifts as well, though not as often. For some reason, Janet only appeared in court twice—for a pretrial motion when the family wore all white—and then on the day of the verdicts. However, sources confirm that the entire Jackson family was very much a comfort and support system for Michael throughout the trial, helping him by working behind the scenes.

Of all his siblings, however, it was Randy who played the most active part in Michael's defense. It was Randy Jackson, working along with Johnnie Cochran, who got Tom Mesereau on board as a replacement for Mark Geragos, at a time when Michael needed a top-flight attorney who could focus entirely on Michael.

Of course, Joe Jackson was there for Michael, perhaps even more than anyone might have expected him to be, given that he kept flying in from faraway places such as Japan. Joe wasn't always at court every day, but he would appear and stay for weeks at a time, usually to hear the most important testimony.

As he sat in the courtroom, Joe Jackson was stoic and looked very much like a statesman. He watched the various people who were trying to put his son behind bars, and his strong character and imposing figure seemed to provide a backbone for the family. Watching him sitting next to his wife, it was apparent that Joe seemed to hold Katherine dear to his heart. Of course, they were far from being lovebirds, but they certainly presented a united front. They were very concerned about their son's well-being, and would not allow anyone or anything to distract them from their support of Michael.

Neither Joe nor Katherine seemed to enjoy the crowds that surrounded the Jackson family. They tolerated Michael's fans, but they certainly didn't like the media. For the most part, Jackson's parents appeared to be tired of the spotlight, anxious to end the ugly criminal accusations against Michael.

The weight of the world was on the Jackson family, and, toward the end of the trial, Joe inadvertently caused a media commotion, arriving to court during jury deliberations, asking people if they had seen Michael. Thinking that Joe Jackson knew something about the verdicts, wondering why Joe Jackson was roaming around on the courthouse grounds, the media swarmed Joe, practically knocking each other down in an effort to follow him. It was one of those moments when the media seemed to go sideways—just desperate for a story, in a complete panic and flurry. It ended quickly when the media pool coordinator was able to clarify the confusion. But by that time, Joe Jackson left the courthouse grounds with his dislike of the media even more solidified.

And then there was Katherine, who, in her quiet and elegant way, brought order to the chaos that surrounded Michael. Always present in the court, no matter what the testimony, no matter how ugly things became, Katherine rarely lost focus, she rarely made any expressions that would allow people to see how she felt about the intrusive accusations. Katherine was a woman, clearly, whose strength Michael could not live without.

As weeks turned into months, there were times when Michael looked disheveled as he sat in court. There were times, early in the morning, when Michael would seem so incredibly weak that he would be helped to the defense table by one of his bodyguards. However, a wink and a smile from Katherine would get Michael sitting with his back straight. A nod from Katherine, who would look at the jury with piercing eyes, seemed to penetrate Michael's soul. No matter how horrible he felt, Katherine's presence was all Michael needed to compose himself each day, as he readied himself for a new battle.

One morning, a psychologist specializing in child abuse was asked to testify on behalf of the prosecution, a gentleman by the name of Anthony Urquizo, who told jurors that he'd been working with abused kids since the late 1970s. The man had done years of clinical work, he had his PhD in clinical psychology, and he was brought in, not to talk about the specific allegations being made in the case, but rather to give the jury an understanding of the "act of grooming," which is common for child sexual predators.

Dr. Urquizo would explain that he'd seen perpetrators who would start off having a relationship with a child that was friendly, then that perpetrator would gradually insert "minor sexual content" into the mix, perhaps an off-color joke or a comment about a girl's breasts, little things that would introduce sexuality. As Dr. Urquizo explained the grooming process, he told jurors that it was something that happened over time. First R-rated movies would be introduced, then X-rated material would be added, then perhaps a back rub or something along that line, all of which would eventually lead to something more sexual—ultimately involving sexual penetration.

Dr. Urquizo explained that a sexual predator would usually start off showing the child something innocuous—a sexy movie, a porn magazine, thus desensitizing the child to sexuality—in order to ready the child for sex.

However, when Mesereau cross-examined the expert, the jury learned that Dr. Urquizo was paid to testify—90 percent of the time—for the prosecution. Though he'd never worked with the Santa Barbara DA before, Dr. Urquizo told the jury that he had extensive experience testifying in criminal cases all across Northern California, and said most of his work involved evaluating children and families as an academic at the University of California at Davis.

"You've published a lot of papers about various aspects of clinical psychology, correct?" Mesereau asked.

"Mostly related to child maltreatment," Dr. Urquizo testified.

"Would you agree that false claims of sexual abuse are made by children?"

"Certainly."

"And none of the papers you've written have ever dealt with that subject, correct?"

"Correct. That's not an area of research that I do," the expert said.

Mesereau wanted to clarify that, unlike Dr. Urquizo, there were many people in the profession of child psychology who had written extensively about false allegations of sexual abuse made by children. The defense attorney mentioned some high-profile criminal cases in California that involved children making false claims of sexual abuse. Mesereau specifically described a case in Bakersfield, where children had testified that they were sexually abused, where adults were convicted, and then years later, these same children had come forward to admit that their allegations were false.

Mesereau also cited the *McMartin Preschool* case, a famous case from Los Angeles County that involved children who made false claims of sexual abuse, who were later publicly exposed. But Dr. Urquizo said he wasn't familiar with the exact details of that case, which was shocking, given that he was called to testify as an expert in that field.

"McMartin Preschool" was a buzz phrase to most child psychologists.

As Mesereau questioned Dr. Urquizo, the jury learned that the expert didn't really have much experience regarding kids who made false accusations. Urquizo testified that he was hesitant to talk about why a child might make up something that was sexual.

Dr. Anthony Urquizo insisted that he was a health care provider who evaluated children regarding mental health, not someone who determined if kids were abused or not. The expert tried to back away from the subject of false allegations, but Mesereau wanted to get down to business. If Mesereau had to pull teeth to get an answer, the defense attorney was ready to perform an extraction.

"Now, you made a comment that parents can put their children up to lying about sexual abuse, correct?" Mesereau pressed.

"I think I made it as part of an example," Dr. Urquizo admitted.

"And you would certainly agree that parents can encourage or induce children to make false claims of sexual abuse, correct?"

"Now, I always hate to go to absolutes," Urquizo said, "though it is possible for a child to be supported in a false allegation by their parent."

"Let me give you a hypothetical question," Mesereau asked. "You've got a mother and three children. There is no father figure present. There has been a traumatic divorce of recent vintage. For whatever reason, the mother and her children pick someone up and adopt that person as the father figure. They refer to that person as 'Daddy,' and the mother encourages the children to refer to the person in that light."

As Mesereau spoke, as he presented a hypothetical scenario, he asked what would happen if a mother and her three children suddenly viewed their adopted surrogate father as someone who was "bailing out" on them, asking if Urquizo could imagine a situation where the mother might encourage her children to make sexual allegations against the former "surrogate dad."

With all eyes staring at him, Dr. Urquizo had to admit that he could imagine such a thing—that a mother could encourage her children to make false sexual allegations. Dr. Urquizo wanted to qualify, however, that the cases in which something like that might happen, were very rare.

"Let's assume, hypothetically, the mother and son have been involved in a prior litigation where the son, at an early age, testified under oath in support of the mother?" Mesereau asked. "Let's assume that lawyers were retained. The mother and son had experience with lawyers, had experience with making the allegations of sexual assault and obtaining money in the process."

Mesereau was on a rant. He was permitted to use a hypothetical, the judge had read the statute which supported Mesereau's ability to do that—and now the defense attorney was going for the jugular.

For Dr. Urquizo, and for the members of the jury, the defense attorney laid it out in very plain English: a family, who had been referring to someone as "Daddy," who had decided that their father figure was a person who would always take care of them, suddenly felt wronged when that father figure was no longer around. Then this family went to see lawyers, not the police—hypothetically—in pursuit of financial gain.

"Given what I've said to you in that hypothetical, you can certainly envision the possibility of false claims of sexual abuse, correct?" Mesereau asked.

But the child psychology expert had "difficulty" answering Mesereau's hypothetical. The PhD from the University of California at Davis testified that he did not have research that would tie in with the lawyer's hypothetical equation. Dr. Urquizo didn't think he could really answer the question.

"Okay. Now, you'd agree that children will sometimes exaggerate claims that they've been abused, true?" Mesereau asked.

"I'm not sure what you mean by the word exaggerate. I know the casual term of exaggerating, but you seem to have a more specific one related to sexual abuse," Urquizo said.

"Well, you know what the word exaggeration means, right?"

"That's what I mean, in sort of casual terms," Urquizo testified. "But I guess I'm asking if you could be more specific."

"Well, certainly you would agree that children can be touched by someone, and at some point in time, exaggerate the touching to be something along the lines of molestation or inappropriate touching, when it isn't?"

"Certainly that would be possible."

Tom Mesereau continued his questioning until Dr. Urquizo admitted two very important things: 1) the possibility of pure falsehood, in which children say sexual abuse happened when they weren't even touched; and 2) the possibility of exaggeration, where a child is touched, not inappropriately, but later claims that the touching was inappropriate.

The child psychologist didn't like the way the questions had been framed, and Dr. Urquizo wanted to be clear that the numbers were small, telling jurors that only 6 percent of kids who made sexual allegations, made allegations that were false. The child psychologist further wanted the record to show that he, personally, was unaware of any false allegations made by children for the purpose of financial gain—but it seemed clear that his testimony was one-sided. Like all experts, Dr. Urquizo had been bought and paid for.

Mesereau cited the number of divorce cases that, over the past fifteen years, had seen an increase in child molestation claims, whether they be true or not. However, Dr. Urquizo said he wasn't aware of the literature on that subject, and could not give any examples, nor could he verify statistics. Mesereau brought up the concept of "autosuggestion," where children are actually induced by parents to conjure up false memories of abuse—and again, the expert had no familiarity with that aspect of his field.

The defense attorney was surprised, given that so many stories had been in the news regarding "recollections" of past abuse that later were proven to be false. He found it shocking that Dr. Urquizo was unable to address the issue, but Mesereau moved onto a more pertinent topic—asking questions about parents having an ability to have an influence over their children. He wanted to know if children who are constantly exposed to parents who are perpetual liars—could adopt the view that lying is acceptable.

On that point, Dr. Urquizo seemed to agree, telling Mesereau that children might have a sense about lying that might be learned from their parents. The expert was uncomfortable making the statement, but he had to admit it, nonetheless.

Regarding children and falsehoods, Dr. Urquizo told the jury about levels of "disclosure," explaining that some victims of sexual abuse never disclose it, others wait for a period of time before they disclose it, and so on. Dr. Urquizo wanted the jury to know that just because a child might have varying stories about the alleged sexual abuse, that didn't mean the child was a flat-out liar. The child psychologist wanted everyone to understand that children weren't perfect—that it was common for children who were abused to include mistakes, errors, to just "goof up on some of the details."

And Tom Mesereau understood that.

But at the same time, the defense attorney wanted the jury to be clear—that being uncertain about details, changing dates and times—could also mean that the child was lying. Moreover, Mesereau wanted the jury to understand that there was no scientific way to determine if a child had been sexually abused, if the child was lying about it.

"Nobody can determine that a child has been sexually abused just based on what the child says, right?" Mesereau wondered.

"I don't know how to answer that. I mean, I could only say that would be a difficult thing to do," Urquizo answered.

The defense attorney asked the expert about the literature, the scientific journals, the professional journals about sexual abuse, asking about the studies and research Dr. Urquizo had done, and Mesereau was able to prove another very critical thing: Dr. Urquizo hadn't personally talked to *one single victim* of sexual abuse.

The reality was, Mesereau's questions proved that the state's expert was dealing in theoretical "studies." By the end of Anthony Urquizo's cross-examination, the jury realized that this expert was talking about sexual abuse from his textbook experience, not from real life.

"Little Bitty Pretty One"

Michael took off his sunglasses to get a better look at a beautiful tall blonde who entered the courtroom: Miss Lauren Wallace, a flight attendant who had served him numerous times. With her long blonde hair and perfect figure accented by a white pants suit and sexy black camisole, Miss Wallace had everyone in the courtroom paying attention. The blonde bombshell was one of the head flight attendants for Extrajet, a private airline that Michael often chartered for himself, his guests, and his three children.

As the gorgeous young woman was sworn in, staring over at Michael with adoring eyes, the pop star looked at her with a curious expression. It seemed like Michael was attracted to her on some level, but then he put on his wire-rimmed reading glasses and began glancing at notes from Mesereau. Apparently, Michael didn't want to be distracted by her beauty. Michael was anxious to hear what she'd been called to talk about.

Miss Wallace was not on the flight Michael had chartered when he brought the Arvizo clan back to Neverland from Miami, but Miss Wallace was able to provide the jury with general details about the Gulfstream 4—the private jet that she'd worked on for over two years, serving celebrities and sports figures, making sure that their service was completely delightful, that their china was polished and their crystal was shining. Just looking at her, people could tell that Lauren Wallace knew how to provide prim and proper catering for a first-class flight.

Miss Wallace identified Mr. Jackson as someone she'd served many times, perhaps as many as twenty flights between 2003 and 2004. She politely explained that her relationship with Michael Jackson was "professional and friendly," and told the jury that Mr. Jackson had some special catering orders and a few special requests, including a penchant for Kentucky Fried Chicken and Subway sandwiches.

People were utterly surprised when they learned that Michael ate such ordinary cuisine—but were even more fascinated to discover that Michael requested that his wine be served out of Diet Coke cans on every flight—which Miss Wallace prepared and kept on ice, ready for Michael when he boarded the plane.

Lauren Wallace was very matter-of-fact when she explained that Michael preferred to drink white wine out of Diet Coke cans, testifying that other adults in Michael's company would drink wine out of soda cans as well. As her testimony evolved, the jury learned that Mr. Jackson did not wish to let his children know that he consumed alcohol. It seemed, at least in her opinion, that Michael was perhaps shy or embarrassed about drinking wine—period. Miss Wallace said she would hide alcohol for Michael, in preparation for his flights, stashing little mini-bottles of vodka and gin in the lavatory to keep them out of the children's reach. The flight attendant testified that it was rare for Michael to drink from those hidden bottles, and told the jury that Michael drank modestly on coast-to-coast flights—usually having some wine, and then perhaps a glass or two of tequila or Tanqueray gin—nothing more.

When the attractive flight attendant was handed over to Mesereau for cross-exam, the defense attorney wanted her to explain more about the Diet Coke cans. Miss Wallace confirmed that Michael requested that white wine be placed in Diet Coke cans on every flight because he wanted to make sure that grown-ups could drink with discretion. Mesereau asked Miss Wallace about her police interview, about her statement in which she explained that "Mr. Jackson didn't want his children to see him drinking at all," but the flight attendant was unable to speculate about why Michael had developed this particular habit.

People in the courtroom later commented about Michael's secretive behavior regarding alcohol. Some felt it was a result of his strict upbringing, speculating that Michael might have learned to hide alcohol as a youth, when he was still active in a religion that strictly prohibited celebrations and parties. Other people chattered about Michael's paranoia, about his experiences with servers and staff members who would "sell" minor details about his private life to tabloids. There was no way for an average person to really understand Michael's thinking. Most people didn't live in a world where confidentiality agreements had become a regular way of life.

"Do you remember telling the Santa Barbara sheriffs that you had never observed children intoxicated on flights when Mr. Jackson was a passenger?" Mesereau asked.

"I never saw intoxicated children on Mr. Jackson's flights," Miss Wallace said.

"And was it your understanding that Mr. Jackson wanted wine placed in cans because he gets nervous on flights?"

"Yes."

"And Miss Wallace, are you familiar with what is called a 'Passenger Profile' for people who fly on Extrajet flights?"

"Yes."

"Would you please tell the jury what a passenger profile is?"

"A passenger profile is a profile based on each passenger with their likes and dislikes, their friend's likes and dislikes, and their family's likes and dislikes. And they're notes, basically, so that if another flight attendant or another person should work with that particular client, they're aware of allergies or preferences."

Miss Wallace explained that the passenger profile on Michael Jackson was not something that he'd given to Extrajet—it was a result of information that was gathered over time. Because Lauren Wallace hadn't seen the profile in a few years, Mesereau handed it over to the flight attendant so she could familiarize herself with the details.

Again, Mesereau asked Miss Wallace to confirm Mr. Jackson's request to keep white wine in soda cans on *every* flight. This had become such a significant issue at the trial, because during Star and Gavin's testimony, both boys claimed that on the flight from Miami to Santa Barbara, Gavin was sharing a Diet Coke with Michael. Each claimed that instead of drinking soda, thirteen-year-old Gavin was drinking wine on the flight. Miss Wallace, however, was not on board for that particular journey, so she could offer no insight about Gavin Arvizo's claims.

For the jury, the Extrajet "passenger profile" document was entered into evidence, providing details about the personal eating habits of Michael, Prince, Paris, and Prince II. This is what it said:

PASSENGER PROFILE

Date: Sept. 1, 2003

Passenger name : Michael Jackson

Food Preferences

1. <u>Breakfast</u>. KFC original chicken breasts, mashed potatoes, corn, biscuits, scrambled eggs with strawberry jelly, gravy and spray butter. Salmon lox, low-fat wheat bagels, low-fat cream cheese. Fruit plate and whole fruit (especially oranges, grapes, apples, and bananas.)

2. <u>Lunch</u>. KFC original chicken breasts, mashed potatoes/gravy on side, corn on the cob, biscuits with strawberry jelly and spray butter. If traveling for a number of consecutive days, will try other forms of chicken, but would still like the KFC.

3. <u>Dinner</u>. KFC original chicken breasts, mashed potatoes/gravy on side, corn on the cob, biscuits with strawberry jelly and spray butter.

4. <u>Desert.</u> Rarely eats desert, but will ask for a Sunday 1 out of 10 times you fly with him. Eats mostly gum and mints for desert. Or will pick at whole fruit.

Beverage Preferences:

White wine in Diet Coke can on <u>every</u> flight. 7-UP, Orange Crush or fruit punch.
* Will sometimes drink tequila, gin, or Crown Royal.

Additional comments:

Likes Big Red gum, and a lot of different gums and mints. Will eat cheese and crackers and fruit plates on very short flights. Very timid flyer but will get out of his seat during take off and landing. Be prepared to clean a lot after he deplanes.
* No chocolate, peanut butter, broccoli, or strong scented foods.

PASSENGER PROFILE

(Prepared as per father and nanny)

<u>Passenger Name</u>: Prince, Paris, and Prince Michael II Jackson
Ages: 6, 5, and 20 months.

Food Preferences:

1. <u>Breakfast</u>. Grilled chicken breasts, scrambled eggs with ketchup, mashed potatoes, corn or corn on the cob with spray butter. 1/4 of a biscuit or a roll. Sugarless cereal with low-fat or skim milk. Fruit—whole or sliced, especially oranges, apples, grapes, and bananas. NO SUGAR!

2. <u>Lunch</u>. Skinless grilled or KFC chicken breasts, mashed potatoes without gravy or gravy on side (changes frequently—ask MJ), corn or corn on the cob with spray butter. 1/4 biscuit or roll. <u>NO CHICKEN SKIN!</u> Turkey Subway sandwiches or regular sandwiches on wheat <u>without</u> lettuce, tomato, cheese or any extras. Will eat with the mashed potatoes and corn to accompany. Fruit or nonfat yogurt for dessert.

3. <u>Dinner</u>. Same as lunch. Typically will ask for the same thing their dad is eating for every meal, but he'll determine what they are allowed to eat. Like crackers.

4. <u>Dessert.</u> Fruit, frozen vanilla yogurt, yogurt raisins.

Beverage Preferences:

Assorted juices, milk.

<u>Additional Comments</u>: Paris loves to bake cookies and will try to eat the sugar. She is good at cajoling for sugar. Kids like sugarless gum before and after flight. OK to eat crackers or honey in tea.

<u>Family/Friends</u>: Ask MJ as per what he would like his children to eat. Nanny (Grace) will also inform you of what you should feed them if Dad is sleeping or busy. If info is conflictive, inform Grace of what MJ has stated and feed them what MJ has requested.

Grace will feed the baby: KFC mashed, corn, cut up grilled chicken breasts, crackers, grapes, apple juice and or milk.

<u>NO peanut butter</u>. <u>NO chicken skin</u>. <u>NO sugar</u>. <u>NO chocolate</u>.

There was a separate note on the profile revealing the contact information for Evvie Tavasci, Michael's longtime assistant, as well as "profile" sheets attached for three other children [not the Arvizos] and a boy named Elijah, who was later identified as Michael's cousin. Food preferences were also noted for Michael's bodyguard, Joe, as well as his nanny, Grace, and his famous Miami-based attorney, Al Malnick, who was reported to have been the attorney for mob boss Meyer Lansky.

Regarding the mini-bottles of alcohol that the flight attendant said she'd "hidden" in the lavatory, Mesereau asked why they weren't mentioned in Michael's profile. When Lauren Wallace explained that stashing the mini-bottles was something that she had thought of *herself*, that it was never a request of Mr. Jackson to stash mini-bottles, the sinister character that the DA was trying to create about Michael completely deflated. Miss Wallace told the jury that she stashed mini-bottles as a thoughtful gesture on her part. The tall blonde said that she informed Mr. Jackson about the secret bottles, just so he'd know alcohol was there "for his own disposal."

When Miss Wallace left the stand, it was obvious that it had been her privilege to serve Michael Jackson and his family. A few days later, when another flight attendant would be called, one who served on the particular flight that the Arvizos took with Michael, suddenly the picture became more vivid. The second flight attendant, Cindy Bell, was also an attractive woman, a blonde with a great smile. She seemed completely capable and sure of herself, and looked like she was very happy to see Michael. Even under the circumstances.

Miss Bell had a sweet expression on her face as she locked eyes with the pop star, who gently rocked back and forth in his seat behind the defense table. Miss Bell began her testimony by explaining that when she served as an attendant on the flight from Miami to Santa Barbara, she served Michael Jackson a bottle of white wine—which he didn't want his kids to know he was drinking.

The young woman testified that she served Janet Arvizo some wine and had also served the girls, Davellin and Marie Nicole, mixed drinks, rum and Coke, which Davellin and Marie Nicole specifically ordered. Michael blushed during Miss Bell's testimony, and he seemed to be embarrassed about it. It was clear he didn't want people to know he consumed any alcohol whatsoever. But Michael's embarrassment about drinking alcohol was overshadowed by information about Davellin Arvizo, who testified that she never tasted alcohol until *after* the Miami trip with Jackson, swearing that Michael Jackson introduced her to alcohol in his secret wine cellar.

Under oath, Davellin swore that the first time she ever tasted alcohol was when Michael came along. Davellin claimed that alcohol was a taste she didn't like, yet the jury heard from Miss Bell, who recalled that Davellin was ordering mixed drinks on the flight without Michael's knowledge.

For the jury, Cindy Bell described the cross-country flight as being crowded, with twelve people on board, and said that Gavin Arvizo was an "odd bird" who acted weird in Michael's presence—not intoxicated—but just very rude and disorderly. Miss Bell characterized Gavin as someone who treated her like a maid. She recalled that Gavin threw his book bag down at her, and said the boy was demanding service from the moment he stepped on board the plane. She described Gavin as being picky, insisting that his chicken wasn't hot enough, asking that his food be separated onto different plates. The flight attendant told the jury that the boy made snippy comments about the passenger towel service, questioning her about how hot or cold the towels should be, and about the amount of towels available in the lavatory, as if he were her boss.

Cindy Bell also mentioned that Gavin started a food fight, throwing mashed potatoes at a doctor who was sleeping at the time, minding his own business. She said Michael Jackson's children and the rest of the passengers on the plane were very well behaved. According to Miss Bell, Michael was extremely polite, talking with the nanny and the doctor, and playing games with Prince and Paris while on board.

The flight attendant was familiar with Michael's children, and said they were always so well mannered, assuring jurors that Michael made certain of that. Miss Bell thought it was unusual that Michael didn't intervene when Gavin acted up, and found it really strange that Gavin's mom didn't try to stop the boy's unruly behavior.

When shown a diagram of the seating chart on the plane, Cindy Bell said that Michael was seated next to Gavin, and recalled seeing a moment when Michael "cuddled" Gavin. According to Miss Bell, Michael seemed to be trying to comfort Gavin, at one time placing his arm around Gavin for a few moments.

Cindy Bell's testimony had everyone laughing when she was asked to describe what cuddling looked like—as if it was a mysterious gesture.

"You want me to show you what cuddling is?" she asked the prosecutor with a look of utter disbelief.

When she was cross-examined, a theme that ran throughout Miss Bell's testimony was that Gavin Arvizo was an intolerable child who was not well behaved.

She did not think the boy was intoxicated, not in the least, though she thought, perhaps, that Michael was feeling the effects of the wine she served him. She said Michael seemed relaxed on the flight and slept part of the time.

As Cindy Bell's testimony continued, it became clear that the flight attendant resented the boy's pushy demeanor, and did not appreciate his attitude toward her. Miss Bell described a moment when Gavin went into the gallery to request an orange soda, showing off the watch Michael had given him. In Cindy Bell's opinion, Gavin was acting like he had Michael Jackson in his back pocket.

Miss Bell had been brought before the jury to testify about the possibility of Michael Jackson being intoxicated and irresponsible on the aircraft, but the tactic backfired. Jurors were raising their eyebrows at the description of Gavin's assertive behavior.

The personable and very pretty Cindy Bell had come to Santa Maria to testify on behalf of the prosecution—but instead had thrown the trial in Michael's favor by describing the pop star as a "soft-spoken," quiet gentleman. Miss Bell said she never saw Michael serving any alcohol, or any kind of drink, to the young accuser.

"The boy [Gavin] was unusually rude, he was obnoxious," Cindy Bell told the jury. "When I served him food, he said, 'This isn't warm, this isn't the way it's supposed to be.' It was embarrassing to have him on board, actually."

"We Are Here to Change the World"

As the trial became a full-blown war, the fight over allowing testimony about past accusations against Michael Jackson became a legal issue that experts couldn't agree about. The rules seemed somewhat broad, and a special hearing was held outside the presence of the jury. The defense team argued that past allegations against Michael were irrelevant, that past accusers lacked credibility.

But the prosecution wanted the judge to let the testimony come into court under a "similar misconduct" provision. If Judge Melville determined that the past allegations had relevance to the current charges, he could allow the testimony for its probative value. Jackson's defense team was outraged by the prosecution's ploy, arguing that any past accusations would only be used to embarrass and demean Michael Jackson.

Legal pundits believed that if the past misconduct allegations were entered into the record, the jury might decide to focus on the past allegations and thus overlook some of the "inaccuracies" of Gavin Arvizo's testimony. The defense team repeatedly claimed that the allegations by Jackson's 1993 accuser were motivated by the *monetary settlement* that the Chandler family desired, and fought vehemently to discredit Jordie Chandler's allegations, insisting that the Chandler boy, who had apparently elicited a settlement of $20 million on behalf of the Chandler family, had presented a story full of holes.

Outside the courtroom, Jackson's longtime music manager, Frank Dileo, would assert that Michael Jackson had promised Jordie Chandler a film career, telling media members that when Jordie's career never materialized, the sexual allegations suddenly emerged. There had been allegations that the Chandlers had admitted that they wanted money, there had been allegations that the Chandlers wanted Jackson to propel them to fame, but no one in the media reported anything about that.

In front of Judge Melville, Tom Mesereau not only argued against the validity of the Chandler family's story, he also argued against the validity of the claims made by Michael's past accusers, promising that he had enough evidence to discredit each one of them. The defense attorney told Melville that "prosecutors are trying to bolster a weak case" by bringing forward boys whose stories were "riddled with problems." Mesereau argued that the witnesses whom the prosecution planned to call about alleged past acts had been involved in their own civil suits against Michael and were people "with axes to grind."

"Why allow them to bring in disgruntled employees who lost their lawsuit?" Mesereau said of the third-party witnesses to these alleged claims. But his arguments fell on deaf ears.

By the end of the special hearing, Judge Rodney Melville ruled in favor of the prosecution, making the decision to allow testimony to be presented about alleged past sexual acts—not only from the accusers, but from former Neverland employees who claimed to have witnessed certain acts as third parties.

It was considered a major "win" for the prosecution. Judge Melville ruled that he would allow the Santa Maria jury to hear testimony concerning Michael's past friendships with five other boys, and on that list was actor Macaulay Culkin.

But Macaulay Culkin, along with two other boys who were named, would eventually cooperate with the *defense* to deny any wrongdoing by Michael Jackson. The only person on the list who agreed to cooperate with the prosecution was Jason Francia, the son of Jackson's former chambermaid, who had been the recipient of a $2 million settlement for allegedly having been "tickled" by the pop star.

As for Jordie Chandler, the young man did not wish to testify, and it appeared that the prosecution could not locate him. According to insiders, Sneddon could not force him to take the stand. In lieu of Jordie's presence, since third-party testimony had been deemed admissible, the prosecution would offer testimony from his mother, June Chandler, a decision legal pundits thought would "devastate" the defense.

Most TV commentators predicted that the decision to allow past molestation allegations would be a huge setback for the defense, one from which they couldn't recover. Chomping at the bit, Tom Sneddon announced that he would begin to present witnesses from prior alleged incidents within two weeks, and journalists promised viewers that the Santa Maria jury would be allowed to hear evidence about five boys who the DA alleged had been "groomed" or molested by Jackson.

It was curious that no one in the media speculated about the strategy of the defense team regarding these past allegations. Mesereau was systematically developing a list of witnesses to show that the two boys who had accepted money from Jackson—Jordie Chandler and Jason Francia—had financial interests at heart and had hired attorneys to file civil suits. In the case of Jason Francia, his mother admitted on the witness stand that she sold her son's story to the tabloids.

To the press, Tom Mesereau once stated that the only reason Mr. Jackson had settled the two prior claims made against him was because his business associates advised him to "pay money rather than face false allegations." The defense attorney told the media that Michael Jackson "now regrets making these payments and realizes the advice he received was wrong."

Outside the presence of the jury, Mesereau would confide that at the time of the Chandler accusations, billions of dollars were at stake for everyone surrounding the "Jackson machine."

To the average person, $20 million would seem like a ludicrous, perhaps an obscene amount to pay to someone who Jackson alleged in his counter-claim was trying to extort money. But to Jackson—who was estimated to be worth about $700 million at the time, who had dozens of corporations banking on him to make huge profits for them, including Sony, FOX, and PepsiCo—$20 million didn't seem like much to pay. The corporations surrounding Michael Jackson wanted to keep his name clear. He was, after all, the world's most famous entertainer.

With the case moving forward at a fast pace, the prosecution called comedian and TV star George Lopez to the stand. Lopez was there to talk about his relationship with the Arvizo family, whom he had formed a bond with in the days when Gavin was first diagnosed with cancer, in the days when the Arvizo kids were involved with the Laugh Factory comedy camp.

Dressed conservatively in a dark blue suit, wearing a starched white shirt with a striped tie, the television star told jurors that he and his wife had tried to organize benefits on behalf of Gavin Arvizo and said they had visited Gavin in the hospital on numerous occasions. As George Lopez began to explain the nature of his relationship to the Arvizo clan, it appeared the comedian had a "soft spot" for the impoverished Latino family. Lopez was certainly making a case for them, trying to show why he sympathized so much with these people.

In court, even though Jackson was hiding behind his glasses, the pop star was listening carefully to the comedian. Michael was studying George Lopez, perhaps wondering how Lopez, who was sitting square and center in front of him, had become the first famous person to have been drawn in by the Arvizo family. In a way, it was George Lopez who led the Arvizos along a path that ultimately ended at Neverland.

Jackson tried to show little emotion, but it was obvious that he was interested to learn about Lopez's experience. The pop star sat motionless, like he was watching the testimony from afar, but in reality, he was hanging on every word.

As he addressed the jury, Mr. Lopez spoke with a pleasant tone, a bright smile flashing across his face. The comedian seemed to like the Arvizos, and Lopez talked about the "comedy camp" at the Laugh Factory, describing a program for underprivileged kids. Lopez explained that participating in the Laugh Factory comedy camp was a chance for him to mentor kids who were "at risk."

George Lopez told the jury he became involved with the comedy camp in 1999, at which time he met the Arvizo kids, and at first, Lopez had nothing but nice things to say about the Arvizo family. He described the three children as being "good kids" and mentioned that their mom, Janet, seemed to be very active in her kids' growth and development. He considered Janet a dedicated mother and was impressed that she was willing to take the bus from East LA in order afford her children the chance to work with top talent.

Lopez had a high opinion of the three Arvizo children, whom he called "fearless." He liked the fact that the Arvizo kids could make fun of their own poverty as a way to discover humor. Apparently, using poverty to as a way to create humor was a trait Lopez had adopted himself.

George Lopez, the star of his own show on ABC, testified that he'd been a stand-up comedian for twenty-five years and said that he'd performed at the Laugh Factory on Sunset Boulevard for over fifteen years. He described his relationship with the comedy club's owner, Jamie Masada, as being a friendship, and he respected Masada for taking an interest in inner-city kids, for making his popular club available to these kids during the day—allowing inner-city kids to study comedy with professionals without having to pay a dime.

Lopez recalled that Jamie Masada had called him to tell him about "a special Latino family" who were underprivileged, who had requested to work with Lopez specifically. The comedian said he worked with Davellin, Star, and Gavin Arvizo in the fall of 1999, meeting with them for two-hour sessions over a period of about seven weeks.

The comedian told jurors that about six weeks after the comedy camp ended, Janet Arvizo called him on his cell phone and was "completely distraught" about her son's condition. Janet was crying because Gavin had been diagnosed with an unknown cancer. When Lopez found out how sick Gavin was, that the boy was barely clinging to life, he visited Gavin in the hospital and found the boy to be "in dire condition."

While at the hospital, George Lopez met Gavin's father, David, for the first time. Lopez said that he and his wife had gone to see Gavin in the hospital on numerous occasions and said he had also visited Gavin at his grandparents' home in El Monte, which Lopez described as a "tract house," a typical low-income home with plastic covers on the furniture and plastic runners on the floor—a place reminiscent of his own childhood home. George Lopez recalled that the modest house was neat and clean, and talked about a special bedroom that had been prepared for Gavin—a sterile environment that Lopez said he had to "wear a robe" to walk into.

As George Lopez continued to answer the DA's questions, the comedian tried to make it clear that he was happy to help the Arvizos and said he had never been approached for money by Janet Arvizo. Lopez testified that he wasn't sure what Janet did for a living. He thought Janet was a waitress. However, as his testimony became more detailed, it was apparent that Lopez didn't really know much about Janet Arvizo at all, that his dealings with her had been limited to a few brief chats at the Laugh Factory. Lopez seemed to think Janet was a nice woman, but he couldn't base his opinion on anything specific.

On cross-examination, Lopez told the jury that in February and March of 2000, when Gavin was very ill, he and his wife went often to visit with Gavin and David Arvizo in the hospital. As he was probed about the specifics, the comedian tried to stay calm, but courtroom observers could see Lopez was becoming a bit uncomfortable with the line of questioning. When he was asked to tell the jury about David Arvizo's money concerns, the comedian said that Mr. Arvizo "made it known that he was strapped for cash."

"Did you find it strange that you never saw Janet at the hospital? "Mesereau asked.

"Well, you know, I knew she was a waitress, or so I thought," Lopez said. "I wasn't there all the time, but every time I went, she wasn't there, so I just figured that she was working."

"You really don't know if she was working, do you?"

"I don't know."

"Okay. And you may have thought she was a waitress, but you really don't know where she was waiting tables, right?"

"She never served me," Lopez said, giving the jury a smile.

"Okay. Okay. Now, how aggressive was David in asking for money?" Mesereau asked.

"You know, it was pretty aggressive," Lopez said. "When you're two guys talking, and the subject always comes up, you know, you kind of get turned off to it. Every time we spoke, it was always about—really about money."

"And he always said he had no way to pay the family bills, right?" Mesereau asked.

"That's right."

"And you gave him little amounts that you had in your pocket at the time?"

"Yeah. I only had little amounts at the time."

"He always wanted money, didn't he?"

"He did," Lopez told the jury. "I literally would give the guy everything I had in my wallet and figure I'd get more later."

Lopez said he'd regularly hand David Arvizo sums of $40, bundles of cash in small amounts of up to $80. He testified that he was asked by David Arvizo to participate in a fund-raiser for Gavin to be held at the Ice House, a comedy club in Pasadena, and said that he was more than happy to take on the project. However, when he got the impression that the fund-raiser "wasn't about Gavin anymore," George Lopez told jurors that he began to change his mind.

"It wasn't about how Gavin was and how Gavin was feeling," Lopez testified. "It wasn't about money for Gavin. It seemed to me that David Arvizo was more interested in money than he was about his son."

George Lopez told the jury that because David Arvizo had indicated that his family had no health insurance (later proven to be a falsehood) and no money to pay medical bills, he agreed to put on a fund-raiser, planning to use his LA-based radio show to draw a crowd. The comedian recalled that when he fell behind schedule in terms of booking other talent, he noticed that David Arvizo suddenly became "pretty aggressive" about scheduling the event, asking questions about how much money he thought Lopez could raise.

"At some point, you thought David was extremely engrossed with money and possessions, true?" Mesereau asked.

"That's correct."

"Because when you visited the room in El Monte, he showed off that room with the DVD and all the rest, correct?"

"That's right," Lopez said.

"Did you ever know who paid to renovate that room?"

"No."

"Okay. Did David ever talk about how that room came to be so nice?" Mesereau wondered.

"No. My assumption was that Jamie Masada had arranged that."

"Now, you told the sheriffs, Mr. Lopez, you thought David Arvizo was particularly enamored with the big screen television and the Nintendo, right?"

"Yes."

"You said you noticed this, to a small degree, with the children as well, correct?"

"Yes."

"Okay. And you told the sheriffs that everything about David, seemed to be about money, right?"

"Yes."

George Lopez testified with integrity and grace, sometimes being funny, and always being candid. The comedian told the jury that in 2000, he was living in a house in Sherman Oaks, and said that when he learned that Gavin's cancer had gone into remission, he invited the Arvizo family to spend time with him at his home one particular afternoon.

Lopez recalled that he'd driven to El Monte to pick up David, along with Gavin and Star, and brought them to his home "so the boys could play in the backyard for a while." Lopez said he took the boys to Pizza Hut, brought them to a mall, took them back to his home for a short while, and later dropped them off in El Monte.

The comedian testified that Gavin looked frail at the time but seemed more energetic than he had been in the past. He said that he felt Gavin Arvizo's behavior was a bit unusual at the mall, explaining that Gavin was pointing to all kinds of items and was asking for "everything" he laid his eyes on. George Lopez thought it was odd that David Arvizo remained "conspicuously off to the side" while his son, Gavin, asked Lopez to purchase expensive items. The comedian found it strange that David Arvizo never once spoke up to enforce any kind of discretion over Gavin's shopping spree.

Lopez said that when he got home later that day after dropping the Arvizos off in El Monte, he looked around his living room, a place he lovingly described as "a room that is very popular with Mexicans—a room that no one's allowed to sit in—where everything stays put." Lopez told the jury that upon his return home, he looked at the mantle over the fireplace and saw a wallet up there, not belonging to him, which held Gavin's ID and a $50 bill.

As he held the wallet, George called over to his wife, Ann, and handed her the billfold. Lopez testified that he immediately called Gavin to let the boy know he'd found his wallet, and he made arrangements to return it to the Laugh Factory, where the Arvizos could pick it up from the club owner, Jamie Masada.

Tom Mesereau wanted a more detailed account of the Arvizos' behavior on that occasion, and George Lopez was asked to go through the specific events of that "shopping" day with the Arvizos. For the jury, Lopez described his adventures with the Arvizos in the San Fernando Valley, culminating with the mysterious appearance of Gavin's wallet.

"You told the sheriffs that David seemed to intentionally stand back and make no efforts to reign in Gavin's requests?" Mesereau asked, referring to the shopping spree.

"That's correct."

"You thought that was strange, right?"

"Seemed odd."

"Did you take them to lunch on that day?"

"Yes, sir."

"And did you take them to lunch on any other day, do you know?"

"No."

"All right. Now, where did you see the wallet?" Mesereau asked.

"The wallet was on the fireplace mantle of my house. It was the only thing on the mantle," Lopez said.

"And when you saw it, how did you think it got there?"

"You know, it never occurred to me how it got there," Lopez said. "Because nobody played in that room, so it was kind of odd that a wallet would end up on that—on that mantle."

"And how high up was that mantle?"

"You know, shoulder height."

"Taller than Gavin, right?"

"At that time, maybe."

"So did it seem peculiar to you that suddenly a wallet's just lying there?"

"Well, being in that room, yeah. Really, nothing's supposed to be in there."

"Had you seen Gavin or David in that room?

"No."

George Lopez told the jury that some days later, he came to discover that David Arvizo claimed to Jamie Masada that there had been $350 in Gavin's wallet. He testified that when David Arvizo went to retrieve the wallet from Masada, the Arvizo dad suggested to Masada that George Lopez somehow "lost" $300 from Gavin's wallet.

It was an accusation that Lopez didn't appreciate, especially when he discovered that Jamie Masada took it upon himself to "replace" the $300 without ever consulting him about it. The comedian said he complained to Masada about replacing money that "supposedly" was lost, but Masada insisted that he just wanted to make peace with the Arvizos.

As the comedian told the story, jurors' ears perked up. Even though the TV star was trying to downplay the Arvizos' strange behavior, to courtroom observers, the Arvizo clan was beginning to look like a family of grifters. The intentions of the Arvizos seemed even worse when Lopez described David Arvizo's constant calls, stating that David Arvizo was hounding him, was pushing him aggressively, trying to get the fund-raiser organized.

Lopez told the jury that David was calling quite often to the radio station where he worked, always asking questions about money. The calls were so pushy that Lopez was thinking that perhaps the fund-raiser event should be cancelled. George Lopez explained that his wife, Ann, had participated in a blood drive held for Gavin at the Laugh Factory, and said that for months to follow, he was still willing to help Gavin Arvizo—until there was an incident in a parking lot that put him "over the top."

For the jury, the comedian detailed an evening in May of 2000, recalling that David Arvizo was waiting for him outside a restaurant where he'd been performing. Lopez testified that when he went outside to the parking lot at 10:00 PM that night, David Arvizo was waiting for him, and David began to get angry and overly aggressive about the fund-raiser event. Lopez told the jury that the two of them "exchanged words" at that time, and said that after their brief exchange, Lopez never wanted to see David Arvizo again.

Lopez told the jury that he called David Arvizo "an extortionist" to his face and made a little joke about using "such a big word." But no one in the courtroom was laughing.

With Tom Mesereau still questioning him, George Lopez described being aggressively pursued by the "Arvizo dad" for money. When Lopez learned that David Arvizo had called his home and had ranted at his wife, Ann, calling her "a fucking bitch" and other ugly names, he basically cut off ties with the rest of the Arvizos as well.

To the jury, George Lopez reiterated that he had a very "heated exchange" with David Arvizo, who had done his best to try to make the comedian feel guilty about not helping Gavin. He mentioned that six months *after* he severed all ties with the Arvizos, Janet approached him somehow, perhaps through Jamie Masada, and sent him a metal key chain that had a mustard seed embedded in it. Lopez knew the key chain was meant to be a "thank you" from Janet, but by then, he said, he really wasn't moved by it.

To Mesereau, George Lopez described the Arvizo family as being "smitten" with Michael Jackson. The TV star recalled David Arvizo boasting about his visits to Neverland Ranch, and indicated that David Arvizo began acting a bit strange after the family had established a firm footing with Jackson.

"At some point, David started bragging to you about Neverland Ranch, didn't he?" Mesereau asked.

"Yes," Lopez said.

"And you thought his attitude changed, correct?"

"Yes."

"You thought he got kind of snooty or snobby, would that be the right word?"

"Enamored," Lopez said.

"Enamored. That's how you described David's attitude after he told you the family had gone to Neverland Ranch?"

"Yes."

"And he told you that Michael Jackson had given a truck to his family, correct?"

"That's correct."

"Okay. And you described him to the sheriffs as 'smitten' with his newfound association with Michael Jackson, correct?"

"Yes."

Before the TV star ended his testimony, people couldn't help wonder why Michael Jackson would not have seen through this family. Clearly, Lopez had decided they were "bad news," but Jackson hadn't noticed anything odd about them. As he left the courtroom, Lopez looked over at Michael and made an effort to smile at the pop star.

But Jackson was not amused.

After witnessing the testimony from George Lopez, the pop star seemed to be realizing that he, of all people, should have had some kind of safety net in place, should have had some kind of screening process to shield him from grifters. Jackson was somehow led to believe that various TV and film stars were embracing this downtrodden Latino family, which, on one level, was true.

However, not one person from the Laugh Factory had informed Jackson about any of the problems or "concerns" with the Arvizos.

"Don't Stop 'Til You Get Enough"

On April Fools' Day, amid a mournful atmosphere and signals that the trial was not going well, the media was outside the courtroom interviewing Michael's fans, who seemed to have mixed feelings about what the future held for the pop star. Many were angry that former accusers were going to be dragged into the current proceedings, certain that the testimony about prior allegations would create more unnecessary prejudice against Michael.

Fans were furious. They felt Michael was being targeted by the court, that he was being treated unfairly. Tired of seeing him being lambasted by the media every day, some of Michael's fans were afraid that the superstar was going to be worn down. Many were convinced that a prison sentence would be the end of the superstar.

People became melodramatic. They speculated that if convicted, Michael would die in a prison cell. Tom Mesereau also agreed with that sentiment, later confiding that he treated the trial as if it were a *death penalty* case. Mesereau felt strongly that Jackson would wind up dead if he was sent to prison.

The thousands of Michael's supporters who made the trip to Santa Maria felt that they were a necessary part of Jackson's fight. Even if the mainstream media tended to ignore them, tended to try to dismiss their significance, fans knew they had a rightful place. Fans made sure their voices were heard, and they kept the media buzzing about Michael's innocence. Some fans were convinced about a conspiracy—and they held up signs that pointed the finger at Sony.

Each day, in Michael's presence, some fans would weep, others would chant. People wanted to tell Michael they loved him and wanted to be near him in any way possible. Fans would wake up every day and stand outside the courthouse at

6:00 AM, waiting out in the cold, in the rain—whatever it took—to land a public seat inside the courtroom.

The fans who were lucky enough to get inside were always interested to hear the twist the media put on things. The witnesses would say one thing, and the media reported only slices of what was coming from the witness stand, none of which supported Jackson. Fans were impressed by the American justice system, but more than anything, they hated the media, who they felt, unequivocally, had sided with the prosecution.

It was on April Fools' Day that an important piece of the puzzle would be revealed. The reported $20 million settlement with Jordie Chandler came under scrutiny as the high-powered attorney, Larry Feldman, made his way into the courtroom to testify. To courtroom observers, Feldman seemed like a demigod. The man had an air of superiority about him that was palpable. Dressed impeccably, standing tall, with a look of money dripping from every pocket, Feldman was asked to tell the jury about his academic preparation, noting that he was number one in his class at Loyola Law School, stating that he'd been in practice as an attorney since 1969.

Larry Feldman worked in a law firm in Los Angeles that housed six hundred lawyers and had offices that spanned thousands of miles—New York, Shanghai, Washington D.C., Chicago—the list went on. Feldman had been a trial lawyer all of his life, claimed he had become the senior partner in the law firm that he joined right out of law school, and said he'd represented injured federal workers, represented labor unions, and had represented a broad range of people—including lawyers who had been accused of malpractice.

When Sneddon asked the attorney to boast more specifically about his vast array of clients, Feldman said he didn't want to be a name-dropper. Larry Feldman had handled everything from suing rock groups to defending oil companies, but the only name that was mentioned was that of Johnnie Cochran. One couldn't help wondering why Sneddon would choose to bring up that particular name. Perhaps he hoped to present Feldman as the lawyer's lawyer. Perhaps he was playing a race card. Maybe it was a little of both.

To answer Sneddon's question, Feldman testified that he represented Johnnie Cochran in a legal matter for ten years—from the day Johnnie became involved in the O. J. Simpson trial until January of 2004. Then, as a list of his credentials was presented to the jury, Feldman confirmed that he was a "Fellow of the American College of Trial Lawyers," a distinction limited to 1 percent of all the lawyers in the United States. He told jurors that he was invited into "the International

Academy of Trial Lawyers," an organization that was, theoretically, made up of the top five hundred lawyers in the world.

Larry Feldman was—as Sneddon pointed out—the cream of the crop.

Once having established that, the DA focused his questions on the infamous lawsuit Larry Feldman handled for Jordan Chandler, the lawsuit everyone in the world seemed to know about. Back in 1993, when the Chandler boy was thirteen, Jordie had initially been represented by Gloria Allred, but the jury learned that the boy "wanted to switch attorneys," and he was referred to Larry Feldman through a series of high-powered hands. When Feldman was shown a photo of Jordie, he identified the young man as the "adorable, good-looking kid" who had filed a lawsuit against Michael Jackson for alleged sexual molestation.

Feldman testified that he filed the case, *Chandler v. Jackson*, in the Los Angeles Superior Court, but said that the case never went to trial because a settlement was reached in favor of Jordon Chandler, back in 1993 or 1994. Feldman wasn't sure about the exact date, and Sneddon didn't quibble. Instead, the DA wanted to fast-forward to 2003, to find out about a time when Larry Feldman had been contacted by an attorney, Bill Dickerman, who had called to refer another family to him—the family of Gavin Arvizo.

Larry Feldman couldn't remember if Bill Dickerman had been with the Arvizos on their first meeting at his old office, then located in Santa Monica, but Feldman assumed Dickerman brought the Arvizos there in person. Though he couldn't recall the specifics of the actual meeting, Feldman testified that in 2003, he met with Janet, Gavin, Davellin, and Star Arvizo, that he used "a process" to determine how he might handle the Arvizo case.

"The process that I follow in my law office at all times is, people come in, they tell a factual story," Feldman testified. "It depends on the case, but generally speaking, we will then do research, legal research, to try to understand what the law is."

Feldman explained that the genesis of Arvizo case was the Martin Bashir documentary, and testified that the Arvizo family wanted to make a claim against Bashir and the British entity he worked for—the fundamental issue being that Mr. Bashir had taped the Arvizo children without any consent.

Larry Feldman said that he tried to made "heads or tails" out of the Arvizos' claims, but when he couldn't, he decided to contact Dr. Stanley Katz, a psychology expert, whom he asked to meet with the Arvizo children. To courtroom observers, it seemed to be a strange coincidence that Dr. Stanley Katz was the same psychologist who Feldman had retained in the case of *Chandler v. Jackson*.

Nonetheless, Dr. Katz was the person who was asked to make an evaluation about the Arvizos, to determine the nature and "severity" of their claims. The Arvizo family, Feldman testified, needed to have an "expert" talk to them—that was a key element in his deciding about whether or not to take their case.

"The course of action was to allow an expert, which I was not, to spend some time with all three of them," Feldman told the jury. "Davellin wasn't really the issue, but Janet, Star, and Gavin [were the issue], and I let some expert figure out, if he could, what was happening."

The jury learned that as a result of Stanley Katz's meeting and "evaluation" with the Arvizos in May or June of 2003, Larry Feldman called the Arvizos back into his office to discuss their options. Feldman said that, based on what Stanley Katz had told him via an oral report, based on the Arvizos' initial discussions with the psychologist, and based on the Arvizo family's state of mind, a decision was made—and the Arvizos went to visit Dr. Katz for a second time.

Larry Feldman explained that after subsequent conversations between the Arvizo family and Dr. Katz, as a result of a report that Dr. Katz had written up regarding the Arvizos, Feldman decided to call the head of the Department of Children and Family Services in Los Angeles County, alerting the agency that a high-profile case might be at hand.

Feldman testified that the reason he contacted the LA County Department of Children and Family Services was to get "absolute assurance" that there would be no leaks about anything in connection with a report that Dr. Katz was going to bring forward. But as it turned out, the DCFS decided that the report should not be turned over to their agency at the time. The DCFS recommended that the report go to a law enforcement agency, and Larry Feldman made a call to DA Tom Sneddon.

As he spoke to the jury in a deep, formal voice, Larry Feldman said that when he contacted Tom Sneddon, he requested that the Santa Barbara DA conduct an investigation. Feldman insisted that he had no plans to file a civil lawsuit against Michael Jackson at the time. Feldman asserted that he was representing the Arvizo family regarding possible claims against Martin Bashir. The high-powered attorney testified that he "terminated" his relationship with the Arvizos by letter sometime in October of 2003.

However, Feldman later admitted that he had subsequently done "some work" on behalf of the Arvizos in 2004. Feldman told the jury that when Michael Jackson was arrested, he decided to file a claim against the DCFS on behalf of the Arvizos because the government agency had "leaked" the Arvizos' name to the press. Feldman believed that the Arvizo family was possibly seeking some form of monetary damages from the DCFS, holding the government agency responsible for "blasting" their names all over the news.

When it came time for Tom Mesereau to begin his cross-examination of Larry Feldman, the tension was so high, it was like watching the start of a professional boxing match. Mesereau wasted no time in getting to the main issue, which in this case was money. Mesereau wanted the jury to understand that, regardless of the outcome of the trial, both Gavin and Star Arvizo would have until age eighteen to sue Michael Jackson. The defense attorney wanted to clarify, for the record, that if a criminal conviction occurred in a child molestation case, the Arvizo boys could use anything they wished from the criminal case, could bring any evidence into a parallel civil suit in order to claim millions of dollars in damages.

"In other words, if Mr. Jackson were convicted of felony child molestation in this case, either Gavin or Star Arvizo could use that conviction to essentially win a civil case regarding similar alleged facts against Mr. Jackson?" Mesereau asked.

"That's correct," Feldman said.

"If there were a conviction for felony child molestation in this case, and if Star or Gavin Arvizo elected to sue in a civil case based on the similar alleged facts of sexual abuse, essentially the only issue remaining would be how much money you get, correct?"

"Probably. I think that's close enough," Feldman admitted. "I mean, nothing is that simple, as just stated. You know it as well as I. But essentially, I think that's what would happen."

Mesereau won on that point. He had gotten a straight answer out of Feldman early on. But as the two attorneys began to go over important details, they couldn't agree on much of anything else. After a while, their banter became a legal sparring session that was difficult for a layperson to understand. Tom Mesereau, who hadn't been number one in his graduating class, who hadn't been named as one of the "top five hundred lawyers in the world," seemed to have prepared himself for a major battle, and Larry Feldman wasn't about to be outdone. Feldman argued with Mesereau on virtually every point.

The bottom line was that Tom Mesereau wanted Larry Feldman to admit that if the DA were to win in the current criminal case, that conviction would save any civil attorney a great deal of time and money toward an investigation involving a subsequent civil suit. Mesereau was indirectly telling the jury that the Arvizos were, perhaps, using the taxpayers' money to cut the costs of a lengthy civil suit. It was an innuendo that Feldman resented, and the two attorneys argued about the issue. While being polite and accurate—they were verbally trying to slit each other's throats.

"Sir, did you tell a grand jury in Santa Barbara County that you had incurred tremendous cost of expenses during your lawsuit against Mr. Jackson in 1993?" Mesereau asked.

"I did. And it was true," Feldman told him.

"And if a liability were established through a criminal conviction, a civil litigator could avoid most of those costs, correct?"

"Some of those costs. Not most," Feldman said. "Some, I mean, certainly some, you would avoid."

"You could avoid a lot of the investigative costs, correct?"

"You know, it's—can I?" Feldman stammered.

"Just answer my question, if you would please," Mesereau insisted.

But Feldman said he couldn't answer the question the way it was being posed. Feldman wanted to explain that the Arvizos wouldn't avoid investigative costs completely, that any civil attorney taking on the case would still incur investigative costs, perhaps to a lesser degree. Feldman admitted that some of the costs would be different but insisted that the legal fees would be the same.

"But if you were to gauge your legal fees at hours, sir, and you didn't have to prove liability, you would save a tremendous amount in legal fees, wouldn't you?" Mesereau asked.

Feldman asserted that Mesereau had it all wrong, telling the defense attorney, "That ain't the way it works." But it was clear to the jury—and to everyone in the courtroom—that Larry Feldman was rattled by Mesereau. As the cross-examination got increasingly heated, Mesereau was able to get Feldman to concede that without a prior criminal conviction, a civil trial would last for months. Feldman began to argue about the fine points and tried to assert that there would still be costs and there would still be a process to obtain a civil judgment against Jackson. But when all was said and done, Feldman finally conceded that with a criminal conviction in hand, the lengthy process of a civil trial would almost be eliminated.

"Now, in the civil case where you represented Mr. Chandler and his parents against Mr. Jackson, there was a cross-complaint, was there not?" Mesereau asked.

"There was?" Feldman said, looking stunned.

"Mr. Jackson sued for extortion, didn't he?"

"I don't know. I know he claimed—I know his investigator, Mr. Pellicano, claimed extortion."

"You don't recall?"

"I'm not saying that it didn't happen. I just don't recall."

As the legal questions flew across the room, Tom Mesereau was able to establish—and break down into layman's terms—the fact that Jordie Chandler's 1993 case had language in the settlement agreement that stated that "neither side admits wrongdoing to the other."

With respect to Arvizo case, Mesereau pounced on the referral arrangement that Larry Feldman had with Attorney Bill Dickerman, insinuating that the two attorneys had a plan to work together in order to get paid as much money as possible. A firestorm of questions came from Mesereau about the amount of money Feldman and Dickerman expected to receive if they brought a case against Jackson on behalf of the Arvizos, but his questions were met with dead ends.

Larry Feldman didn't seem to recall the terms he had worked out with Dickerman. Feldman knew that Dickerman wanted money—he was sure of that. But Feldman couldn't pinpoint the exact financial terms he and Dickerman had agreed to. When pressed on the subject, it was Feldman's contention that since the Arvizo case "never went anyplace," he had no particular reason to recall the exact details. Feldman tried to make light of his connection to Bill Dickerman. He clearly didn't want to be portrayed as an ambulance chaser.

When Mesereau brought up a series of faxes and letters that had gone back and forth between the two law offices after Dickerman referred the Arvizos to Feldman, Larry Feldman admitted that he had agreed to pay Bill Dickerman something if Feldman took the Arvizo case. Feldman told jurors that he would be the lead lawyer on the case, that Dickerman would have had very little work to do except perhaps a small task here or there.

As words got heated inside the courtroom, as feathers got ruffled, Mesereau continued to pounce on Feldman on two points: 1) Larry Feldman had made a career of suing high-profile people. 2) The Arvizo family, along with Bill Dickerman and Larry Feldman, all stood to make a lot of money from Michael Jackson—if the jury believed a sexual molestation had occurred.

"Now in Los Angeles County, you're known as one of the most successful plaintiff's lawyers, correct?" Mesereau asked.

"Say it again for the press. I want to—that's the nicest thing anybody's ever said about me in this case," Feldman quipped.

"Is that true?"

"I think so."

"You've had numerous multimillion-dollar awards that you have obtained for your clients, correct?"

"I have."

"And in most of those situations, you had what is called a contingency fee arrangement, correct?"

"Oh, I'm sure. Over the course of my legal career, that's absolutely right."

"And generally speaking, in a contingency fee arrangement, the plaintiff's lawyer in these cases, namely you, get a percentage of whatever is recovered for the client, true?"

"Yes."

Feldman was forced to admit that in a contingency fee case, there was an incentive for the attorney to obtain the largest settlement possible. As he asked pointed questions, Mesereau looked down at two documents signed by Jordie Chandler's parents, who had each consented to Feldman's contingency fee agreement. Without going into the exact dollar amounts of the settlement, Mesereau established that both of Jordie's parents, who were divorced long before 1993, had received settlement money from Michael Jackson. Having Evan and June Chandler each collect their own separate monies was Jordie Chandler's idea—according to Feldman's testimony.

Mesereau brought out details about Evan Chandler's criminal defense, because Evan Chandler was being sued for allegedly trying to extort money from Michael Jackson. As the two attorneys bantered back and forth, testimony would show that, not only did Jordie's parents receive separate payments, but, June Chandler's new husband at the time, David Schwartz, decided to file his own suit against Michael Jackson—seeking his own monetary damages as well.

"You have represented the parents of Janet Arvizo in this case, correct?" Mesereau wanted to know.

"Her parents?" Feldman asked.

"You represented them in an attempt to prevent us from seeing if she deposited money into her parents' account, true?"

"I prevented you from getting into their—these parents' bank records," Feldman responded.

"And in doing that, sir, you tried to prevent us from seeing if Janet got checks or David Arvizo got checks, whether they deposited them into her parents' account?"

"No, Mr. Mesereau. I prevented you from dragging in these poor parents, who don't even speak English, into this melee."

"Sir, you can't prevent the parents from being subpoenaed as witnesses in this case, can you?"

"No."

"And you haven't even tried to do that."

"And I wouldn't."

"The only thing you tried to do was stop us from seeing whether Janet put money into her parents' account."

When Mesereau's volume raised, Tom Sneddon objected, telling the court that the witness was being attacked. However, Mesereau was standing on proper legal grounds. Mesereau was relying on court documents, and through them, the defense attorney was able to prove that Larry Feldman had represented Janet Arvizo's parents from December 2004 through January 2005. Throughout that time period, Mesereau had served Janet's parents with a subpoena to view all of their checks and financial records.

From the stand, Feldman admitted that he had prevented Mesereau from pursuing the possibility that Janet was funneling money. When Mesereau took a poll about the work that the high-powered lawyer had done, pro bono, on behalf of the Arvizo family, Feldman admitted that he'd had acted on behalf of Janet Arvizo, her three children, her parents, and had also advised Janet's new husband, Major Jay Jackson, in connection with a search warrant on his military records.

"How many times do you think you've spoken on the telephone with Prosecutor Sneddon about this criminal case?" Mesereau wondered.

"Well, I don't know. At least two or three times," Feldman said. "We haven't had a lot of calls. Frankly, I called him when I called him to say, 'Here's the case. Do what you want with it.' And maybe—I don't know, five, six [other times]. Not a lot. I mean, I don't know. Something like that."

"How many times do you think you met with Mr. Sneddon regarding your representation of Mr. Chandler in 1993?" Mesereau asked.

"I don't know that I ever met with him in 1993. With Mr. Sneddon?"

"Yes."

"In 1993, I was on my own, without—I was handling," Feldman's voice trailed off.

"You certainly spoke to him," Mesereau insisted.

"I was handling the case. I'm sure I spoke with him, but I don't think I ever met with him. Maybe I did. I could have. I just can't remember, Mr. Mesereau. It's so long ago. I mean, that's twelve years ago. I just don't have an independent memory of whether I did or whether I didn't. Because the case was also in LA, and you know, I was dealing with the LA lawyers, criminal lawyers."

"Would it be accurate to say that you at least talked to Mr. Sneddon a number of times about your representation of Mr. Chandler?"

"You know," Feldman said, "Not mister—Mr. Chandler now is little Jordie, who's now a mister. Or is it his father we're talking about? When you say Mr. Chandler, [you mean] Jordie? Who are we talking about?"

"Any of them."

"You know, I don't think—it could have happened. I can't deny it. I just have no recollection of it one way or the other. I don't remember having many—any—real discussions with Mr. Sneddon on the case."

Courtroom observers watched carefully as the high-powered attorney evaded questions. Some sat silently, wondering to themselves exactly what the merit of the Jordie Chandler suit was.

"BE CAREFUL WHO YOU LOVE"

Jesus Salas, employed by Michael Jackson for twenty years as his personal house manager, was a humble man. Testifying on behalf of the prosecution, Mr. Salas rarely looked over in Michael's direction. The gentleman seemed uncomfortable in court. Like many of the witnesses who came before him, Mr. Salas looked like he was anxious to answer the questions, to end the public ordeal as quickly as possible.

For starters, the house manager talked about children being frequent guests at Michael's home. Mr. Salas told jurors that Michael expected "the best" for every guest who visited Neverland, that his young guests were provided pretty much, with whatever they wanted. If kids wanted candy, they were given candy. If kids wanted their dinner served in the train station, that was fine. If they wanted to eat in the main house, that was fine too.

Children had constant access to all of Michael's prized possessions, including all of his rides and games, an alphabetized video library, two separate zoos, and a movie theater that was open 24/7. Salas testified that Michael had a full-sized theater where he maintained a staff to serve guests from a free candy concession and ice cream stand. The jury was shown a photo of the theater, which had plush velvet seats and two rooms downstairs, each room equipped with hospital beds so children could lie down and watch movies, if they chose to. The only rules Jesus Salas knew of at Neverland had to do with safety. Children were not permitted to drive 4-wheelers without permission, and they were monitored whenever they drove golf carts, Quadrunners, scooters—things of that nature.

As for the security set up at Neverland, Salas testified that all of Michael's guests were given the combination to the main house, that all of the guests at

Neverland were able to enter the main buildings on the property freely, including the Arvizo family, who were invited by Michael in the spring of 2003.

Jesus Salas recalled picking up the Arvizos from the Santa Barbara airport and said the family stayed at Neverland for about two weeks, then left for a while, then returned to Neverland for another two weeks. Salas said that there was a time when he was asked to drive the Arvizos to LA, which he did, and testified that the Arvizos returned to Neverland for a third time, staying for about a week. During these three visits, Salas said, Michael was "on the property" most of the time.

Mr. Salas confirmed that there were two German men on the property, whom he referred to as "Deiter" and "Ronald," and said that these men were having "meetings" with Michael during the time that the Arvizos were at Neverland. Salas testified that he had no idea what the meetings were about, explaining that he had no knowledge about Deiter or Ronald's connection to Michael Jackson. Salas told the jury that Frank Casio was also a regular guest at Neverland when the Arvizos were staying there, stating that Frank was "practically living there."

When asked about the Arvizos' sleeping arrangements, the house manager said there were times when the Arvizo boys slept in the guest units next to their mother and sister and other times when they slept in Michael's bedroom. Salas testified that throughout the years he'd seen "other kids" sleep in Michael's bedroom, both upstairs and downstairs in Michael's two-story master suite.

Salas said it was not unusual to see kids in Michael's bedroom, explaining that Michael would play games with his own kids and with other kids, all of whom would join Michael in his room, whenever he had spare time. Salas said that Michael also entertained adults in his master suite, telling jurors that he'd seen adults being served food and alcohol on the lower level of the suite, which had a sitting room area, a grand piano, and a large fireplace.

When asked specific questions about alcohol, Salas said that he believed Michael drank wine and vodka. Salas testified that, in his opinion, Michael exhibited the effects of drinking on a regular basis but pointed out that he rarely saw Michael Jackson actually consume any alcoholic beverage. Salas also confirmed that Michael had once had a prescription drug problem, which stemmed from Michael being severely burned during the filming of a Superbowl Pepsi commercial. Salas testified that he had been aware that Michael had gone through "treatment" for that problem, but also noted that Michael had a back problem and also had broken his leg in the year 2003, testifying that Michael had been seeing doctors, and was on prescription medications at times.

In the twenty years that he served as Jackson's chief domestic worker, running Michael's home, Jesus Salas said he had not witnessed the entertainer drinking alcohol in front of children—ever. Salas was asked specifically about Gavin, who Salas thought was acting drunk one night—however, Salas told jurors that Michael wasn't with Gavin that night. Moreover, Salas said he wasn't even certain that Gavin was intoxicated.

Mr. Salas was also asked about a group of local boys from Los Olivos who'd been caught coming out of the wine cellar in the arcade, causing an issue at Neverland in the fall of 2003. Salas described the incident with the Los Olivos boys and told the jury that the local boys were Michael's guests who had spent many days enjoying Neverland. Salas recalled seeing these boys sneaking out of the wine cellar, but insisted that Michael was not with them.

Jesus Salas said it was Michael's policy not to allow children into the wine cellar. He told the jury that the Los Olivos boys were neighbors who frequented Neverland, often when Michael wasn't even home. He said that the boys were young teens who had taken liberties around Neverland, playing hide-and-seek in the house, getting caught in rooms that were off-limits. Salas said the boys were "known" to Neverland staff because they often got themselves into trouble. In terms of the allegations that the Arvizo boys made—claiming that they were always intoxicated at Neverland—the prosecution asked about a particular evening when the Arvizo boys were in Michael's bedroom with Frank Casio and his siblings, asking if Michael Jackson had ordered a bottle of wine to be delivered to the room with four wine glasses.

For the jurors, Salas confirmed that Michael had indeed placed a wine order on the night in question. But as the house manager thought back to that particular evening, Salas inadvertently added that Michael had also ordered regular sodas to be delivered along with the wine that night—which made people on the jury roll their eyes.

It was a blow for the prosecution, because Salas was their witness, and the man was very sincere in his responses. He was being honest about things, as he recalled them, and when Salas told the jury that he recalled soda being delivered to the room for the Arvizo boys—in light of the Arvizos' testimony, both boys claiming that they drank alcohol with Michael in his bedroom every night—the facts weren't adding up at all.

Jesus Salas was a credible witness, and his answers were heartfelt. When repeatedly asked about the alcohol served at Neverland, Salas recalled only one other occasion that Michael ordered wine with the Arvizo boys present—and told the jury that Michael had requested just one wineglass.

For the jury, Salas was asked to identify various "adult" magazines that Michael had in his office, to identify tiny S&M dolls that Michael had in his office, photos of which were entered into evidence and flashed on a large screen for the courtroom spectators to stare at. It was quite awkward, looking at the sadomasochistic figurines flashing boldly on the screen. People later wondered what that had to do with anything. There was never any testimony that linked these obscure objects to Michael and children. Some courtroom observers felt it was gratuitous. Others found it amusing that Michael was into female sex objects.

In furtherance of the conspiracy charge, Jesus Salas was asked to talk about a time when Janet called him and asked him to drive her home. Janet was crying, Salas recalled, and she was insisting that she wanted to leave Neverland. Salas felt sorry for Janet, so he took it upon himself to drive the Arvizo family to their home in LA, using one of Michael's cars—a Rolls-Royce—to transport them. Salas told the jury that when Janet made the request, it was late at night, and explained that before he drove the Arvizos off the property, he informed Chris Carter, one of Michael's bodyguards, about the situation, just so someone would be aware that he was escorting the Arvizos off the property.

According to Salas, it was Michael's friend, Frank Casio, who was angry that the Arvizos were gone. Salas told jurors that a short time after he brought the Arvizos to LA, perhaps within a week, the Arvizos returned to Neverland—though he could not say why. Salas testified that upon their return, Janet approached him a second time, perhaps a week later, and asked to be driven to LA again. But this time, Salas told her that he couldn't make the drive. A few days after that, Salas recalled, Janet and her children left the property for good, never to be seen at Michael's home again.

As Tom Mesereau began his cross-examination, the first thing he asked Mr. Salas about was the Arvizo boys' sleeping arrangements. The boys claimed they slept with Michael all the time, yet Salas saw the Arvizo boys sleeping on the ground floor of Michael's bedroom suite. Salas told the jury that was the only place he saw the boys sleeping. Salas had not seen the boys sleeping in Michael's bed, which was located on the second floor of his master suite.

Mr. Salas talked about the first-class service that was given to the entire Arvizo family, who ate in the kitchen or dining room when they chose to, who ordered room service when they desired, who had food service available to them at all hours of the day and night. The Arvizos, he said, were afforded the "classy service" that all of Michael's guests enjoyed. Mr. Salas said the Arvizo boys roamed the grounds of Neverland freely, spent time on the rides, played games at the arcade, and watched movies in the theater. Mr. Salas said Janet spent most of her time in her guest unit. She was not outside with her children—not on the train, not on the rides, not at the zoo. According to Salas, the only times Janet would appear was to have a meal in the main house. Janet seemed preoccupied, Salas recalled, and he testified that she often would walk around the Neverland grounds by herself.

The house manager testified that Janet Arvizo stayed in the most beautiful room on the property—the same guest suite that Elizabeth Taylor and Marlon Brando always requested. Salas said Janet was given the same level of service that Liz Taylor and Marlon Brando received, telling the jury that the theater, the main house, and all of the grounds were available to her.

As for Janet's request to have someone drive her off the property with her children, Mr. Salas explained that he drove the Arvizos to LA because Janet seemed upset at the time. He assured the jury that Janet and her children were never forcibly kept at Neverland, blowing the DA's conspiracy theory completely away.

"At no time was Janet ever kept at Neverland against her will?" Mesereau asked.

"That is exactly what I said," Salas testified.

"She called you, upset, and asked you to take her home, and you did so, right?"

"Yes."

"You took her yourself, is that correct? Do you remember what month you took her in the Rolls-Royce?"

"It was December or January. Somewhere around there. Pretty bad on dates," Salas said.

"And then she came back, what, in less than a week?"

"I would say in a couple of weeks, thereabout."

"She came back, and then a few weeks later wanted to leave again, right?" Mesereau asked.

"That is correct."

"And you arranged for transportation for her to leave again, right?"

"Yes, I had to call a limo."

As Mesereau questioned Jesus Salas, the jury learned that Janet Arvizo never complained about the way she was treated at Neverland, that her only comments were directed toward her dislike of the two German men, Deiter and Ronald, as well as toward her dislike of the media attention her family had become subjected to—all because of the Bashir documentary.

To Salas, Janet had only good things to say about Jackson. She respected Jackson and liked him very, very much. And that seemed to be Jesus Salas' opinion of

Michael as well. Salas said that Michael was very generous with gifts—and would sometimes send him to Toys "R" Us to purchase as much as $11,000 worth of toys to be handed out to children at Neverland. Salas testified that Michael would sometimes personally arrange to bring a busload of children and their parents to the property and then have them assemble in an area so that staff members could hand out toys to them. Whenever possible, Michael would come out to see the children in the middle of the toy distribution, and all the children and their parents would run to hug and kiss Michael, to thank him for his random act of kindness.

In the twenty years that Jesus Salas worked there, he'd seen thousands of children arrive in busloads to visit Neverland, many of whom came from Los Angeles. He told jurors that Michael's property was visited by children from all around the globe, and estimated that he'd seen hundreds of thousands of children visit Neverland, each of them having the time of their lives.

Jesus Salas talked about "Family Day" at Neverland, which Michael put on at least once a year for all of his employees. It was a big event that lasted the whole day, and all other groups would be kept off the property so that employees and their children could enjoy the rides, the zoos, the total Neverland experience—where everyone could be a kid again, and everything was always "compliments of the house."

As Mesereau switched away from happy talk, he decided to ask about the mischievous situations that certain children at Neverland would get into. Jesus Salas told the jury that over the years, children were often caught going beyond limits. Sometimes kids would try to access closets and maids' quarters. Sometimes they'd be caught handling expensive antiques and art objects. Other times, kids were caught trying to access the locked wine cellar—a room that already existed on the property when Michael first bought Neverland.

Jesus Salas said that as much as Michael enjoyed playing and having fun with kids, the pop star often liked to be left alone in his dance studio or in his recording studio to work on his music. Salas said that Michael would spend "hours on end" doing his creative work—allowing the day-to-day operations at Neverland to be handled by his employees. Salas confirmed that Jackson let his employees take care of the twenty-seven-hundred-acre property, mentioning that Michael had a full security patrol unit on the grounds because there were no fences around Neverland. For the record, Jesus Salas told the jury that even though intruders sometimes were caught on the property, none of the Neverland security people carried a gun.

Michael didn't want any weapons at Neverland.

Michael was more concerned about children's safety.

"Black and White"

"I love you."

"God and the truth are on our side."

—The voice of Michael Jackson via telephone, addressing hundreds of fans who gathered for a vigil during his trial in Santa Maria.

When two former employees of Neverland Ranch testified that they witnessed various forms of lewd conduct between Michael Jackson and young boys, the King of Pop stared over at the jury and studied their faces. Michael was making a deliberate effort to connect with them, and it looked like he was trying to read their minds. Former employees alleged that Jackson was seen naked with young boys and was seen kissing and touching boys on several occasions, and for the first time, members of the jury looked completely disturbed.

To Michael's family, these claims by former employees were completely disingenuous, especially given that both of Michael's employees, Ralph Chacon and Adrian McManus, had chosen to sue Michael in a civil court and had lost. To some courtroom observers, these former employees seemed bitter, as if they were holding a grudge against Michael, but nonetheless, when Ralph Chacon began to describe his version of the lurid details, journalists took fast and furious notes. As the testimony became graphic, Tito Jackson walked out of the courtroom. Tito seemed angry. He clearly felt that Michael was being betrayed, sold out, by disgruntled people.

Ralph Chacon was a former security guard at Neverland, having worked there from 1991 to 1994. He told jurors that he'd spied on Jackson through a window, and claimed he had witnessed the pop star naked in the shower with a young boy.

Chacon alleged that he'd seen more than one incident where Jackson was kissing and caressing the young boy, and said he'd been subpoenaed to testify at a 1994 grand jury hearing involving Jordie Chandler, where he told those jurors the same story.

When Tom Mesereau questioned Ralph Chacon, the jury learned that back in 1994, the former security guard was desperately trying to get his bills paid. Chacon was in financial trouble and was working with a Santa Barbara attorney to try to extract money from Jackson. They discovered that Chacon and other former Neverland employees had hired a "media broker" to try to sell Michael Jackson stories to the tabloids. As he answered questions, Ralph Chacon came off as a man who had an axe to grind. He appeared to be defensive, and was angry that he was being portrayed as someone who was trying to make a fast buck.

According to Mesereau, not only was Chacon desperate to pay his rent at the time that he sued Jackson, he had actually bragged to neighbors that he was going to get rich by being a "star witness" against the entertainer. Though Chacon denied it, the former security guard was already counting his millions before the civil law suit went to trial. Back in 1994, he allegedly told neighbors that he planned to be driving a 450 Mercedes-Benz in the near future.

As the defense attorney grilled Ralph Chacon, he asked about the counter-claims made by Michael Jackson in the civil suit, which resulted in a $25,000 judgment against Chacon for maliciously transferring Jackson's personal property. As sparks flew, courtroom observers realized that Ralph Chacon had no leg to stand on in his civil suit, that Chacon had decided to sue Michael Jackson—just because he could. The more Chacon tried to defend himself against Mesereau's attack, the more the former Neverland security guard seemed to have been motivated by greed and media attention.

In his civil suit, Ralph Chacon claimed he suffered "damage" because Michael Jackson stared at him. From the stand, when Chacon assured Mesereau that he was "hurt" because Michael stared at him, many of the jurors looked at each other with smirks. When Chacon testified that he thought his phones were tapped at Neverland, that he'd filed an additional claim against Jackson because he'd been "emotionally damaged" by having his phone calls listened to, a few of the jurors looked like they were about to burst out laughing.

Under cross-examination, Ralph Chacon admitted that he told an attorney that he thought Michael Jackson should compensate him for the rest of his life. Mesereau was reading from Chacon's deposition, so the disgruntled employee couldn't deny that he wanted Jackson to give him a free ride in perpetuity. Looking at Chacon with utter disbelief, the jury listened as Mr. Chacon went into a sob story about his wife's problems, about a death in his family. The man actually shed tears while on the stand, crying about the problems he had in his own life. But the jury didn't seem to care.

Chacon was forced to admit that he had asked Michael Jackson to pay him $16 million in damages—for hang-up calls and supposed threats made by Michael's other security guards. When jurors learned that a previous Santa Maria jury had rejected Chacon's ridiculous claims back in 1994, people looked at Ralph Chacon with different eyes.

This was a man who claimed he witnessed sex acts between Jackson and Jordie Chandler, yet he decided to go to lawyers and tabloids rather than being helpful to police. This was a man who testified that he never had stolen property from Michael, even though a previous jury had found him guilty of theft and had awarded Jackson substantial compensation for damages.

At one point, in the heat of the moment, Mesereau elicited spontaneous testimony from Chacon, who admitted that he left Neverland because he didn't like the new set of security guards that Michael had hired in 1993. To the jury it seemed that Chacon's civil lawsuit was vindictive. In front of God, the judge, and all the courtroom observers—the man was totally discredited.

That same morning, just before the noontime break, Adrian McManus, Michael's former chambermaid, took the stand to talk about Michael's bedroom and his most personal habits. She reported seeing a number of boys in Michael's room and explained that she spent a lot of time there, since it was her job to wash Michael's clothes, to make his bed, to clean his bathrooms. According to McManus, who worked at Neverland for a couple of years until July of 1994, she witnessed Michael kissing boys on the cheek and touching them on the outside of their clothes.

McManus testified about boys getting very wild and destructive while visiting Neverland, claiming some boys would dump soda and popcorn on Michael and leave big messes for her to clean up. Among the things she told the prosecutor that got people whispering during the next break: Michael had chimps running around his bedroom, whose droppings she was required to clean up after.

Everyone laughed about that.

Back on the stand, as McManus continued to tell her story, the jury learned that she had joined forces with Ralph Chacon and three other Neverland employees to sue Jackson for monetary damages, claiming they were pressured to quit their jobs by a new set of bodyguards who were hired in 1993. McManus alleged that she quit her job because Michael's security team had harassed her for over six months. She told the jury she received a few threatening phone calls at her home and said she was subject to menacing comments by the Neverland security staff. McManus claimed she was sexually harassed by Michael's body-guards—though the only detail she could report was an offhand comment some-one once made asking her what kind of underwear she had on.

Sizing up McManus, who was a pretty woman, fair skinned, yet clearly plump, her claims seemed totally out of place. Unable to offer any details, McManus spoke in generalities about receiving anonymous hang-up calls, but the chambermaid seemed to be reaching. She claimed that she'd been abused at Neverland, however, she couldn't relate one specific instance of abuse to the jury.

Under direct examination, Adrian McManus admitted that instead of collect-ing millions of dollars from her former employer, a civil jury found in favor of Michael Jackson and ordered her (and four other former employees) to pay *him* $1.4 million in legal expenses. In addition, because Jackson had filed a counter-suit claiming that the five disgruntled employees had stolen from him, a judge ordered McManus and the others to pay an additional $40,000 in damages, find-ing that his former employees had acted with "fraud, oppression, and malice" against Jackson.

The whole time that Adrian McManus testified, Michael looked straight at her, taking notes and whispering to his attorneys. Michael sat up tall, his eyes fix-ated on McManus as she told the jury that she'd seen Jackson touching a series of boys—among them, Macaulay Culkin. Weeks later, these same boys would take the stand to testify that nothing sexual ever happened when they were with Michael.

As Mesereau questioned Adrian McManus, the defense attorney established that she had spoken to authorities about the alleged molestation of Jordie Chan-dler in a deposition taken December 7, 1993. At that time, McManus had not mentioned anything about sexually inappropriate acts in Michael's bedroom. Then, approximately one year later, on December 2, 1994, when McManus filed her civil complaint against Jackson, the chambermaid conveniently "recalled" witnessing sexual acts that she'd never spoken of before. Suddenly, with big money at stake, McManus had stories to report about Michael being in his Jacuzzi with young boys, about Michael being involved in three "incidents" with boys.

Once Tom Mesereau established this time line, he came down hard on Adrian McManus. He was tearing into her, just ripping her to shreds, and the woman was not prepared for it. For one thing, the defense attorney made sure to let everyone in the courtroom know that a 1994 civil jury believed Adrian McManus was a fraud. Mesereau brought out details that made McManus look like a malicious and conniving woman, and the former chambermaid was clearly shocked by this attack.

Mesereau showed McManus a deposition filed in the civil suit by Jordie Chandler, in which McManus said that she'd never seen anything suspicious in Michael's bedroom, that she'd never seen Michael sleeping with any children at all. In that initial deposition, McManus went so far as to state that she would allow her own ten-year-old boy to stay alone with Michael.

Mesereau repeatedly pointed out that McManus did not say one word about three alleged "incidents" until a year later, when she decided to bring forth this information during a deposition with Larry Feldman. Mesereau simply couldn't understand why McManus would claim that Jackson was innocent in 1993, then turn her story around 360 degrees and label herself as a potential witness against Jackson in 1994. As Mesereau approached the subject from different angles, McManus became more defensive. But rather than gaining sympathy for herself, her responses seemed to irk the jury.

"In that lawsuit, you were suing Mr. Jackson for a number of different claims, and one of the claims said that you were a potential material witness against Jackson in both the civil suit and a criminal investigation, right?" Mesereau asked.

"I believe so," McManus said.

"And what that really meant was, by filing that complaint with that language, you were essentially threatening Mr. Jackson that you would change your testimony unless you were paid, right?"

"I'm not familiar with a lot of attorney language," McManus said. "So I really don't know how to answer that."

"How much money do you recall you were seeking from Mr. Jackson in that lawsuit?" Mesereau wanted to know.

"That's another question I cannot answer. That was dealing with my attorney."

"Well, you were in court when he argued to the Santa Maria jury for millions of dollars, right?"

"I don't even know if I was there at the time," McManus stammered. "I could have been. I don't remember."

"You certainly must have discussed with your attorney during that six-month trial how much money you were trying to get for yourself from Mr. Jackson, right?"

"Honestly, I don't believe anybody knew how much money anybody would be getting out of a trial," McManus said.

"But how much did you want?"

"I really didn't want anything. I just wanted justice for what I had been through."

McManus told the jury that she had also sued a few of Michael's personal security people, one of whom, Jerome Johnson, had decided to jump over to her camp, to join in her suit against Jackson. At some point, when the jury learned that Jerome Johnson had written a letter to Michael Jackson, asking the pop star for three million dollars, the idea that Michael's staff was so eager to betray him started to weigh on everyone's minds.

"You didn't want millions of dollars in that lawsuit?" Mesereau asked.

"I wanted justice," McManus answered. "I don't—whatever—I just wanted justice."

"But your idea of justice was millions of bucks, right?"

"Well, that's not what I call justice," McManus quipped.

"You file a lawsuit, you go through approximately eight days of depositions, all sorts of paperwork, and you're in trial for six months. You wanted millions, right?" Mesereau persisted.

"Honestly, a simple, 'Sorry for what we did to you' would have been great for me," she told him.

"Did you ever write a letter to Mr. Jackson saying, 'Mr. Jackson, I don't want to sue you. Just tell me you're sorry?'"

"No. I did not."

"Ever call Mr. Jackson and say, 'Mr. Jackson I don't really want to sue you. Just say you're sorry?'"

"I didn't have a number to contact Mr. Jackson."

The defense attorney asserted that McManus hoped that by going to the Santa Barbara sheriffs with "information," perhaps she could put pressure on Michael Jackson to pay money to settle her civil case. When Mesereau fired more questions at McManus that pointed to her own inappropriate behavior, the former chambermaid seemed to go completely numb.

"Do you know someone named Francine Orosco?" Mesereau asked.

"Yes, she was a maid for Neverland Valley Ranch," McManus testified.

"And at some point, she was a personal friend of yours, was she not?"

"We became friends, yes."

"Now, you know that she became a witness against your claims in the lawsuit, right?" Mesereau asked.

"Yes, I believe so," McManus told him.

"Didn't you repeatedly tell Francine Orosco that Michael Jackson was innocent of any charge of sexual molestation?"

"No, I did not."

"Do you remember telling Francine Orosco that you were going to get big-time money in your lawsuit against Michael Jackson?"

"No, I did not."

"And you tried to convince her to say that she had seen acts of sexual harassment involving you, right?"

"No, I did not," McManus insisted.

"While you worked at Neverland," Mesereau asked, "Francine Orosco visited you at your home, did she not?"

"Maybe one time."

"And you showed her a room in your house filled with watches, posters, clocks, sunglasses, T-shirts, and other items you had taken from Neverland, correct?"

"No," McManus insisted.

"You showed her laundry baskets filled with Michael Jackson's clothes that you had taken from Neverland, right?"

"No."

Michael's former chambermaid denied ever having taken anything of his, with the exception of a few candy bars from the movie theater. When Mesereau offered proof that the 1994 civil jury had found that McManus had stolen from Mr. Jackson, the former chambermaid admitted to having a sketch that belonged to Michael, which she claimed she found in the trash. It was a sketch that Michael had drawn of Elvis Presley, which McManus sold to a tabloid for a thousand dollars.

"You and the other plaintiffs in that lawsuit decided that you would go to the show *Hard Copy* to try and sell a story, correct?" Mesereau asked.

"Not that I ever recall," she told him.

McManus did not want to admit it, but the woman was forced to testify that there was indeed tabloid money, which the five employees collected from shows such as *Inside Edition* and other media outlets—it added up to about $32,000, of which, $1,000 went to her. Though she tried to minimize her involvement, McManus couldn't deny that she and other employees at Neverland "possibly" tried to sell additional stories to the tabloids about Michael Jackson's relationship with Lisa Marie Presley.

Adrian McManus blushed when she was asked questions about a contract she signed with *Star* magazine to provide details about Michael's relationship with his then-wife, Lisa Marie. Apparently, she had also signed an agreement with Splash, an agency that was retained by this group of former employees to help them find other media sources and outlets that would pay cash for Jackson stories.

As McManus tried to deny her participation in the tabloid scandals, Tom Mesereau brought out the news clippings, showing the jury that Adrian McManus was quoted in an issue of *Star* magazine in which she bragged about having a key to Michael's bedroom. The tabloid issue was headlined, "Five of His Closest Servants Tell All: Kinky Sex Secrets of Michael and Lisa Marie's Bedroom."

"Do you recall being quoted in any Australian newspapers about Mr. Jackson's private life?" Mesereau wondered.

"I have no idea."

"How many television shows do you think you've appeared on where you purported to give private information about Michael Jackson?"

"The only thing I can recall that I appeared on was maybe—I think it was *Inside Edition*," McManus said.

Shifting gears, Mesereau wanted to return to the subject of the deposition Adrian McManus had given in 1993 regarding Jordie Chandler. Reading pages of her deposition to refresh her memory, McManus admitted that back in 1993, she had reported that she'd seen Jordie Chandler's mother repeatedly in Michael's bedroom, that she'd seen Jordie Chandler and Michael riding around the property on a Jet Ski, that she had seen Michael having water-balloon fights with Jordie and other children. The jury got the message: prior to her 1994 civil case, Adrian McManus swore that she'd never seen Michael as much as holding hands with any child at the ranch.

As they listened to the "revelations" from both former employees, jurors were thinking about the curious testimony they heard from Jason Francia, the son of a Neverland housekeeper, who testified that he'd been tickled by Jackson, that he'd been tickled three times by Jackson, on the outside of his clothing.

It was because of these tickling incidents, Jason Francia told the jury, that he decided to go into therapy. But Francia failed to testify about certain things. According to Mesereau, Sneddon was actually present for the first therapy session, but that was never mentioned in court. That Sneddon was so involved in obtaining evidence against Jackson—was information that would later come out on cross-examination.

Initially, when Jason Francia took the stand, his much-anticipated testimony seemed authentic. Francia told jurors that the "tickling incidents" took place in the early 1990s, claiming that he was still suffering over the alleged incidents.

Francia seemed truly upset, but then the jury became confused when they learned that Francia (who received a $2 million settlement) had changed his story at least once. At first, Francia reported that he was not touched near his private area. Another curious thing that Jason Francia claimed: he was unaware of the financial terms that his mother reached regarding the alleged "incidents."

"When did you learn that your mother got twenty thousand dollars to give an interview with *Hard Copy* in the 1990s?" Mesereau asked.

"I think it was last Sunday," Francia testified.

"Okay. And I guess she told you that?" Mesereau wondered.

"No."

"She's never told you that?"

"That she received twenty thousand dollars? She's never told me that," Francia insisted.

"Did you know before last week that your mother had been paid to go on the television show *Hard Copy*?"

"I think I assumed it."

"Okay. All right. Now, you admitted that at the beginning of your first interview in 1993, you said that Mr. Jackson had not touched your genital area, right?" Mesereau asked.

"I said that in the very beginning," Francia admitted.

"It was only after you were pushed real hard by the sheriffs that you began to say anything like that, true?"

But the question was not answered.

Jason Francia had done his 1993 police interview on tape, so Mesereau then quoted the sheriffs, who seemed to be forcing Francia into making an accusation.

"Even after the sheriffs said to you, 'He's a molester. He's a great guy, makes great music, bullshit, he has lots of money,' you still said he had never touched your genital area, right?" Mesereau asked.

"I believe so," Francia told the jury.

"Okay. Did you tell the sheriffs in your first interview, you had never spent the night with Mr. Jackson, right?"

"I never slept in his bed with him," Francia said.

"Okay. Without going into any amounts, do you know if your mother has received any money from Mr. Jackson?"

"She has."

"Do you know approximately when she received money from a settlement?"

"I don't."

"Do you know if it was before you did [receive money]?"

"Yes. I think it was."

"Now, in the interview [with the sheriffs], you indicated that you were aware that another boy [Chandler] had sued Mr. Jackson, seeking money, right?" Mesereau asked.

"I don't remember," Francia said blankly.

"Looking back, when is the first time that you recall you knew someone else had sued Mr. Jackson looking for money?"

"I was probably sixteen, because that's when money started being an issue for me."

Money was an issue for Jason Francia. The jury heard that. However, the media seemed to get caught up in Jason Francia's claim that he was still suffering psychological damage from the tickling incidents. Most reporters focused on the emotions Francia displayed in court. News reports failed to inform the public that just maybe—it was all about the money.

"People Make the World Go 'Round"

Bob Jones, who joined Motown records in 1969 as a publicity manager, later signed on as vice president of MJJ Productions, Michael's company, where Jones worked for about twenty years. Among other things, Bob Jones was responsible for community and public relations. Jones took care of everything about "image" where Michael was concerned. It was Jones, the public relations guru, who was called on to put a positive spin on PR nightmares such as the infamous allegation that Jackson slept in an antiaging hyperbaric chamber, and the endless rumors that Jackson wanted to buy the bones of the Elephant Man. Having become a fixture in Michael's life, it was Jones who came up with the title "King of Pop."

About Jackson's preference to spend his time with children, Bob Jones had nothing to say. Jones, who had been a friend and business associate for decades, who had been honest and loyal to Michael, had no unkind words regarding Michael's closeness to children. He would say that Michael Jackson was someone who believed in children as "the future," who believed that children "could heal the world."

However, upon his sudden termination in 2004, Bob Jones began to have a new attitude toward Jackson. No longer the spinmaster of Michael's PR, he didn't seem to care about Michael as a person. Since he was not receiving regular checks from MJJ Productions, Bob Jones felt the need to earn money another way. Part of the problem was the way Jones had been terminated. Michael had insulted Bob, had chosen not to deal with Bob in person, which created some very hard feelings. After so many years of service, Michael had sent a one-line note thanking Jones, letting him know that he was no longer an employee. Not only had Jones been terminated via courier, but he was told by Jackson's attorneys that there would be no severance pay, no retirement package. A note was written to Bob Jones that reportedly said, "It should have been enough of an honor just to work with Michael Jackson."

Not long after his termination, Jones decided to write a book. It was an expose that he coauthored, entitled *Michael Jackson: The Man Behind the Mask*. In it, Bob Jones presented a portrait that promised to further tarnish the once-promising legacy of Michael Jackson. Written in collaboration with Stacy Brown, a longtime journalist and self-proclaimed friend of the Jackson family, *The Man Behind the Mask* attacked Michael for his ever-changing looks and described Michael's marriage to Lisa Marie Presley as "farcical." The book tried to discredit Jackson's respectable musical legacy by asserting that Michael was "a crazed, confused, and angered addict."

To balance out the nasty allegations, Bob Jones' epilogue made a special effort to note that, during the time that he worked with Michael, Bob considered Jackson "the world's leading entertainer." Even as he was attacking the pop star, Jones reminded readers that in his opinion, Michael Jackson was "bigger than Elvis Presley." He noted that because Jackson performed to hundreds of thousands of people around the world, because his reach extended far beyond America, Michael was the world's biggest star. Jones mentioned that Michael Jackson had a global population that adored him. Apparently Jones felt he needed to say that.

The book was a paradox. On the one hand, Jones spoke of Michael's life being a farce, picking on his marriages and his "blonde-haired children." On the other, Jones offered details about Lisa Marie Presley having "a thing for Michael," insisting that when Michael suddenly announced his marriage to the nurse, Debbie Rowe, Lisa Marie made repeated attempts to win Michael back.

According to his book, Lisa Marie was furious when Michael told her that Debbie Rowe offered to give him a child. Bob Jones asserted that Lisa Marie Presley had made Michael the same offer, hoping to have a child shortly after the pair married. Jones asserted that Lisa Marie Presley was "freaked out" when, immediately following her divorce from Michael, the pop star announced that Debbie was pregnant with his child.

There were so many paradoxes in the book, too many to mention, but the most prominent insult was Bob Jones' assertion that Michael Jackson, who had been the most celebrated musical performer—ever—was suddenly nonexistent as a musical influence. As for the "dish" that Jones had to offer about Jackson's personal life, Jones implied that Michael's Neverland estate was a place "designed to lure innocent children." The book made attempts to knock Jackson in every chapter, yet, at the same time, Jones mentioned various people who supported Jackson, such as activist Dick Gregory and comedian Steve Harvey. Jones said there were people who believed that Michael had been "set up" by families looking for cash payouts.

To Michael, the Bob Jones book was an act of ultimate betrayal, regardless of the feeble attempts to appear fair and balanced. The book was poorly received by the public, selling only about ten thousand copies, and reading it, people learned that Bob Jones sided with the people whose "minds were made up" about Michael from the days of the Jordie Chandler allegations. Bob Jones was actively condemning Michael for paying a $20 million settlement to Jordie Chandler and his parents, and Jackson fans found this assertion to be especially distasteful.

Because he didn't want to be viewed as yet another disgruntled employee, Bob Jones told his readers that his sudden termination had been a "sore spot" for him, stating that he felt that being terminated via FedEx was just plain shabby. Jones wanted to assure readers that he was being totally honest. He didn't want readers to think that his termination had any bearing on the subtext of his book, although anyone reading between the lines could see that Jones intended to bash Michael.

Bob Jones and Stacy Brown had cowritten the book before the Santa Maria trial began, and when they were each questioned on the witness stand, both men admitted that the manuscript was being edited and would be released in time for the trial verdicts. On the front inside cover of the book, Jones wondered, "What would happen if Michael Jackson were to be found guilty of child molestation?" He reminded readers about what La Toya had claimed in her book about the little boys being around Michael. All through the text, Jones seemed to blame Michael's parents and siblings for not paying closer attention to the pop star. He seemed to be happy to condemn Michael, hoping to remove the crown from the King of Pop—forever.

Bob Jones sounded bitter, both on the stand and in his book. To readers, the PR guru scoffed at the notion that the world viewed Michael Jackson as royalty. In his book, Jones called the Jackson clan "a different breed" who had "weird and wacky ways." Jones portrayed the Jackson family in the worst possible light and trashed them in subtle ways.

"There was indeed a time when the Jacksons were compared to the Kennedys as America's royalty," Jones wrote. "That time seems like eons ago now as the actions of the family, particularly Michael, have successfully destroyed what once appeared to be an untouchable legacy."

On the morning that Bob Jones took the witness stand, there was a hushed courtroom waiting to hear every word the PR man had to say. Jones identified Michael Jackson as the man seated behind the defense table, the man with the long black hair, and Michael looked at him with piercing eyes. Michael seemed to be in disbelief that one of his most trusted employees could turn on him so openly. Jones was there to testify on behalf of the prosecution—and everyone was curious to learn what secrets he was about to share.

Gordon Auchincloss, himself a distant member of the Kennedy clan, was the prosecutor handling the direct examination, and, as an opener, he asked Bob Jones to talk about his book, which Jones referred to as the "memoirs" of his years with Michael Jackson. It was surprising to hear Jones say that he seldom saw Jackson in person, telling jurors that he'd only been with Michael on three or four music tours and had accompanied Michael to a few special events that he'd arranged, such as the World Music Awards that were held in Monaco in 1992.

Moving on to more relevant matters, Bob Jones testified that he'd flown with Jackson and the Chandler family from Los Angeles to Paris, then from Paris to Monte Carlo, and said that he'd witnessed Michael having physical contact with Jordie Chandler only once—when the pop star held Jordie on his lap during the music awards. What followed was a line of questioning that had to do with the allegation that Michael had licked the hair on Jordie Chandler's head—but Jones denied ever having witnessed such a thing.

When Auchincloss presented Jones with an e-mail where Jones allegedly wrote about seeing "licks on the top of the head" at the World Music Awards, Jones didn't recall writing the e-mail. The PR man was hesitant about saying that he'd written it, though Jones couldn't deny that the quote referring to Jackson licking Jordie Chandler's hair, had been sent from his e-mail address.

The "hair licking" allegation was another crazy little detail that came out during the trial, and in this case it became an issue because Janet Arvizo had made a similar claim, stating that she witnessed Michael licking Gavin's hair while Gavin was asleep, as they flew on Extrajet with Michael from Miami to Santa Barbara.

The image of Michael licking someone's hair, like a cat, was something that had everyone cracking jokes and making funny gestures. It was something people didn't even try to report on news broadcasts. Rather than making it a television sound bite, for the media covering the trial, it became yet another background story that caused people to speculate. People wondered if Janet Arvizo could have learned about this "hair licking" allegation somewhere. Janet might have decided to throw it into her testimony, foolishly, to spice things up.

Of course, Janet's testimony didn't need any spicing up. Not at all. When Janet Arvizo would later come into the courtroom, she would put on a show for three days that was not to be believed. Not only was she snapping her fingers at the jury, Janet would insist that she was "God chosen" to testify, promising that she wasn't in it for the money.

In front of courtroom observers, Janet made a sign of the cross over her chest, swearing that she didn't need Jackson's money. Janet seemed like a multiple personality, jumping in and out of different characters, yet at times, her performance was worthy of an Oscar. In retrospect, Janet Arvizo was the antithesis of Bob Jones, who was steadfast and sure of himself as he sat on the stand.

As he testified, Bob Jones was so comfortable, it was as if he was sitting on the couch in his living room. Jones was completely at ease when he spoke about Michael's private life to the judge, the jury, and the courtroom observers. Jones revealed details about Jackson without seeming to have a care in the world about the criminal charges the pop star was facing. It was obvious that Michael was no stranger to him. But for Bob to be so calm and cool about Michael's life, with Michael's freedom on the line—was striking.

At certain points during his testimony, Jones decided to look over at Jackson, but the King of Pop gave him no visible response. Bob Jones spoke to the jury with a very polite manner, and he was unshakable in his responses, even though his memory wasn't all that clear. As Mesereau questioned Jones, it seemed the defense attorney decided to be deliberately gentle with the witness. Mesereau was not looking to get a rise out of Jones, he just wanted the PR man to clarify a few things.

Mesereau reminded Jones that in his interview with Santa Barbara police, there had been a specific question about "hair licking," to which Jones responded he hadn't seen such a thing—ever. About that statement, Bob Jones had no clear recollection. The PR man took no responsibility for the discrepancy between what he'd told police and what he'd told Stacy Brown for the purposes of their book.

"The reality is, Mr. Jones, you repeatedly said you don't recall any hair licking on the plane with Jordie, do you?" Mesereau asked.

"It appeared in an e-mail. I did not recall seeing it, but it—apparently so, because it appeared in an e-mail that came from my machine." Jones testified.

"Well, in response to the prosecutor's questions, you said you had reservations about that statement?"

"Yes."

"And what are your reservations about that statement?" Mesereau wanted to know.

"That I just don't recall exactly seeing that. I truly don't," Jones said.

"And would you agree that when you're working with a cowriter and publisher to prepare a book about Michael Jackson, there's pressure to make things sensational when you can?"

"Yes."

"Okay. And certainly, having worked with Michael all those years, you've seen numerous attempts by numerous people to sensationalize aspects of Michael's life, right?"

"Correct."

Mesereau wanted Bob Jones to admit that his book, written with Stacy Brown, had been written with the intent to sensationalize Jackson's life in every way possible. The prosecution objected to the line of questioning as being argumentative, so Mesereau rephrased, but later dropped the issue. Mesereau decided to take another tack, asking Jones about his personal experiences with Michael, offering the jury a more intimate portrait, trying to humanize the superstar.

"Did you not go to Neverland very much?" Mesereau wondered.

"I went to Neverland when I brought groups up, such as the Challagers Boys and Girls Club, such as the First AME Church, et cetera. I was not a regular visitor at Neverland at all," Jones told him.

"Okay, now, you indicated at the music awards, the World Music Awards, that at one point you saw Jordie on Michael Jackson's lap and his sister on Michael Jackson's lap together, right?"

"That is correct."

"Okay. And where was Michael Jackson sitting in that event?" Mesereau asked.

"He was seated on the front row next to Prince Albert of Monaco on one side, and Linda Evans, the actress, on the other side," Jones testified. "And I had arranged for the Chandlers to sit directly behind Mr. Jackson because I did not feel that the royalty wanted to be bothered with those guests. But he insisted that they sit with him, so I left it alone."

At the time, Michael was being honored at an annual awards show in Monte Carlo, which was being televised around the world. Bob Jones confirmed that Jordie's mother, June Chandler, was sitting directly behind Michael throughout the show, prominently seated in the second row. Jones said that the two Chandler children were initially seated in the second row with June, but Michael had insisted that Jordie and his sister join him in his seat. At one point, Jordie sat on Michael's lap, and his sister sat on Linda Evans' lap. According to Jones, at no time did Michael try to hide the children, nor did he touch the children in any inappropriate way.

Bob Jones told the jury that Michael brought June Chandler and her children with him to a reception hosted by His Royal Highness Prince Albert, which was held at the palace for visiting dignitaries. As Jones described the trip, it became evident that Michael treated the Chandlers like family. It also became clear that, while Jones wasn't crazy about having children around, Jackson seemed to enjoy the company of children more than the company of adults. There was nothing Bob could do or say to change Michael's mind about that.

Immediately following Bob Jones was Stacy Brown, the coauthor of *The Man Behind the Mask*, who told the jury that he'd known Bob Jones for years, saying that he'd covered stories about Michael Jackson for the *LA Daily News* and had a long history of writing "Jackson" stories. An affable guy, good-looking, shy, and charming, Stacy Brown said he had called Bob Jones for comments over the years about personal things regarding Michael's life, and their relationship had flourished. Stacy Brown told the jury that Bob Jones had approached him about collaborating on a Jackson expose, and reported that they had first talked about the idea on the day of Michael's arraignment in Santa Maria, in January of 2004.

Brown testified that he and Jones worked together by e-mail and said that he had interviewed Bob Jones extensively in order to write the book. An African American journalist, Stacy Brown claimed that he'd been a friend of the Jackson family for years, but as he spoke, Brown deliberately avoided any eye contact with Michael. In fact, Stacy Brown stayed clear of the Jackson clan throughout his time spent in Santa Maria.

Like Bob Jones, Brown was a witness for the prosecution. He testified that he recalled Jones telling him about the "hair licking" incident with Jordie Chandler, though he stated that Bob Jones had been hesitant to testify about that particular detail because Jones had "fuzzy recollections" regarding the issue of hair licking.

The more Stacy Brown was asked questions about alleged "hair licking," the more people in the courtroom were shaking their heads and smiling. People were trying to keep from laughing, and no one knew if there was any truth to the allegation because Jordie Chandler never testified, and Gavin Arvizo had never mentioned it during his testimony. It was bizarre to think about the "hair licking" allegations, and people stared at Michael, hoping to catch his reaction to the journalist's testimony. But Michael's face was hard to read. As Stacy Brown spoke,

Michael seemed to keep still. Only once or twice did he shake his head, as if to discredit Brown's relationship to him. And that was about all.

When asked about his book deal and how it came into being, Stacy Brown testified that Bob Jones was in financial need, that Jones was "broke" at the time that he proposed the idea to write the Jackson expose. When asked about monies he expected to make from the enterprise, Stacy Brown claimed that he and Jones hadn't thought about the money.

Mr. Brown told the jury that he really enjoyed writing, that he wasn't counting on any promises about how his Michael Jackson book would do, but he affirmed that he was hoping to bring the book to the stands before the end of the trial. The author thought the combination of Bob Jones and Michael Jackson would generate a buzz, and he later gave a free copy of his book to every media person covering the trial.

"Would you agree that the more sensational the book, the better the chance of making money on it?" Mesereau asked.

"Well, obviously," Brown said. "We've been told things that nothing surprises them about Michael Jackson, so—but it's not our intention to write a book of scandal, if that's what you're implying. It's certainly not mine, and I have to write it. And I have people in his family who I happen to love very much, who I'm not going to disappoint."

In the last days of the trial, just before the verdict, *Michael Jackson: The Man Behind the Mask* was released. As media members read passages from it, they gave each other sideways glances. Most people never looked past the inside flap, reading a statement that said: "Jackson's recent arrest on child molestation charges ... could ... bring down the curtain on show business' longest running freak show."

Whether they intended to create a scandal or not, Bob Jones and Stacy Brown had published a book that offered an insider's view about a lot of gritty subjects, about rumors and innuendos that persisted in Michael's life. Among the things that the book claimed to expose were Michael's "decadent fraudulent marriages," his "poisonous family relations," and his "voodoo ceremonies."

The book was poison.

The book was vicious.

In the end, the effort to place it into the hands of readers around the world, failed miserably.

"With a Child's Heart"

The air in the room felt heavy when June Chandler took the stand. Tom Sneddon greeted Jordie's mom and asked her to go back to 1992 and 1993, to the time when she and her son met the pop icon. A soft-spoken woman, a very elegant lady, June Chandler was alluring. She was, perhaps, younger and more beautiful than people might have expected, and as DA Sneddon asked his questions, he was being sweet and folksy with her.

As she began to testify, June Chandler seemed completely authentic and believable, and jurors were paying close attention. June was all class. She was grace personified. Dressed impeccably, Ms. Chandler looked like a vision, like she just stepped off the pages of *Vogue*. It was obvious that Sneddon was impressed by the exotic-looking woman. He fully expected her testimony to move his case into high gear.

However, as June Chandler began to give the details about being married and divorced from her first husband, Evan, as she talked about being married and divorced from her second husband, David Schwartz, it became evident that her life wasn't quite as glorious as her appearance made it seem. When June told the jury that she and her son met Michael through Schwartz's business, a place called Rent-A-Wreck, it seemed likely that before she met Michael Jackson, June Chandler's life wasn't very glamorous at all.

June told the jury about how much she adored Michael, explaining that she implored the entertainer to wait at Rent-A-Wreck for a few minutes to meet Jordie. Ms. Chandler said their first meeting with Michael lasted a mere five minutes, but then described a friendship that she and her two children had with the pop star, testifying that their relationship became very close, that she and her kids traveled with Michael to glitzy places like Las Vegas, to elegant resorts in Europe. They had a fabulous time with the King of Pop.

June said that she stayed in the Neverland guest units with her children, Jordie and Lily, and described Michael as being "a regular guy." She spoke of Michael as someone who was nothing like the superstar image he projected, and said Michael was surprisingly down-to-earth. During all of their visits to Neverland, June testified, Michael treated the Chandlers like family. She talked about the time when Jordie began to sleep with Michael in his room, showing no indication that anything unusual had happened to her son while he was in the presence of Michael Jackson.

When questioned about the lawsuit, June Chandler said that she had been named in her son's lawsuit but wanted it known that she had not sued Michael Jackson herself. June Chandler told the jury that Larry Feldman handled the civil lawsuit on behalf of her son, Jordon, reiterating that Jordie was the only person who sued Michael. Still, June Chandler had to admit that both she and her son received monetary compensation from that litigation, and said that she had signed a confidentiality agreement, which resulted in her inability to write a book or grant any interviews about Michael Jackson.

To the amazement of the media covering the trial, under cross-examination by Mesereau, June Chandler testified that she hadn't talked to her son Jordie at all, for over eleven years.

As Tom Mesereau laced into her about the Chandler lawsuit, asking questions about the alleged debt David Schwartz was in, Mesereau indicated that June's ex-husband was millions of dollars in debt at the time of the Chandler lawsuit. But in her responses, June denied any allegations about past financial struggles.

Ms. Chandler tried to keep her composure regarding the money issue, but then, as the questions got more heated, the woman began to shut down. To some courtroom observers, Chandler appeared to be a gold digger. As she squirmed on the witness stand, it became painfully clear that this elegant woman, dripping in designer clothing, had purchased that lifestyle with Michael Jackson's cash.

The defense attorney asked her about specific dates and numbers, but the more he grilled Chandler about her alleged financial crisis back in 1993, the more the jury could see that June Chandler was not about to be pinned down. Above all else, Mesereau was unable to get Chandler to admit that she was looking for a cash payout.

Courtroom observers found it odd the way June Chandler sometimes didn't have a mind for remembering things. Watching June Chandler testify that she "couldn't recall" certain particulars relevant to the Chandler lawsuit seemed completely surreal. For example, June couldn't recall whether Michael Jackson had ever countersued the Chandler family for extortion.

June Chandler seemed to have a selective memory. She had vivid recollections about all her travels with Jackson, from Los Angeles to Florida to Europe and back again, but couldn't recall even the simplest details about Jordie's lawsuit. When she was asked questions about her personal financial needs and wishes in 1993, June Chandler recalled her ex-husband, Evan, had once asked Jackson to finance a wing on the Chandler house. But as for herself, though she had accepted a few expensive gifts from Jackson, a Cartier bracelet among them, June Chandler swore that she wanted nothing monetary from the entertainer.

When she spoke about her son's friendship with the pop icon, Chandler testified that she never suspected anything inappropriate was going on between Michael and Jordie. This response aroused consternation among media because everyone was waiting for Chandler to say something—anything—that would implicate Jackson.

Instead, June sat very proudly and spoke about her son's friendship with Michael as being something special. She told the jury that Jordie had dressed like Michael, had tried to emulate the pop icon from the time that he was a very young child, before Jordie ever met the pop star. She also admitted that back in 1992 and 1993, Evan Chandler was busy writing a screenplay, telling the jury that because Evan wasn't spending much time with Jordie back then, she was happy to have Michael around their home. Michael was devoting time to her son, and June said she was grateful for that.

June Chandler testified that Michael Jackson had spent approximately thirty nights at their home in Santa Monica, and admitted that she had encouraged the friendship between her son and the pop star. As she spoke, the courtroom became very still. People had strong preconceived notions about Jordie Chandler. Some had issues with Chandler and his family using Jackson as a pawn, others felt Jackson had been the mastermind of a cover-up. Media people knew that after the financial settlement was made, Jordie Chandler had refused to cooperate with authorities, which had everyone offering opinions. During breaks, media people gossiped endlessly about Jackson's friendship with young Jordie Chandler.

Not interested in gossip, not interested in the quiet whispers going on in courtroom hallways, Tom Mesereau wasn't going to let the infamous Chandler lawsuit compound the serious criminal case confronting Michael Jackson. Mesereau didn't want the jury embroiled in gossip. He didn't want the jury to get caught up in speculation and rumor.

At one point, the prosecution had asked that the jury be shown 1993 photos of Jackson's blemished penis, a motion that was denied. Mesereau had good reason to ask the judge to keep the jury away from scandalous evidence, evidence that had been used to sensationalize the very claims that Michael Jackson had repeatedly denied.

As he proceeded, Mesereau explored other avenues in Michael's life. The defense attorney not only wanted to discredit all of the negative rumors from more than a decade prior, he wanted to remind the jury of the Peter Pan myth that had always been synonymous with Jackson. Mesereau wanted the jury to understand why Michael felt so close to Jordie and his family. He asked June to confirm that Michael Jackson was a very lonely person, a person in need of true friends.

June Chandler told the jury that Michael had become a part of their small family, and said the pop star shared dinner with them at their home in Santa Monica each of those thirty nights. When Mesereau asked if Michael ever helped Jordie with his homework, when he asked about Michael playing video games with Jordie, Ms. Chandler acknowledged that yes, Michael had helped with homework and had been a good friend to her son.

She told the jury that she considered Michael to be "like a child," and testified that Jordie was the one who had insisted on staying in Michael's room at Neverland, which she described as being "filled with dolls" and a lot of play toys. Ms. Chandler said she'd been in Michael's bedroom many times, and described it as "a boy's room, a big boy's room."

"When was the first time that your son, Jordon, asked if he could sleep with Michael Jackson?" Mesereau wondered.

"I would say around the second visit to Neverland, second or third visit to Neverland, because there were always boys around staying in his bedroom, and why couldn't he? And that's when he started asking," Ms. Chandler said.

"And it was your understanding that there were a lot of kids hanging around Michael Jackson's bedroom?

"Yes."

"Okay. Did you meet Macaulay Culkin at Neverland?" Mesereau asked.

"Yes."

"Did you meet Macaulay's parents?"

"His father."

"Was anyone else from Macaulay's family there, do you know?"

"His brothers were there."

June Chandler answered Mesereau with a staccato that was palpable. She kept it short and tried to be nonchalant when she spoke about flying on the Sony jet, about flying on billionaire Steve Wynn's jet, about traveling to Orlando and Las Vegas and other resorts around the world.

Though Ms. Chandler was being very matter-of-fact in her responses, Michael watched her with an intense closeness, and his stare seemed to transcend her cavalier attitude. As June Chandler testified, the jury watched her very intently, and people were trying to read her body language. When Ms. Chandler casually stated that she *never* had an issue with Michael being around her son, courtroom observers seemed stunned.

"Michael said to you that he wanted a family just to treat him like a regular person, right?" Mesereau asked.

"Correct," Ms. Chandler said.

"He said he didn't want to be like a stranger, right?"

"Correct."

"And he asked you to trust him, right?"

"Yeah."

"Do you remember telling the district attorney in Los Angeles that when you talked to your ex-husband, Evan, about Michael Jackson's relationship with your family, that Evan saw this as a wonderful means for Jordie not having to worry for the rest of his life?" Mesereau asked.

"Would you repeat your question?" Ms. Chandler stammered.

"Didn't you tell the Los Angeles district attorney that your ex-husband, Evan, the father of Jordie, told you that the relationship with Michael was a wonderful means of Jordie not having to worry for the rest of his life?"

"Yes," Ms. Chandler said.

"And to you, that meant Michael Jackson supporting you for the rest of your life, correct?"

"No."

"That's what your ex-husband meant by it, true?"

By then, DA Sneddon was jumping up and down, objecting to the line of questioning with fervor. With Sneddon's face turning bright red, the judge gave a signal for Sneddon to quiet down. Judge Melville sustained the objection, and the judge used a sarcastic tone that had some of the people in the courtroom laughing out loud. Melville had a personable style, and he was using a hint of sarcasm to keep Tom Sneddon coolheaded. But Sneddon was steaming, and everyone in the room could feel Sneddon's rage. The DA was furious that Mesereau had been able to turn a star witness around. Mesereau had been successful in making June Chandler look money hungry.

Even with the objection sustained, Mesereau wouldn't let the matter of the civil lawsuit drop. Mesereau didn't want laughter. He didn't want people sidetracked from the gravity of the Chandler lawsuit and the mentality of the Chandler family. Mesereau wanted the jury to understand that the Chandler family wanted Michael Jackson to provide a permanent meal ticket for them. When he brought up details, Mesereau let everyone in the courtroom know that through Jackson, the Chandlers had a doorway leading to people such as Elizabeth Taylor, Nelson Mandela, and the royalty around the world.

The more June Chandler tried to argue with Mesereau's portrait of the Chandler family, the more it appeared that she was protesting too much. It seemed that Jackson had given the Chandlers a sense of the good life, had exposed them to a life of fame and fortune, and, having tasted a bit of Jackson's world, the Chandler clan wasn't willing to give that up. The Chandlers had developed champagne taste, and they wanted more.

Mesereau asked June Chandler about her meetings with famed private investigator Anthony Pellicano. Mesereau wondered if she recalled telling Pellicano that "Evan wanted money." He asked if she'd ever told Pellicano that "Evan's concerns could only be about money."

But June Chandler didn't recall.

Ms. Chandler testified that she'd met with Anthony Pellicano at least three or four times, but had no recollection of what went on during those meetings. Ultimately, the substance of Chandler's conversations with Pellicano were deemed to be speculation, not admissible in court. But with Mesereau's questions remaining unanswered, the secret meetings between June Chandler and Anthony Pellicano just hung in the air, looming, making everyone more suspicious about the motivations behind the Chandler lawsuit.

"Do you remember telling Michael Jackson, 'You're like Peter Pan. Everybody wants to be around you and spend twenty-four hours?'" Mesereau asked.

"Yes," Ms. Chandler said, almost in a whisper.

"Okay, do you remember at your meeting with Mr. Pellicano, that Mr. Pellicano said, 'This is all extortion'?" Mesereau asked.

With that, Tom Sneddon jumped up and objected. The objection was sustained on the grounds that it was hearsay, and Mesereau moved on.

"Do you recall meeting with attorney Robert Shapiro?" Mesereau asked.

"Yes," Ms. Chandler testified.

"And when was that?"

"In Larry Feldman's office."

"How many meetings did you have with Robert Shapiro?"

"I don't recall."

"Do you know why he was at the meeting?" Mesereau asked.

"I think he was part of Michael Jackson's legal team," Ms. Chandler said.

"Who? Robert Shapiro?"

"I think so. I don't recall."

"Well, he was there because Michael Jackson's attorneys were claiming extortion, right?" Mesereau pressed.

"I don't recall."

"Robert Shapiro was there because he's a criminal defense lawyer, right?"

Tom Sneddon tried to prevent further questions about Shapiro, about extortion, about the claims Michael Jackson was making against the Chandlers back in 1993, but Judge Melville overruled his objections. The witness was directed to respond to the questions, but June Chandler could not recall the details regarding the counterclaim of extortion by Michael Jackson.

She said she was unaware that Robert Shapiro had been part of the Chandler's legal team, unaware that Shapiro was counseling the Chandler family as a criminal attorney. Ms. Chandler was also unaware that Robert Shapiro had represented another Chandler attorney, Barry Rothman, who had been accused by Jackson's attorneys of unethical conduct regarding Michael Jackson. Rothman was not charged with anything.

Mesereau wanted it known that the Chandler family had received legal advice from a top criminal attorney, that they were being briefed in the event that Jackson sued them for extortion. But June Chandler said she only had a limited memory of meeting with the famous O. J. Simpson attorney.

Ms. Chandler testified that she had no definite recall about any of her conversations with Robert Shapiro, and acted like she hardly knew who Shapiro was, which seemed like a stretch.

Though the Chandler clan had met with Robert Shapiro in his Century City offices, and June had met with Robert Shapiro at the offices of Larry Feldman, somehow, the famous Robert Shapiro hadn't left an impression on her.

As the beautiful Ms. Chandler left the stand, many of the jurors seemed unimpressed. From the looks on their faces, it was obvious that June Chandler had not been a good witness. The females on the jury, in particular, seemed to see right through her.

"She's Out of My Life"

On the first day that the accuser's mother walked past photographers, she covered her face with a hood. As the woman entered the courthouse, Katherine Jackson sat alone in the front row, facing Janet "Jackson" Arvizo without Joe, without Tito or Jermaine, and without Randy or Jackie, all of whom had been regulars in the courtroom during the proceedings. Michael's mother looked displeased, unhappy at the very sight of Janet, and she closed her eyes for a good thirty seconds as the hooded woman made her way to the front of the room.

As Janet slowly made her way to the witness stand, the thirty-six-year-old woman looked nothing like the video version of Janet Arvizo, the woman on the rebuttal tape. The rebuttal tape, showing Janet and her three kids praising Michael for helping cure Gavin of cancer, had never aired on TV. But the tape had been played to the jury so often that, by the time Janet actually testified, courtroom observers felt they knew her.

Jackson fans had the rebuttal video memorized, and people had fun repeating key lines from the interview, in which Janet claimed she was neglected and "dejected." In the video rebuttal, Janet Arvizo couldn't have been more melodramatic. She had all kinds of sad anecdotes to report, insisting that before Michael had taken an interest in her family, she was living in near poverty, forced to feed her children cereal for dinner, often having no secure place to live. Throughout the rebuttal interview, Janet made outlandish statements. She claimed that she and her kids had been forced to sleep in a barn. She claimed that her ex-husband was pretending to be a wonderful father.

On the tape, Janet spent a good deal of time bashing her former husband, David, the biological dad to her three kids. But she spent even more time praising

Michael Jackson for being a person who had come to her rescue, calling Michael a godsend, a good person, and a "family man."

The rebuttal tape had created certain expectations and impressions for the jury that Janet had not really anticipated. On the tape, she appeared as a glamorous young woman with long, wavy hair, red-glossed lips, and a beautiful hourglass figure. But the person she had been in the past, the person who Janet was when she was around Michael Jackson, was nothing but a video memory.

Janet's presence in the courtroom was disjointed and disconcerting. Not only had her looks faded, but her whole personality seemed to have changed. No longer the glamour girl, Janet Arvizo was an enigma. On the witness stand, she sometimes looked like a child and would often act infantile.

As she spoke, she seemed to shape-shift, projecting different images and different personas. There were times when the thirty-six-year-old looked like a dowdy housewife, presenting herself as an overburdened mother who was too tired to keep up with her appearance. In any other case, that tactic might have worked, might have gained her some sympathy, but Janet knew she was in the spotlight.

Certainly she could have worn a business suit, knowing the worldwide media was very interested in seeing her, that people from all corners of the earth were there to report every detail about her courtroom appearance. As Janet shrank down in the witness chair, a roomful of media were taking copious notes.

Everyone in the courtroom was shocked to see how much Janet's physical appearance had altered in two years, and people remarked about it, gossiping about the fact that she had gained quite a bit of weight, had chosen not to wear stylish clothes, and had forgotten her beauty secrets, wearing no makeup whatsoever. Janet's hair was shorter, her face was wider, and she dressed like a little girl, wearing a pink sweatshirt and donning hairpins with cheap, sparkly stars.

As for her personality, Janet was rather a mess, no longer the confident woman who had appeared on the video. In front of the jury, rarely did she make sense, and rarely did she answer direct questions reasonably. Oftentimes, Janet would cry to the jury. Her tears, however, did not seem real.

When she first began to testify, Janet was sobbing, asking the jury not to judge her. She was inappropriate, and people saw that Janet was making some of the jurors feel uncomfortable. She was an odd person who made odd choices. For the duration of her testimony, Janet chose not to look at Michael Jackson, and chose not to look at Ron Zonen, the prosecutor handling her direct examination.

People found it bizarre that Janet refused to look anywhere else, that she wished to vent and testify entirely to the members of the jury. In some strange way, it seemed Janet thought she could win the case by pleading directly to the jurors, but the court system didn't work that way. To make matters worse, often-times Janet would get angry, and the woman would point her fingers and snap at the jury panel. Outspoken members of the jury would later say that they found Janet's behavior to be offensive and bizarre.

Janet Arvizo made people cringe.

The accuser's mom testified for three days in a row, always covering herself with a hooded sweatshirt as she made her way into the courtroom. Each day, she was escorted through a throng of reporters who were never able to get a clear shot of her. Because Janet had gotten remarried to a man named Jay Jackson, she requested that the court recognize her as "Janet Jackson," but Judge Melville refused to allow that. The judge said it would be too confusing, and for the pur-pose of the trial, Janet would be known as Janet Ventura Arvizo.

Before she had entered the courtroom, the defense team argued against Janet's assertion of her Fifth Amendment right not to testify about welfare fraud, telling the court that Janet Arvizo should not have the right to pick and choose what she would testify about. The defense pointed out that Janet had made an emergency welfare application, applying for welfare, food stamps, disability, unemploy-ment—all while she had a personal bank account with thousands and thousands of dollars available to her.

But Janet's Fifth Amendment right was upheld, and in a California court, she did not have to assert her claim against self-incrimination in front of the jury. Of course, Sneddon hoped that the jurors would hear nothing about the details regarding Janet's alleged welfare fraud. The DA hoped there would be no men-tion that Janet Arvizo had pled the Fifth regarding false welfare applications.

To be fair to both sides, Judge Melville decided that *he* would inform the jury about Janet Arvizo's decision to assert her Fifth Amendment privilege, and fur-thermore, Melville ruled that he would allow the defense team to present evi-dence about Janet's alleged welfare fraud during their case-in-chief. The defense team would later call a certified public accountant, as well as a welfare fraud expert, in order to prove that Janet Arvizo was using every possible government source to receive money that she wasn't entitled to.

As Janet Arvizo was sworn in, Judge Melville informed the jury that Ms. Arvizo had pled the Fifth regarding alleged welfare fraud and perjury. Instantly, the jury panel looked at her with disapproving glances. Before Janet ever opened her mouth in court, the mother of Gavin Arvizo had gotten off to a bad start.

There was more than a hint of disdain.

Because the Santa Barbara DA had not granted Janet immunity from prosecu-tion on the welfare fraud issue, a year and a half after the Jackson trial ended, in

November of 2006, Janet Arvizo pled guilty to defrauding the American taxpayers by falsely applying for welfare. Apparently, welfare fraud was something that Janet Arvizo never thought she'd be held accountable for. Apparently, she was too focused on a criminal judgment against Michael Jackson, which would be followed by a civil judgment in her favor. Janet Arvizo seemed to be blinded by million-dollar signs. She seemed to have little concern about exposing her private life. Anything unsavory that might be revealed was, perhaps, overshadowed by the prospect of becoming very rich.

Janet Arvizo agreed to testify without immunity, and Ron Zonen was quick to try to establish for the jury that Ms. Arvizo was a God-fearing woman, a woman who lived a hard life, who had suffered through sickness and poverty, who had lived through many bad times. Zonen wanted to garner as much sympathy for her as possible, and he asked Janet to provide details about being the mother of four children, about her having recently given birth to an eight-month-old baby with her new husband. He then asked Janet to tell the jury about Gavin's serious cancer and the near-death experience that had led the Arvizo family to the home of Michael Jackson.

No stranger to high-profile cases, Santa Barbara Deputy District Attorney Ron Zonen was the strongest of the three-member prosecution team. He was well prepared and clear headed, never exhibiting the rage of Tom Sneddon, never out of control. Ron Zonen was sharp—as smart as they come, and he had the added benefit of being down-to-earth, unlike Gordon Auchincloss, who came off as arrogant and highly self-important. Of the three, Zonen was the most likeable character. He had presence. He had wit. When Zonen spoke, people listened.

But having Janet "Jackson" Arvizo on his hands left Zonen with a very tricky tightrope to walk. Janet Arvizo was the kingpin of the prosecution's conspiracy charge against Jackson. The prosecutor was putting Janet on the stand in an attempt to prove that Jackson and his associates had conspired to hold Janet and her children at Neverland against their will. To that end, Janet testified that her family was coerced and held captive at Neverland for weeks following their trip to Miami—until they agreed to tape a rebuttal video in response to the Bashir documentary.

Janet told the jury that her "captivity" began when she received a call from Michael, who requested that the family join him in Miami to hold a press conference in response to the Bashir piece. According to Janet, it was Michael himself who called to report that she and her family might be "in danger." Janet claimed that Michael was the one who wanted the Arvizos to join him in Miami so they could be protected from alleged "death threats."

Janet told the jury that when she arrived in Miami on February 7, 2003, Michael Jackson had decided that no press conference was needed. Janet claimed that Jackson and his "people" had kept a close eye on her, refusing to allow her to watch the U.S. airing of the Bashir documentary, which ran on the ABC network during that same time period.

As Janet ran through the details regarding her trip to see Jackson in Miami, she said that in early February 2003, she and her kids flew across the country with movie star Chris Tucker on a private jet. They went to the Turnberry Resort in North Miami, where she checked into her own room with her kids and then met with Michael Jackson in his presidential suite. Janet told the jury that her kids were treated to massages at the spa at Turnberry, but she complained that most of their time was spent with Michael, locked away in his large hotel suite.

While in Miami, Janet claimed she didn't really have the chance to enjoy the facilities at the swanky hotel. She spent her days with Michael, Prince, and Paris, who were accompanied by Frank Casio and his young sister, Marie Nicole, and his young brother, Aldo, whom Jackson called "Baby Rubba."

Janet had multiple complaints about her stay with Michael at the Turnberry Resort, which she felt was like a business trip. Janet indicated that her kids were happy to be Michael's guests for a few nights, but in a roundabout way, she was complaining to the jury that she and her kids didn't spend any time outside because of the intense media interest.

Later, an exhibit was entered into court, showing the media calls that Jackson had received on February 6, 2003, the day following the British airing of *Living with Michael Jackson*. It included a barrage of messages from *Extra!* and *Entertainment Tonight*, the *CBS Early Show* and *Good Morning America*, SkyNews London, as well as personal calls from Larry King and Barbara Walters. The list was astonishing.

To the jury, Janet confirmed that she had been overwhelmed with media requests, but insisted that she wasn't interested in taking tabloid money, claiming that she had "zero" conversations with reporters, that her contact with media was "double zero." Janet testified that she agreed to fly to Miami to meet with Michael and his "people" while they were figuring out what to do about the PR nightmare created by the Bashir documentary. She asserted that Michael's associates were scripting a media response for her. Throughout her testimony, Janet said that all of her statements in the rebuttal tape were inaccurate and were just plain made up.

But that didn't sit well with the jury.

"Now, Ms. Arvizo, you said that you and your children were neglected and spit on, right?" Mesereau asked.

"Yes," she responded.

"And who were you referring to?"

"They took elements of my life and my children's life which were truthful, and they incorporated them into their script. And this happened in the initial meeting in Miami. They were already in the works on this. It took me a while to find out."

"Who neglected your family?" Mesereau wondered.

"In this script, everything is scripted," Janet told him.

"When you say your family was spit on, who were you referring to?"

"On this rebuttal thing, everything is scripted. They took elements of mine and my children's life which were true, and incorporated them here."

"When you said, 'We weren't in the right zip code, and we weren't the right race,' what were you referring to?"

"This was all scripted," Janet insisted.

As her testimony continued, Janet made assertions that became difficult to swallow, just impossible to believe. For one thing, she swore that she'd never seen the entire Bashir documentary, ever. She claimed that at the time the Bashir documentary was taped at Neverland, she had not been informed that her children were taping anything that would be aired on TV.

Janet told the jury that she learned about Gavin and his siblings filming "something about Michael helping Gavin with his cancer" only after the Bashir documentary aired in Britain. Upon further questioning, Ms. Arvizo admitted she had joined Michael Jackson in a suit against Granada Television for using images of her children without permission.

It seemed the more Janet Arvizo testified, the more she dug a hole for the prosecution. The jury was not believing her, not at all. Like her sons, Janet was asserting that Gavin was inappropriately touched by Jackson *after* the Bashir documentary scandal, not before.

According to Janet, the first time that Mr. Jackson had decided to act inappropriately with Gavin was on the way back to California from Florida, just after the Bashir documentary aired. It was Janet's testimony that she never saw Michael Jackson do anything sexually inappropriate to Gavin, though she claimed to have seen Michael lick the hair on her son's head—during the plane ride back from Miami to Santa Barbara.

With Mesereau cross-examining her, Janet's version of Gavin's alleged molestation made less and less sense. Janet Arvizo's claims began to seem increasingly outrageous. The defense attorney cut Janet to pieces, particularly about her alleged captivity at Neverland. If there was any kind of conspiracy, Mesereau made it seem like there was a conspiracy aimed at Michael Jackson.

Having Janet testify that Michael had plotted to abduct the Arvizos and then had acted inappropriately with Gavin immediately after the Bashir documentary, would open up a Pandora's box that Tom Mesereau would have a field day with. Mesereau would show that in the weeks following the Bashir documentary, Janet Arvizo and her kids were voluntarily spending time at Neverland, taking advantage of Michael's fully stocked home.

The defense attorney would prove that while Janet was taking her time about deciding whether or not to tape a rebuttal video, Ms. Arvizo kept herself busy by having Michael pay for everything from Gavin's dental work to Janet's full-body waxes. When Janet and her kids finally did make their rebuttal tape, it was taped long after the Arvizos arrived back to California, way past the deadline to be able to air on the FOX rebuttal show, *The Michael Jackson Interview: The Footage You Were Never Meant to See.*

As for her comments about Jackson in the rebuttal footage, Janet kept insisting that she and her kids were reading from a script and told jurors that none of them meant any of the loving things they said about Michael. Janet asserted that she and her kids had been forced to say that Jackson had acted like a "father figure" to Gavin. She said she and her children had been spoon-fed every word they uttered during the interview. But her testimony seemed disingenuous.

It was interesting to watch Janet become so irate about having been forced to use a script for the entirety of the rebuttal video, especially since everyone in the courtroom had seen the outtake footage from that video, and had seen Janet telling her kids to sit up straight, to behave themselves, spontaneously suggesting that she and Gavin hold hands for the camera.

When asked if the outtake footage was scripted as well, Janet told the jury that it was. The more Janet insisted on it, the more she looked like a bad liar. As Mesereau questioned her, he was getting his point across to the jury: Janet Arvizo was a woman with an agenda.

"I'm not a very good actress," Janet testified.

"Oh, I think that you are," Mesereau said.

The defense attorney had reason to believe that Janet was putting on a show. But sometimes, Janet couldn't always control her emotions, and she would become explosive and antagonistic on the stand. Her emotional testimony was so unbalanced, that, throughout her direct examination, Mesereau deliberately refused to object. An intuitive attorney, Mesereau sized Janet up instantly, and was happy to let her go off on tangents. As Janet told the jury about her zany conspiracy theory, she claimed that she once planned to escape from Neverland in a hot-air balloon.

In furtherance of the conspiracy theory, a taped phone conversation between Janet and Michael's close friend Frank Casio was played for the jury. In that conversation, Frank asked Janet to return to Neverland with her kids, mentioning his concern for Janet's safety. However, Frank said nothing about people allegedly threatening Janet's life. As the jury listened to the taped phone call, they heard Frank Casio say he was worried about the safety of the Arvizos because of all the paparazzi.

There was no mention of death threats.

There was no mention of killers.

The only person who alleged that the fallout from the Bashir documentary had created a life-threatening situation—was Ms. Janet Arvizo. It was a claim that her two sons, Gavin and Star, tried to corroborate—without success. Early in the trial, both boys testified that they heard something from their mom about "killers," but their memories were vague. Under cross-examination, both Arvizo boys admitted that they loved being at Neverland, testified that they never felt frightened by anyone, and told the jury that they really didn't want to leave Jackson's ranch at any time.

Janet's allegation that she was being held as a prisoner at Neverland, her assertion that she and her kids were being kept hidden from mysterious "killers," seemed far-fetched and nutty, especially since records were brought into evidence that proved that Janet Arvizo was charging thousands of dollars worth of makeup, beauty products, and beauty treatments to Michael Jackson's Neverland Valley Entertainment business account during February of 2003.

The conspiracy theory that the prosecution had thrown into the mix was the weakest link in the case. It would cause many people to think twice about the DA having a vendetta against Jackson, about Sneddon trying to ruin the entertainer in any way possible. Of course, Tom Sneddon vehemently denied this. When the prosecution asserted that Michael Jackson had created a plot to ship the Arvizo family off to Brazil, the allegation seemed preposterous.

The prosecution produced the passports and visas showing that Jackson's "associates" had obtained these items together with Janet Arvizo, hinting that Jackson's "people" were arranging for the Arvizos to take a permanent trip to Brazil. But the prosecution was unable to establish that the Brazil trip was anything more than a vacation offer. And DA Sneddon was unable to prove, by any means, that Michael Jackson was even aware that a trip to Brazil was ever in the works.

The more testimony there was about the Brazil trip, the more the conspiracy plot seemed like a trumped-up scenario by the prosecution. It seemed strange that the prosecution put such an emphasis on it, especially since the Arvizos never made any such trip at all.

To the jury, DA Sneddon made the argument that Michael Jackson was so completely desperate after the Bashir documentary aired that Jackson's whole career and financial status was at stake—thus the pop star needed to abduct, imprison, and extort the Arvizo family in order to maintain his "image." To many folks, it was the most absurd claim in the entire trial. Courtroom observers scoffed at the notion.

People thought the conspiracy theory was just ludicrous.

At the end of the day, Tom Sneddon was unable to prove that Michael Jackson had any knowledge about a conspiracy to send the Arvizos anywhere. The prosecutorial team was arguing, unsuccessfully, that Jackson, through his "associates," had a hand in the Arvizos' abduction and captivity. The DA asserted that Jackson engaged in a criminal plot in order to save himself from financial and professional ruin. It was a theory that had most people in the courtroom puzzled. People began wondering if the prosecutors were serious, if the prosecutors had lost their minds.

"Never Can Say Good-Bye"

Beyond the absurd conspiracy theory, the most damning thing that Janet testified about was her prior civil claim against the JC Penney Corporation and her $152,000 settlement for allegedly having been physically and sexually molested by JC Penney security guards in a parking lot. Among the things Janet claimed was that one of the JC Penney guards allegedly twisted her nipple up to twenty-five times.

"And please tell the jury how you were sexually assaulted in that public parking lot?" Mesereau asked.

"Okay. I was laying on the floor while they're beating on me, one of the Tower Records guys, who—incidentally, this can be verified. I think he was also fired for doing this to some other people after this," Janet explained. "But, this person, while I was laying on the floor getting beat up, he had his hand over on my breast and on the front area of my private area."

"Do you remember testifying that your nipple was squeezed ten to twenty-five times?" Mesereau asked.

"Yes," Janet said. "And again, it was, he wanted to humiliate me, like he's trying to do at this moment, and making me to say it millisecond by millisecond."

"You testified to these facts to get money, true?"

"Yes. It was a civil lawsuit, yes it was."

"Now, you claim in that lawsuit that Gavin's cancer was made worse by the security guards, true?"

"I don't think so. I think I said something that Gavin was having the chemotherapy at this time when they wanted the deposition to occur."

As Mesereau grilled Janet about her prior allegations, Janet was becoming visibly flustered. She admitted that there were "inaccuracies" in her JC Penney deposition, claiming that she tried to get her attorney to make corrections in the deposition before a settlement was reached. The more Janet admitted to inaccuracies, the more she stated that parts of her JC Penney deposition were untrue, the less people were listening to her.

Mesereau pointed out that the allegations Janet made against the JC Penney guards were corroborated by her two sons, Gavin and Star, who each said, in sworn depositions, that they witnessed their mother being assaulted in the JC Penney parking lot. Both Star and Gavin's depositions had been brought into evidence early on in the trial, and Mesereau had established that Star, at age nine, told attorneys that he put his mommy's breast "back into her bra" after the alleged nipple-twisting incident occurred. Star Arvizo, who claimed he witnessed Jackson inappropriately touch his brother, had previously testified that he saw a JC Penney guard touch his mother's private parts.

As Mesereau sorted through Janet's JC Penney deposition, he was able to suggest that Janet had coached her kids about how to testify. Mesereau brought up real doubts about the alleged JC Penney attack, and the jury was in a quandary.

"In the JC Penney case, you claimed under oath that you were punched with closed fists in the parking lot of JC Penney, correct?" Mesereau asked.

"Yes." Janet said.

"In the JC Penney case, did you claim under oath that you were punched with handcuffs as if they were brass knuckles?"

"I remember seeing the female having her fingers inside the handcuffs, like this," Janet said, gesturing to the jury.

"And after being punched all these times in the parking lot, you said you thought you were going to die, and it was like you were in a cave in a tunnel. Do you remember that?"

"Yes, it did feel that way."

"You said the security guards were punching Gavin and Star, correct?"

"Can you please read me, bring me where it says that?" Janet asked.

"Okay," Mesereau said, walking over to Janet to show her the quote.

"Oh, yes, because my son, both of my sons were hurt," Janet testified.

As Janet answered uncomfortable questions, becoming highly nervous on the stand, she confirmed that on the day of the JC Penney incident, she and her husband, David, were eventually brought down to the city jail, both of them having been arrested in the JC Penney parking lot in West Covina. After they had their cell phones and other property items taken from them, after they were fingerprinted and photographed, they each put up $250 bail and were released within a matter of hours. The West Covina police booking information from the incident, dated August 27, 1998, described Janet Ventura Arvizo as having no visible physical oddities, as needing no special medical attention.

But some time after, Janet Arvizo showed up at an attorney's office making claims of having been physically and sexually assaulted by JC Penney guards. She offered a half-dozen color photos of her bruises as "evidence." As Tom Mesereau continued to ask Janet about her previous civil claim, he gave the jury an opportunity to see the pattern that Janet Arvizo and her family had established many years prior.

The Arvizos and their kids were in the habit of using lawyers.

At an early age, Gavin had learned how to sue people for "damages."

When Mesereau brought up other abuse allegations made by each member of the Arvizo family, people on the jury looked mortified. At first, Janet tried to deny that David had been violent toward her and her children. But later, she testified that there had been other allegations of abuse within her family, that she had been granted multiple restraining orders against her former husband. As Janet was forced to verify the documented reports of abuse that Mesereau held in his hands, jurors were frowning with tightly pursed lips.

"You were investigated by the Department of Children and Family Services in the 1990s when Gavin alleged you had abused him. Remember that?" Mesereau asked.

"Yes, I do," Janet said.

"Okay. Did you have a good relationship with the Department of Children and Family Services at the time?"

"Yes, I did."

"Okay. He accused you of abusing him and then changed his mind, right?" Mesereau asked.

"No, that's inaccurate," Janet said.

Janet tried to explain about the investigation in the 1990s, trying to downplay the significance of prior abuse allegations made by Gavin. But Janet's explanation didn't really make sense.

Janet told the jury that Gavin, when he was in kindergarten, had gone to the school nurse to say that he didn't want to go home because he didn't want to get into trouble. Janet wasn't very clear; she had a conveniently foggy memory of the kindergarten event. However, she admitted that because of Gavin's complaint to the nurse, someone from the DCFS came out to her home to verify that Gavin lived in a safe environment.

Though Janet tried to put a positive spin on the incident, calling the DCFS visit "another positive experience," no one on the jury was buying the idea that a visit from the Department of Children and Family Services was a good thing.

"Gavin had accused you of abusing him and then changed his story, didn't he?" Mesereau pressed.

"No. It's inaccurate what you're saying," Janet told him.

"You just said that to the jury, that he accused you of abuse, right?"

"And it's okay. He was a kindergartner. And the way the nurse or teacher, whoever it was, had communicated it that way to the Department of Children and Family Services, and that was it. It's okay," Janet testified.

But it wasn't okay. Janet's story was breaking down. As she spoke, her sentences were becoming unintelligible. To Mesereau, Janet was trying to deny other tawdry anecdotes. As Janet hastily argued with Mesereau, courtroom observers recalled hearing about abuse allegations from other Arvizo family members. For instance, Janet's daughter, Davellin, had already testified that she had once been sexually approached by her father. The more the Arvizo mom told the jury different versions of the truth, the more people saw that Janet was living in a world of false accusations and sexual innuendo.

While Janet Arvizo continued to tell jurors her version of her personal history, Michael Jackson stared at the woman, looking straight through her. Once or twice, Janet took her eyes away from the jurors, directing her comments right at the pop star. Janet was trying to have a personal conversation with Michael from the witness stand, and Michael gave Janet a few disapproving looks.

But mostly, he seemed tired of her antics.

It was surreal, watching Janet trying to have one last chat with Michael from across the crowded courtroom. As Janet spoke out of turn, as she refused to abide by the rules of the court, people began to wonder about Janet's comprehension of fact versus fiction.

Realizing that Janet Arvizo had a hard time giving a straight answer about anything, courtroom observers exuded a silent contempt. At times, Janet was telling the jury she thought she had "imagined things," which people were apt to believe. Janet testified that she never witnessed any act of molestation, and claimed that she learned of Gavin's allegations after the family had gone to see Dr. Stanley Katz. As for inappropriate touching, Janet claimed she "thought" she witnessed Michael licking her son's hair on the private airplane but told jurors she couldn't be sure. At one point, Janet testified that she might have been "seeing things."

When Janet talked about observing this alleged act, an act which Gavin never mentioned, it seemed strange that Gavin would have slept though it, that the young man wouldn't have felt *something*. Moreover, it seemed implausible that Jackson would lick someone's hair in front of the Extrajet personnel, not to mention all the other passengers on the private flight.

As Mesereau switched gears, asking Janet about hiding from the media, he wanted to show the jury that Janet had gone to Miami in order to get away from LA reporters. But Janet denied this completely. She told jurors that she was only worried about mysterious "killers" who made death threats and claimed she was unmoved by the media people swarming around her East LA home.

Upon further questioning, Janet finally admitted that she did, indeed, make a complaint about media harassment, that she did want to get away from the throng of reporters who were hounding her in Los Angeles. But Janet's admission came only when Mesereau played a portion of an audio tape where jurors could hear Janet Arvizo complaining to Frank Casio.

In order to get Janet to stick to the facts, Mesereau was forced to refer to Janet's taped conversation, which often conflicted with Janet's prior testimony.

"You say here, 'I know we're family, Frank. Me, you, me, my kids, are family. You, Marie Nicole, my kids, Baby Rubba, are family. Michael, Marie Nicole, you, me, are family, and my parents. That's all I got.' Do you see that?" Mesereau asked.

"That's correct," Janet said, reading over the transcript of her conversation with Frank.

"Now, this conversation is taking place after you say you escaped from Neverland with Jesus [Salas], true?"

"Correct."

"You're still calling Michael your family, correct?"

"That's correct, yes."

"You didn't escape from Neverland at all, did you?" Mesereau quipped.

"Oh, yes I did," Janet insisted.

"How many times did you return to Neverland after your first escape?"

"After I was convinced by Frank that they were good people, I went back with Chris immediately," Janet told him. "I came back that same day, and then Vinnie took me back, and that's it. I think. I'm trying to be summarizing those two days' worth of information."

"Well, it's a total of three escapes, isn't it?"

"Are you including the one where I permanently left and never went back?"

"Yes. And maybe it's four escapes. How many times did you escape from Neverland?" Mesereau asked.

But Janet Arvizo couldn't answer. Janet seemed to have a storyline about her escapes and returns to Neverland, and, at times, she spoke about Neverland as if she had been in a dream world. Either she was trying to evade the questions, or she was confused about her facts. In terms of her "escapes" from Neverland, Janet begged Tom Mesereau to please tell *her* the answer. As she became frazzled and dazed on the stand, everyone in the courtroom was stunned.

Courtroom observers gossiped furiously about Janet during the breaks, wondering why the prosecution would have put this witness on at all. Janet had become a joke, and most people thought the woman was out of her mind. People commented that Janet Arvizo seemed out of touch with reality. Media people laughed about the fact that Janet testified with more certainty about her leg wax treatments, her bikini wax treatments, and her eyebrow wax treatments, than she did about Michael Jackson, his associates, and her family's alleged captivity.

The idea that everyone was writing notes about bikini waxes—had most media members chuckling to themselves. For a moment, Janet had become the star of the trial, and people watched with amazement, waiting for the next crazy thing to come out of her mouth.

Janet kept telling the jury about Michael's associates, who she called "the Germans." But she testified that she had no concrete knowledge about what Deiter Weisner or Ronald Konitzer had to do with Michael Jackson's life. Regarding "the Germans," Janet seemed to think they were in charge of Jackson's affairs, and insisted that Deiter and Ronald were trying to control her. She told the jury that "the Germans" were causing her problems, but when asked to elaborate, Janet could only say that she didn't like having Deiter and Ronald around.

Janet claimed that the German men scared her and asserted that "the Germans" once said that they could make her disappear. When asked why, if she felt so threatened, she never made an attempt to file a report with police about the German men, Janet avoided the question. Mesereau wondered why Janet would set foot at Neverland at all, if in fact, she was afraid for her life. But Janet had no answer.

"Are you still telling the jury that everything nice you said about Michael on the rebuttal tape was from a script?" Mesereau wondered.

"Yes," Janet insisted.

"You've told the jury that when you did the tape, all the good things you said about Mr. Jackson were scripted, correct?"

"In the rebuttal that they did, the whole entire thing, from the beginning to the end, including outtakes. It was all scripted material, all of it," Janet testified.

"Ms. Arvizo, was what you said about Michael Jackson being fatherly, was that the truth?"

"Everything on here was choreographed by Deiter and Ronald," Janet insisted, "and it's all acting."

"Are the words you spoke true or false?" Mesereau asked.

"The words I spoke were part of a script."

"Were you telling the truth or not?"

"I was acting."

"Was it your belief that Gavin was acting in this tape?" Mesereau wondered.

"Yes, because I had seen Deiter work with my children prior to Jesus taking us back to my mom's house. I had seen Deiter work with me and my children."

"Did you believe what Gavin said was the truth or not?"

"I believe what he was saying was keeping to the script."

Mesereau asked about the subject of Michael as a father figure, and curiously, Janet admitted that even during her alleged attempts to escape from Neverland, she had referred to Michael Jackson as "family." Janet's testimony was extremely contradictory. As courtroom observers judged her, people decided that the woman was living in a world of paranoia. After a while, everything Janet said seemed to be invalid, and certain members of the jury were rolling their eyes.

Filled with conspiracy theories and allegations that Michael Jackson was a mastermind of a plot, people were looking at her like she had six heads.

Janet Arvizo was a disaster for the prosecution.

By the time Mesereau was through, the defense attorney was able to show that Janet used Michael for blood drives and fund-raisers and had found other ways to use Michael to help bring money to Gavin's cause. Mesereau reminded jurors that Jackson had opened up his home to the Arvizo family and had allowed Gavin and Star to stay at Neverland when Gavin was a bald, scrawny kid in a wheelchair. No other celebrity made such offers.

From the witness stand, Janet did her best to deny that Michael had helped cure her son of cancer. She questioned Michael's motives and denied that he acted out of love and goodwill. But the fact was—Jackson had devoted a lot of time and effort to Gavin Arvizo, and with prayers and help from Michael, Gavin's stage-four cancer had gone into remission. There was no denying that Jackson had played a part in the child's miraculous recovery. No doubt in anyone's mind.

"One Day in Your Life"

Michael wore mostly black suits accented by a different vest every day, his clothes made from unusual fabric and often adorned with gold buttons. Sometimes he polished off his look with a gold medallion draped around his shirt collar; other times he wore a gold ornamental belt, reminiscent of ages gone by. There was always a matching armband emblazoned on his suit, which no one seemed to know the significance of, but some thought the armband was meant to look "military," indicating a sign of rank, like a military leader. For sure, the armband had become a way for Jackson to distinguish himself, a way for him to convey his pop star status to the world.

Not that Jackson needed to do anything special to attract fans. His mere presence caused a swirl of excitement that transferred into a rhythm. Whenever he appeared, people would play his music loudly. Some would sing and imitate the artist. Jackson created an intensity in the air that made everyone feel a thrill, and that thrill carried over to sheriff's deputies and Jackson naysayers, whether they admitted it or not.

No matter how intense the media got, no matter how loud the fans seemed to be, Michael carried himself well, moving at a slow and steady pace, particularly aware of the media scrutiny, acutely aware of his image. Even in the face of serious criminal charges, Michael exuded a sense of jubilation that he fought to maintain. His energy was undeniable, and it sparked people, so much so, that many of Michael's fans couldn't control their outbursts. In his darkest hour, fans couldn't get enough of Jackson, and he couldn't resist them.

Nonetheless, Tom Mesereau didn't want Jackson to get caught up in anything that would distract him. Mesereau didn't want Jackson to get sidetracked by adulation and loud music and fans dancing all around him. To keep Jackson on course, the defense attorney made sure to greet the pop star outside the courthouse each day, whisking the icon away from the cameras and the fanfare that followed Michael daily.

Previous attorneys had made the mistake of allowing Jackson to hold lavish parties and press conferences in Los Angeles, of allowing Jackson to travel by private jet back and forth to Santa Maria, of allowing Jackson to get so bombarded by fans that the star was forced to stand on top of his SUV in order to avoid being crushed in a pretrial hearing. Mesereau knew that the media had fun with all of that—describing Jackson as someone who was out of touch with reality, twisting the SUV incident into something it wasn't—claiming that Jackson was trying to perform on top of his car in front of the courthouse. Mesereau also knew that Jackson's previous attorneys had a strong desire to get their own "face time" in front of the cameras. From Randy, Mesereau heard about the antics of Mark Geragos, Michael's attorney who reportedly shoved Randy Jackson out of the way, just after the first arraignment. Apparently, Mark Geragos pushed his way next to Michael's side, so he could be there for the "photo op."

People didn't know that Michael wasn't happy with "Hollywood" attorneys. People didn't know that Tom Mesereau became involved with the Michael Jackson case because Michael and Randy personally called Johnnie Cochran in the hospital to ask for Johnnie's advice. It was Johnnie Cochran who told Michael and Randy that Tom Mesereau was the man who would "get the job done."

Early on, when Mesereau took the case, he put a stop to all the rumors, eliminating any "Hollywood moments" and eliminating any people who would be fodder for media speculation. This included the Nation of Islam folks, who had attached themselves to Jackson as part of an ever-growing entourage.

The defense attorney didn't see how parties and press conferences and Hollywood hype would help Jackson win over a jury in Santa Maria, nor did he see how the Nation of Islam would serve to help Jackson win in a criminal trial. More than anything, Mesereau didn't want the trial to become more of a spectacle than it already was. He was careful to keep the "race card," and any type of politics, out of the mix.

Mesereau was all business, and from the moment he signed on to represent Jackson, the defense attorney made Michael understand that he was in the business of winning. Mesereau was not interested in personal press, in media friends, in "support group" parties, or any of that nonsense. Mesereau was there to fight for Jackson's life. He believed wholeheartedly that the superstar was the victim of false charges. He believed if he could humanize Jackson, strip away the "Hollywood" and the "entourage," the Santa Maria jury would see the truth for themselves. To keep the trial from becoming a circus, Mesereau supported the gag order imposed by Judge Melville. He was glad the media had no direct access to witnesses and key players.

Inside the courtroom, Mesereau tore apart key witnesses, bringing up details that discredited important pieces of the prosecution's theories. Mesereau was able to point out huge discrepancies in so-called "eyewitness" testimony, which created doubt about the case against Jackson. The longer the trial went on, it seemed, the more the jury connected with Mesereau and Jackson.

The state's case against Jackson was actually in trouble early on, but most of the media covering the trial didn't seem to notice. The majority of the media pool seemed convinced that there would be a conviction of some kind. This was especially true of the legal analysts, who seemed to be quite biased against Jackson.

Instead of being fair and balanced, many legal pundits seemed to be talking about the DA's strategy, seemed to think the DA was doing a good job. That pro-prosecution sentiment had a trickle-down effect, causing other media members to report details that amounted to a smear campaign against Jackson. Courtroom observers understood the lack of credibility that surrounded the accuser and his family, but still, many reporters were caught up in all the hoopla and sensationalism that the negative press created. The media covering the trial was interested in giving the public "dish," and was often ignoring the plain facts being presented in court.

The discrepancies between Janet Arvizo's recollection and the actual events at Neverland became completely clear when a former Neverland security guard, Officer Brian Barron, took the stand and described the three-week period that Janet and her children were guests of Michael Jackson in early 2003. For example, Janet claimed that she was hidden away in a guest unit throughout the duration of her visit, but Officer Barron told jurors that Janet Arvizo was seen walking all over the property, that she spent numerous nights sleeping with her children in one of the dance studios at Neverland, and ate her meals in the main house on a regular basis.

The former security guard, whose job it was to maintain safety at Neverland for children, whose job it was to supervise Michael Jackson's young guests, testified that when the Arvizo family stayed on the property in February of 2003, at least thirty other guests were visiting Neverland at the same time. Officer Barron mentioned Nikko Brando, the son of acting legend Marlon Brando, as well as

Aldo and Marie Nicole Casio, the siblings of Michael's friend Frank. The list of Neverland guests was long. The place seemed to have revolving doors.

A local police officer who had worked part-time security for Jackson, Brian Barron insisted that he'd never seen any wrongdoing at Neverland Ranch, assuring jurors that he would have reported it if he had. According to Barron, Neverland was a "fun place to go" where kids did pretty much whatever they wished, where kids "were treated quite well."

When Brian Barron told the jury that he was given no indication, at any time, that the Arvizos were trying to run away from Neverland, his testimony was devastating to the conspiracy charge against Michael Jackson. Officer Barron was asked to look over the exit logbooks from Neverland Ranch, shown to the jury on a large screen, and he was quite certain about the comings and goings of the Arvizos. According to the police officer, the Neverland security logs indicated that on February 12, 2003, Janet and her kids were driven off the property by Jesus Salas in Jackson's Rolls-Royce, without any incident whatsoever. Barron recalled that the family stopped at the guard booth and followed normal procedures as the Rolls-Royce left the ranch.

There was no "spiriting away" of the Arvizo family.

There was no "panic" at the gates of Neverland.

When the police officer told the jury that there were two private schools right across the street from Neverland, people became curious as to why, if Janet felt she was in such danger, she wouldn't have run across the road to a school to get help.

Officer Barron confirmed that there was plenty of activity going on at Figueroa Mountain Road, explaining that he saw parents and teachers and administrators coming and going every day in early 2003, during the same time period that Michael Jackson was allegedly involved in a conspiracy to hold the Arvizos as prisoners.

The gist of Officer Barron's testimony was: he heard no one complaining, he heard no one crying for help. Not one person in the Arvizo family acted like there was any problem at Neverland. If anything, the Arvizos seemed to be quite happy and content. The Arvizo kids were free to play and roam the grounds all day, and Janet Arvizo was enjoying a lifestyle that included regular "cash expense" payouts for her beauty treatments and other amenities.

Jurors seemed shocked when the former Neverland security guard testified that Janet and her kids took short trips to local towns surrounding Neverland, showing them where he had logged their daily movements at the Neverland gates. When a document was produced that showed two pages of Janet's petty cash expenditures, thousands of dollars of bills all paid for by Michael Jackson, it was impossible to believe Janet's claim that she ever made any serious attempt to escape from Neverland.

With another witness turned around by the defense, courtroom observers began to realize that the conspiracy charge was unwarranted. A few media folks reported their doubts about the state's case, but those people were in the minority. Behind the scenes, certain people were speculating that the prosecution team was grasping at straws, but no reporter had the guts to say it on the news.

The prosecution was drowning in a conspiracy theory, and as the insanity of the conspiracy charge against Michael Jackson became more evident to the jury, the child molestation charges became more questionable as well. Though the media kept focusing on the peculiarities of Jackson's personal life, though the prosecution was hell-bent on seeing Jackson go to prison—the stories and scenarios that were presented to the jury were not ironclad.

The prosecution tried to present Janet Arvizo as an unsophisticated mother who was blinded by Jackson's celebrity. They wanted the jury to ignore her unseemly past. They wanted the jury to think that Janet was a simple victim. However, they failed to see that Janet's constant lying made the prosecution look like *they* were in "Never Never Land." The more they learned about Janet, the more they heard testimony from Neverland staff that contradicted Janet's claims—the more the jury found themselves in the position of having to pick and choose what Janet was lying about.

Janet had repeatedly insisted that she had been held hostage, that she and her children were pretending to be "family" with Michael because she felt pressured by Michael's associates. She insisted there was a conspiracy.

Ms. Arvizo testified that she was too afraid to call authorities. She said that she was too scared to challenge "this Goliath," Michael Jackson. But to courtroom observers, it seemed Janet was incapable of telling the truth—not for one day in her life.

(left) Michael Jackson signals to an army of fans as his trial opens.

(Reprinted with permission from the Santa Barbara News-Press.)

(right) Famed attorney Tom Mesereau Jr., surrounded by the Jackson family, addresses the media as he prepares his defense strategy.

(Credit: AP Images/Phil Klein)

(left) Michael Jackson, flanked by bodyguards and defense attorneys, leaves the Santa Maria courthouse during a break in jury selection.

(Reprinted with permission from the Santa Barbara News-Press.)

(left) District Attorney Tom Sneddon had been investigating Michael Jackson for over a decade. Although Sneddon denied it, many thought the DA had a vendetta against the pop star.

(Credit: AP Images//Phil Klein)

(right) Superior Court Judge Rodney Melville acted with grace under pressure as he presided over the most high-profile trial in recent history.

(Credit: AP Images//Nick Ut)

(above) Jackson's SUV is mobbed by fans at the gates of Neverland.

(Reprinted with permission from the Santa Barbara News-Press.)

(left) British journalist Martin Bashir, the first witness to testify, enters the court with his attorney, Theodore Boutrous.

(Reprinted with permission from the Santa Barbara News-Press.)

(left) Michael Jackson responds to loud supporters on the day that jurors watch the British documentary that sparked the criminal case.

(Reprinted with permission from the Santa Barbara News-Press.)

(below) Jackson is supported by security, staff, and his father, Joe, on what became the infamous "Pajama Day."

(Credit: AP Images//Hector Mata)

(left) When Michael Jackson wanted to change attorneys, he turned to Johnnie Cochran. Reportedly, it was Cochran who thought Tom Mesereau would "get the job done."

(Credit:AP Images/Stephan Savoia)

(left) TV star George Lopez told the jury that he'd been a friend to Jackson's accuser, visiting the boy in the hospital while he underwent chemotherapy. During cross examination, Lopez admitted that his friendship with the accuser and his family ended when the accuser's dad became greedy and money hungry.

(Credit: AP Images//Mirek Towski/DMI via AP)

(left) Jackson's former wife, and mother to two of his children, Debbie Rowe testified for the prosecution. Her testimony became tearful when she spoke about what a good father Michael has always been.

(Credit: AP Images//Aaron Lambert)

(left) Angry that media made sexual innuendos about their association, *Home Alone* star Macaulay Culkin told jurors that he has enjoyed a lifetime friendship with Jackson.

(Credit: AP Images/Tammie Arroyo)

(left) CNN star Larry King testified outside the presence of the jury. The talk show host claimed that the accuser's attorney said the accuser's mother "was in it for the money." King's testimony was not allowed into the trial.

(Credit: AP Images/Manuel Balce Ceneta)

(left) TV mega-star Jay Leno took the stand to tell jurors that Jackson's accuser had called *The Tonight Show* looking for an in-person meeting with the talk show host. Leno recalled that he had a phone conversation with Jackson's accuser, a boy who Leno described as being "overly effusive" and "scripted."

(Credit: AP Images/Nick Ut)

(left) Comedian-actor Chris Tucker became a key witness for the defense. The *Rush Hour* star had befriended Jackson's accuser and his family, and later warned Jackson about them, telling jurors that he felt Jackson's accuser was "cunning."

(Credit: AP Images/Michael Mariant)

(left) TV host Nancy Grace propelled herself to super fame by using the Jackson trial to launch her new show at CNN Headline news. Many people believed that because Grace was so overtly pro-prosecution, her trial coverage was biased and one-sided.

(Credit: AP Images/Jennifer Graylock)

(above) Michael Jackson leaves the courtroom, a free man, and then disappears from public sight.

(Reprinted with permission from the Santa Barbara News-Press.)

(below) Jackson's defense team, from left, Thomas Mesereau Jr, Robert Sanger, Susan Yu, and Jesus Castillo, as they await Jackson on the day of the verdicts. Later, victorious lead defense attorney, Thomas Mesereau Jr, tells the press that "justice is done."

(Credit: AP Images/Michael Mariant)

(above) Members of the Jackson jury were jubilant on the day of the verdict. However, two jurors later said they were coerced into voting to acquit. Insiders felt that these jurors hoped to profit off the Jackson trial, especially when the media exposed the fact that both jurors were trying to land book deals.

(Credit: AP Images//Aaron Lambert)

(below) As word of the "Not Guilty" verdicts reached them, Jackson fans roared approval outside the Santa Maria courthouse.

(Reprinted with permission from the Santa Barbara News-Press.)

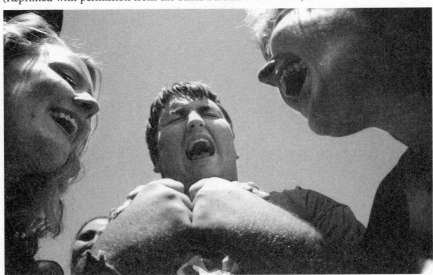

"Beat It"

Trial proceedings took a backseat on the day that Mesereau fired Jackson's long-time family advisor, Brian Oxman. Oxman, an attorney who was often seen with his eyes closed in court, certainly wasn't adding anything to the defense strategy. If anything, he was hurting the defense by looking bored and disinterested half the time.

When the attorney was sent packing by Mesereau, who filed a "notice of disassociation" with the superior court on April 21, 2005, the scene was caught by photographers in the court parking lot. Newspapers showed Mesereau pointing a finger at Oxman, chastising the family legal advisor. Even after the notice of disassociation had been filed, Brian Oxman marched into the courthouse, only to be escorted away by a bailiff when he tried to sit behind the defense table.

Up until that point, Oxman had only a limited role in the trial. He was a hand-holder more than anything else. Trial witnesses were handled exclusively by Tom Mesereau and Bob Sanger, with Mesereau taking the bulk of the work on his shoulders, assisted by his cocounsel, Susan Yu. Courtroom observers believed that, had it been up to Michael, it would have been his choice to have Tom Mesereau, along with the beautiful Susan Yu, handle the whole trial by themselves.

The tabloids made a big deal out of the public firing of Brian Oxman, but Tom Mesereau later confided that he was trying to avoid any public embarrassment for Oxman, who had been a family attorney for the Jacksons over the years. Mesereau insisted that Brian Oxman had been told to stay away from the courthouse, that he had been warned that an official notice of termination was about to be filed. Brian Oxman could have avoided the tabloid gossip had he not been so insistent on hanging onto the Jackson family's coattails, but Oxman felt it was his right to be present in the center of the limelight.

A family confidant who had represented Randy Jackson and other family members, Oxman claimed he was the lawyer who initially helped broker the deal to have Tom Mesereau replace Jackson's original defense attorney, Mark Geragos. To some observers, it was ironic that Mesereau was forced to have a public scene with Oxman out in the courthouse parking lot, but Oxman wasn't the criminal attorney in charge of the case. Oxman was extra baggage, and his public showboating with the media was not sending a message that Mesereau appreciated.

After their heated exchange, Oxman and Mesereau parted ways with a hug and a handshake. It would be the first shake-up for the defense team, but before the trial ended, Ramone Bain, Michael Jackson's gorgeous publicist, would also get a letter of termination. No one could confirm why it happened, but people put two and two together when they saw that Ms. Bain's departure was seemingly in conjunction with the ousting of the Reverend Jesse Jackson, who had come to Santa Maria to talk about Michael's state of mind, to talk about Michael being the victim of an overzealous prosecution team.

Apparently, Mesereau felt strongly about the trial coverage staying pure. He wanted the media to stick to the facts, and didn't need any outside opinions. It was odd that when the Reverend Jackson pulled out of Santa Maria, it was done quietly, without much media speculation. If, behind the scenes, the defense team was happy to remove any mention of civil rights or racial discrimination from the equation—no one in the media picked up on that.

Still, it seemed there were always "issues" around Michael Jackson that continued to pop up. For instance, an Extrajet stewardess, Cindy Montgomery, was initially disqualified as a potential witness because she was planning to assert her Fifth Amendment privilege on matters related to a secret taping of Michael Jackson on a plane. Ms. Montgomery had her own attorney present to assert that anything she might say would be potentially incriminating.

As it happened, Ms. Montgomery did testify and was never formally accused of any wrongdoing. But a few months after the Jackson criminal trial ended, two other parties involved in secretly taping Michael Jackson on an Extrajet flight were prosecuted, convicted, and were sentenced for conspiracy to violate Jackson's privacy.

Such was the world of the superstar.

It was always a big ordeal—anything to do with Michael Jackson, and that was highlighted by the testimony of his ex-wife, Debbie Rowe, who had already given up her parental rights to the two children she gave birth to, Prince and Paris, who would find herself in a very difficult emotional situation when she took the stand to testify on the behalf of the prosecution.

Debbie Rowe was expected to testify that she had given a "scripted performance" on the Jackson rebuttal video, which eventually aired on the FOX network. Rowe was expected to say that Michael was not a good father, she was expected to complain about her visitation rights.

All sorts of gossip was fueled in the days before Debbie Rowe took the stand, especially since she was publicly battling Jackson in a custody dispute over Prince Michael I, age eight, and Paris, age seven. Debbie Rowe, who had been married to Jackson from 1996 to 1999, had changed her mind about Prince and Paris, and she made a bid for custody in 2004—just after Jackson cut her off from the annual $1 million payment she had been receiving.

With a custody battle looming, with an appellate judge having ruled that Rowe's surrender of her parental rights was "invalid" due to "procedural problems," the media salivated over the potential bombshells Rowe would offer in her testimony against Jackson. Hoping that Rowe would say scandalous things in an effort to help gain custody of her kids, the media intensity was at an all-time high.

But when she was questioned by Assistant DA Ron Zonen, Debbie Rowe kept her cool. She spoke of taping the rebuttal film for Michael, a taping which lasted for almost nine hours, and said her attorney was present with her the entire time. When asked if she ever looked at a script—Debbie Rowe said flatly, "No."

Rowe told the jury that Ian Drew, the man conducting the interview, had a huge set of questions for her, asserting that she was truthful in her responses. She was insistent that her answers were spontaneous and honest, and admitted that she had misrepresented herself on the issue of "still being a part of Michael's family." Rowe claimed she had fibbed about that in order "to protect the children, and to try to keep the media questions away."

Debbie Rowe was perky, describing her efforts to participate in the rebuttal interview as something she enjoyed and was "excited" about. She testified that she was happy to answer questions on Michael's behalf and stated that she agreed to do the interview, in part, because she had hoped that she would be able to see her children—whom she hadn't seen in over two years. Rowe said she also hoped to "possibly renew a relationship with Mr. Jackson."

Ms. Rowe testified that she was promised a trip to Neverland that didn't materialize, and explained that after nine months of phone tag, she decided to go to family court, where she had her parental rights reinstated. As she was cross-examined by Mesereau, he wanted her to be more specific about her dispute with Michael Jackson in family court, but Debbie Rowe didn't want to call it a dispute. Debbie didn't want to anger Michael, and she looked at him with misty eyes in a way that made her seem remorseful.

When Mesereau asked Ms. Rowe about her "pretext phone calls," Debbie Rowe admitted that she had agreed to work with Santa Barbara sheriffs, telephoning Michael's "people" while allowing the sheriffs to secretly record her calls. She recalled making about a half dozen calls, specifically to Marc Shaffel, Ian Drew, and Deiter Weisner, all of whom had participated in the making of Michael's rebuttal video.

But rather than allow her to hurt the defense, Mesereau was able to focus on Rowe's reaction to the conspiracy investigation and to explore her view of the "unindicted coconspirators" surrounding Michael Jackson. It did not take much prodding for her to admit that she didn't really trust any of Michael's associates. Apparently, Rowe's pretext calls to these alleged coconspirators didn't help law enforcement establish that Michael was directly involved in any of the interviews being conducted for the purpose of the rebuttal documentary. If anything, under cross-examination, Rowe gave jurors the impression that Michael's "people" were operating without the pop star's knowledge.

"You told the sheriffs that, in your opinion, Marc Shaffel was continually trying to take advantage of Michael Jackson, true?" Mesereau asked.

"Correct," Rowe said.

"And you thought he was manipulating Michael Jackson to make lots of money, right?"

"Yes."

"You've also made statements to the sheriffs that you thought Dieter and Ronald Konitzer were manipulating Michael Jackson, correct?"

"Yes."

"Was it your perception, based upon what you observed of Shaffel, Deiter, and Konitzer, that those three were working together?" Mesereau asked.

"Oh, yeah," Rowe testified.

Debbie Rowe told jurors that, in her opinion, three men were working together—Shaffel, Deiter, and Konitzer—trying to find ways to use Michael Jackson's name so they could profit. To her knowledge, the three men had plans for "Jackson" enterprises in America and in Europe. Rowe said she was convinced that Michael wasn't aware of all of their endeavors, explaining she had seen this type of pattern with "handlers" in Michael's life before.

"And at one point, you told the sheriffs that you thought Michael Jackson was, in some ways, very removed from what those guys were doing, right?" Mesereau asked.

"In my past knowledge, he's removed from the handlers, the people who are taking care of business, and they make all the decisions, and there's a number of times that they don't consult him," Rowe explained.

"And you thought these three guys, Shaffel, Deiter, and Konitzer, were doing just that, didn't you?"

"Very strongly," Rowe insisted.

The more he questioned her, carefully and softly asking Rowe to tell the jury about Michael's private world, the more Debbie Rowe began to break down, struggling to answer the questions. She assured the jury that her responses on the rebuttal tape were spontaneous and confirmed that she gave honest, favorable reviews about Michael. About allowing herself to be taped for over nine hours, she explained that she had cooperated freely, without pay, because she heard about the "negative, twisted, and misunderstood" Bashir footage that aired in England.

For the jury, Debbie Rowe wanted to clarify a few issues. Perhaps she wanted a clean slate with Michael. For whatever reason, she was full of praise for him. Among the things Debbie Rowe communicated in her testimony:

Michael was a good father.

Michael was a family man.

Michael was a man whom she still cared about.

Debbie insisted that she still considered Michael to be her friend, and told the jury that she had given Michael full custody of the children at the time of their divorce. Looking over at Michael with tears welling up in her eyes, Debbie described having to communicate with Michael through attorneys because of the custody dispute.

As she sat on the stand, Debbie couldn't seem to take her eyes off Michael, but her pleading glances were virtually ignored by the pop star. Under the circumstances, it was clear that Michael was hurt by her betrayal. Debbie was a witness for the prosecution. Any positive comments she made about him, any of her testimony that was pro-Michael, didn't change the fact that she had cooperated with police, that Debbie had agreed to assist law enforcement in the criminal prosecution of her ex-husband.

When Mesereau questioned her, Debbie Rowe told the jury that she was worried about the "characters" around Jackson in early 2003, testifying that she was warned to "be careful" around certain men. Rowe mentioned her old boss, Dr.

Arnold Klein, whom she had contacted with the hope of having direct contact with Michael, to no avail. Rowe told the jury that she contacted Dr. Klein because she wasn't sure Jackson's "associates" were being honest with her, and indicated that she felt she was being used as a commodity.

"How did you learn that Mr. Shaffel was trying to make millions of dollars from the footage of your interview?" Mesereau wondered.

"He told me he was paid for it. He told me that part of the money that was made from it went for a debt Mr. Jackson owed him," Rowe testified.

"Did Shaffel, in your mind, ever ask you to help him in his business dealings with Mr. Jackson?" Mesereau asked.

"No. He just bragged about either how he took advantage of an opportunity that I'm sure he knew nothing about. And he talked about how he was going to do this, that, or the other thing to make sure that Michael's career was saved, and things of that nature," Rowe said.

"Okay. And did you ever get the impression that Shaffel was not giving Michael Jackson all the information about what he was up to?" Mesereau asked.

"He was like everybody else around Mr. Jackson. Yeah. He wasn't telling him everything," Rowe explained.

As courtroom observers listened to Debbie Rowe, as they heard her call all of Michael's associates "liars," her anger and resentment about the people who encircled Jackson became crystal clear. Through Debbie's eyes, courtroom observers learned that Michael had precious few people he could trust. Even his closest advisors, the people who were trying to "save" him, seemed to be hoping to cash in on the superstar's name.

"Did Shaffel tell you that he and Deiter and Konitzer were going to make a lot of money off of the problems that came out of the Bashir documentary?" Mesereau pressed.

"They said that they were going to fix the problem and bragged that they had made money," Rowe testified.

"And that bothered you, didn't it?"

"Yeah," Rowe said.

Debbie Rowe called Michael's associates "opportunistic vultures." She testified that Shaffel had bragged that he'd personally made over seven million dollars off of her rebuttal tape interview. She insisted that she didn't believe anything Shaffel boasted about and said that his attitude annoyed her.

As people listened to Debbie Rowe speak, what stood out to courtroom observers was how Michael Jackson could be easily manipulated by people. Somehow, through the years, the superstar had become completely vulnerable.

"HIStory"

When prosecutors produced a forensic accountant to prove that Michael Jackson was sinking into a multimillion-dollar hole, people had a hard time believing that Jackson was losing control of his financial empire. The prosecution was asserting that the pop star's money problems directly related to the conspiracy charge, claiming that his financial troubles were a direct result of his tarnished overall image.

For the jury, the prosecution had a certified public accountant explain the forensics of Jackson's vast spending habits as they pertained to the pop star's lagging earning capacity. According to their expert, J. Duross O'Bryan, who had worked dozens of forensic accounting investigations, Michael Jackson had been consistently spending an overage of $20 million to $30 million dollars a year, adding to his increasing debt, which had skyrocketed since the year 1999.

The expert accountant seemed very sure of himself when he testified that Jackson's estimated debt in 2003 totaled $224 million. O'Bryan told the jury that in order to fill in the gap between his $11.5 million annual earnings and his lavish spending habits, Mr. Jackson borrowed extensively against the properties he owned, specifically, the SONY/ATV catalogue.

O'Bryan surmised that in 2003, Michael Jackson was mired in "an ongoing cash crisis." He explained that the SONY/ATV catalogue had an estimated value of $1 billion dollars and said Jackson had been borrowing steadily against the value of the catalogue for years, calculating that Jackson's stake in the Sony catalogue would add up to no more than "a couple hundred million dollars." O'Bryan explained that, if he sold the catalogue, Mr. Jackson would owe Sony money, would have to pay off a $200 million loan to the Bank of America. He told jurors that Jackson would owe millions in capital gains taxes as well.

"He'd end up with nothing," O'Bryan testified.

Pointing to a string of warnings from Jackson's financial advisors over the years, O'Bryan detailed Jackson's use of a line of credit in 1999, which paid for the pop star's annual expenses. That included $5 million for legal and professional fees, $5 million for security and the operation of Neverland, $2.5 million for insurance, and $7.5 million for personal expenses. O'Bryan explained the balance sheets that listed Jackson's assets and liabilities, claiming at a certain point, Jackson's net worth had been in the negative of over $200,000.

But O'Bryan's facts and figures couldn't be verified, given that Jackson had not provided all of his bank statements and ledgers to the prosecution. O'Bryan was relying primarily on five boxes of correspondence between Jackson and his financial advisors, and he didn't have the complete data. In terms of tangible assets, O'Bryan told the jury that the primary holdings Jackson owned consisted of three things: the MIJAC catalogue, which contained publishing rights to Michael's songs and personal performances; the SONY/ATV catalogue, which contained a library of songs copyrighted by both Sony and Michael Jackson, and Neverland Valley Ranch, which was estimated to be worth about $50 million.

As O'Bryan continued to detail Michael's outstanding obligations versus Jackson's cash holdings, the amount of money being talked about—all in the millions of dollars—seemed to overwhelm the jury. Most people couldn't wrap their brains around that much money, nor could they understand how Michael could possibly overspend in the amount of $20 million to $30 million dollars a year. It was crazy to think that Jackson would allow himself to get into financial debt, especially since he had a steady income revenue that was well over $10 million a year. Jackson had the world's top financial consulting firms working for him, keeping track of his spending, loan documents, vendor invoices, and cash flow.

To Jackson and his family, the idea that the state was allowed to put on such evidence, the idea that the state was permitted to expose Michael's personal finances, was outrageous. The prosecutors were able to make Michael look fiscally irresponsible. They were able to drag his financial history into the picture because Jackson's financial "state of mind" at the time of the Bashir documentary was deemed to be part of the motive that led him to conspire to commit criminal acts.

Out of the presence of the jury, Mesereau had argued that Jackson's financial status in February and March of 2003 was the only possible relevant information that should be allowed into court. The one concession Judge Melville made was that Jackson's current financial status would not be revealed.

The prosecution argued, successfully, that Jackson's earlier financial statements would prove the "genesis" of the problems that existed in 2003, and thus a five-year history of Michael's financial condition was laid bare to the jury, shown to them in charts and on balance sheets. Jurors were exposed to Jackson's vast financial empire, with all its entanglements and all of Jackson's convoluted loans. Frankly, the information became quite confusing for anyone who was not used to dealing in the multimillion-dollar arena.

"Let me ask you the following. Let's assume that your conclusions are correct. In February of 2003, let's assume that your conclusions about Mr. Jackson's financial crisis are true, okay?" Mesereau prodded.

"Okay," O'Bryan said.

"As of February of 2003, how much was he in debt?"

"Well, the Sony Bank of America loan had a balance of $200 million. The MIJAC loan had a balance of $24 million. There was apparently an additional ten and a half million owing to vendors that had not been paid," O'Bryan testified. "Those are the large liabilities that I can think of as I sit here right now."

"Let assume that's all correct, all right?" Mesereau said. "And let's assume he doesn't want to sell his interest in the SONY/ATV catalogue. Let's assume he doesn't want to sell his own catalogue, which was estimated to be worth $128 million in 1999, okay? Let's assume he decides to sit there and just keep living with these obligations that you've identified, all right?" Mesereau asked.

"Okay," O'Bryan said blankly.

"Now, let's assume he has an opportunity to make a documentary for television that can generate about seven million dollars, all right?"

"Okay."

"Let's assume FOX is doing what is called a rebuttal documentary, okay? Now, that seven million isn't going to make much of a difference, is it?" Mesereau wondered.

"No, it's not," O'Bryan conceded.

"Wouldn't be worth committing a crime over seven million in that situation, would it?" Mesereau quipped.

As the cross-examination became heated, Mesereau was clearly annoyed with the audacity of the state's financial expert, who was basing Jackson's net worth on incomplete information. Mesereau was insulted by the state's attempt to make Jackson look like he was in the poorhouse. The defense attorney seemed infuriated, and though he retained his composure, his tone shifted.

"You've given the jury your opinions about Mr. Jackson's expenditures, liabilities, and liquidity, correct?" Mesereau asked.

"That's correct," O'Bryan said.

"You were not here to tell the jury what all of his assets were worth during that particular time period [of 2002 and 2003], correct?"

"We don't know exactly what they were worth during that particular time frame," O'Bryan admitted.

Mesereau pointed out that O'Bryan had seen a 2003 letter confirming that the SONY/ATV catalogue was worth an estimated $1 billion dollars, asserting that Jackson could have solved any 2003 cash crisis by selling his interest in the Sony catalogue that same year. O'Bryan argued that Jackson's interest in the Sony catalogue was only half of the estimated worth, informing jurors that in 1995, Jackson had already sold half of his interest in the Sony catalogue for $90 million dollars. Nonetheless, Mesereau pointed out that in 2003, Michael Jackson had the potential to borrow against his half of the Sony catalogue, which was valued at $500 million and maybe more.

"In 2003, you see an estimated value in this particular letter of one billion dollars, right?" Mesereau asked, showing O'Bryan the letter.

"That's correct," O'Bryan testified.

"And that catalogue contains ownership interests in all of the Beatles' music, true?"

"I don't know that it's all the Beatles' music," O'Bryan stammered. "I think it's some of the Beatles' music."

"Do you know whether it's all of it or not?" Mesereau asked.

"I don't know."

"Do you know any other recording artists whose copyrighted music is contained within that catalogue?"

"Yeah, I saw a memo on that. I don't recall the specifics, but I saw there were others involved," O'Bryan testified. "I think Sony's copyrighted music was in there, which I think initially was country-western. But I think there were other artists in there, as well as the Beatles."

"Okay. That catalogue today has been estimated to be worth a couple of billion dollars by some, even four to five by others, are you aware of that?" Mesereau wondered.

"I'm not aware of that."

"Your job was not to appraise the value of the SONY/ATV catalogue, correct?"

"No," O'Bryan told him. "But we certainly considered the value in coming to our opinions."

"Did you hire an appraiser to give you appraisal of the value of that catalogue in the year 2003?"

"No."

"Are you aware of any efforts between the years 1999 and March 2003 by any third party to get Mr. Jackson and Sony together so they could purchase Mr. Jackson's interest in that catalogue?" Mesereau asked.

"No, I have not seen any document like that," O'Bryan said.

"If Mr. Jackson sold his interest in March of 2003, in the SONY/ATV joint venture, okay?" Mesereau asked.

"Yes, I gotcha," O'Bryan followed.

"That's assuming all parties got together and all agreed Mr. Jackson could sell his interest, all right?" Mesereau wondered.

"That's what I believe would have to happen, yes," O'Bryan agreed.

"Yes. He could have paid off the Bank of America loan, he could have ended up worth two hundred million dollars after taxes, excluding royalty income, true?" Mesereau quipped.

"I've never seen that document, so I couldn't tell you if it was true or not," O'Bryan testified, his body shrinking down on the witness stand.

Mesereau reminded the state's expert witness that an entertainer of Michael Jackson's caliber didn't check with his accountant every time he was offered an opportunity somewhere around the world. The defense attorney wondered if the forensic accountant was aware that Michael Jackson had been offered $100 million to do a national tour in 2002—but O'Bryan had no such knowledge. The expert seemed to be at a loss for words.

The forensic accountant had to admit that he wasn't an expert in the music industry. O'Bryan told the jury that he had no idea what opportunities Michael Jackson might have regarding music licensing and "Jackson-related" products to be sold in the entertainment industry throughout the world. The expert testified that to his knowledge, Mr. Jackson had never gone bankrupt, and he squirmed in his seat when he was forced to agree with Tom Mesereau that it was entirely possible that a worldwide entity like Michael Jackson could solve his "liquidity problems" in just one day.

"Ebony and Ivory"

In the presence of the jury, as the prosecution was nearing the end of its case, there was a hearing about the admission of evidence that pertained to the conspiracy charge. Gordon Auchincloss asked to submit certain e-mails, seized under search warrant, that revealed communications from Jackson's "crisis management team"—e-mails that made specific references to the Arvizo family. The prosecution wanted to show "the panic that existed at the time."

The documents that the Santa Barbara DA's office submitted was their attempt to piece together circumstantial evidence. It was their contention that Michael Jackson was the person who wanted to cool down the negative press, that it was Jackson himself—who was the mastermind of a criminal conspiracy. Prosecutors felt that there was enough circumstantial evidence to show that the conspiracy was being spearheaded by the pop star. To bolster their charge, prosecutors entered the FOX TV contract into evidence, showing how much money Jackson and his "unindicted coconspirators" were being paid to release Jackson's rebuttal documentary.

The fact that Jackson was never directly linked to any of the e-mails, nor could the pop star be linked to any of his coconspirators' phone records, was never addressed by the DA's office. But that came later, when Tom Mesereau pointed out that Michael Jackson didn't own a cell phone, that there was no way to know exactly who Mr. Jackson ever spoke to. That Jackson could not be traced to any of the communications whatsoever made an indelible impression on the jury.

"The defense have attempted, through the introduction of evidence, through cross-examination, to show that Mr. Jackson was an unknowing party to this conspiracy," Auchincloss argued. "Then, in some respects, [they] seem to concede that there was something nefarious going on, but not involving Mr. Jackson."

Auchincloss told the court that Jackson's continued "association" with the unindicted coconspirators (specifically Marc Shaffel, Ronald Konitzer, and Dieter Weisner) showed that Jackson was, indeed, tied to the conspiracy. The $3 million FOX contract was relevant, Auchincloss said, because it showed the financial motive on the part of various coconspirators to continue their relationships with Michael Jackson. There was also a second FOX agreement, stating that another FOX rebuttal documentary would produce $4 million in income for Jackson and his "crisis management" team.

"This is all about money," Auchincloss contended. "We don't dispute that among the coconspirators. They're interested in financial gain. But the financial gain they are seeking is from the success of Mr. Jackson, not from his fall."

"[Item] 406 is the contract for the FOX rebuttal. There's been quite a bit of testimony about the amount of money that was going to be made from this endeavor," Auchincloss said. "This [document] is corroborative of that testimony. It's offered to show that this was a money-making enterprise, that Mr. Jackson was going to personally profit from it, as well as the coconspirators."

The prosecution team wanted to show, circumstantially, that Marc Shaffel was in control of the making of the rebuttal film, that Shaffel stood to earn $600,000—his cut of the $3 million. Auchincloss successfully entered into evidence the contract for the FOX rebuttal, as well as proof of cash disbursements to members of Jackson's alleged coconspirators paid from Jackson's company, Neverland Valley Entertainment.

The strategy of the prosecution was to show that there was a "consciousness of guilt" among Jackson and his people "and knowledge of the criminal purpose of this conspiracy."

But there was not even a single document that showed that Jackson was aware of any "strategies" regarding the production of the FOX rebuttal film. There was no direct evidence, no documentation, that showed that Jackson knew anything about the state of mind of the people who were handling his "crisis management." Sure, there was evidence that Jackson paid people to create a rebuttal film—but that didn't mean that Michael Jackson knew anything about a conspiracy plot.

The more the prosecution pushed the conspiracy charge against Jackson, the more ridiculous Sneddon's team appeared. They couldn't see themselves, but courtroom observers were shaking their heads about the allegations being made by the Santa Barbara DA's office. Tom Sneddon and his team were so caught up in minutia, they were missing the big picture.

The conspiracy charge made the prosecution seem desperate.

Before Mesereau began the defense's case-in-chief, his cocounsel, Robert Sanger, made an argument that all charges against Jackson should be dismissed.

Out of the presence of the jury, Sanger pointed out falsehoods in the testimony of Janet, Star, and Davellin Arvizo, and told the court that at issue were "the willfully false" statements of the Arvizos, including those of the accuser, Gavin.

Referring to Gavin's testimony, Sanger asserted that the accuser made willfully false statements about the dates of the alleged incidents, citing Gavin's grand jury testimony, where Gavin Arvizo claimed that the first sexual "incident" occurred on or about February 7, 2004.

Sanger argued that, when the Arvizos discovered that they were on tape with Brad Miller in early February, praising Jackson to the hilt—Gavin changed the dates of the alleged incidents, claiming that his "recollection" was that first sexual incident occurred toward the end of his stay at Neverland—sometime in March of 2003.

"For one thing, what the Arvizos did is, they decided to move the dates," Sanger told the court. "They moved the dates to the point where it happened at the end of their stay [at Neverland]. They moved the dates. It's willfully false."

Sanger insisted that Gavin Arvizo was fabricating his testimony. The defense attorney provided specific instances where it seemed clear that the boy lied on the stand, that Gavin was making things up as he went along.

"He's lying," Sanger insisted. "That's all there is to it."

But Judge Melville saw no cause for dismissal. Melville requested that the jury be brought in—and asked the defense to call their first witness.

Unlike other high-profile criminal lawyers, without being flamboyant, without being "Hollywood," Mesereau used a style that abandoned most conventions of trial practice, referring to the prosecution team as "the government" and introducing himself to each witness with the words:

"Hello. My name is Tom Mesereau, and I speak for Michael Jackson."

It was brilliant.

Mesereau began the defense case with a young man who had been a friend of Michael's, twenty-two-year-old Wade Robson, who started teaching dance at the age of twelve, who had started choreographing music videos from the age of fourteen. Wade Robson had become successful. The young man was known in the music industry and was one of Britney Spears' personal choreographers.

Under direct examination, the jury learned that Robson met Michael Jackson when he was five years old. At the time, back in 1987, Robson lived in Australia and had entered a dance contest that Jackson held during his "Bad" tour. Robson said that he won the contest, and the prize was to meet Michael backstage. Robson testified that the pop star was impressed by his dance style, and told the jury that Jackson pulled him up on stage that night, happy to have the five-year-old perform with him.

Two years later, Wade Robson and his mother pursued Jackson, hoping that Jackson would help Wade's career. They met Jackson at a recording studio in California and showed the pop star some videotapes of Wade's latest dance routines.

Wade testified that by 1989, he and Michael became friends. Wade recalled that he and his entire family went to visit Michael at Neverland when he was age seven. Robson said that after that initial visit, he stayed in touch with Jackson via telephone, and told the jury that in 1991, he moved from Australia to Los Angeles, where he lived with his sister, Chantel, and his mother, Joy.

"How many times do you think you've stayed at Neverland?" Mesereau asked.

"It's got to be somewhere in the twenties, or something like that. Mid twenties," Robson said.

"And you've stayed there for varying periods of time?"

"Yeah. And most of the time, it's like a weekend, you know. Friday, Saturday, Sunday."

"What's the longest amount of time, do you think, that you've ever stayed at Neverland?" Mesereau wondered.

"You know, I would say a week to a week and a half," Robson testified.

"Do you consider Michael Jackson your friend?"

"Yes."

"You're aware of the allegations in this case, are you not?"

"Yes."

"And are you aware, as you sit here today, that there's been allegations that Mr. Jackson molested you?"

"Yes."

"Mr. Robson, did Michael ever molest you at any time?" Mesereau asked.

"Absolutely not," Robson responded.

"Mr. Robson, did Michael Jackson ever touch you in a sexual way?"

"Never. No."

"Mr. Robson, has Mr. Jackson ever inappropriately touched any part of your body at any time?"

The answer was no.

Wade Robson told the jury that he stayed in Michael's room on numerous occasions, saying that he and Michael would watch movies, play video games, and have a pillow fight every now and then. As for taking showers with Michael, Robson said that never happened. Robson said that he'd been in the Jacuzzi with Michael, testifying that both he and the pop star wore swimming trunks, that nothing inappropriate ever happened in the Jacuzzi, or anywhere else.

Of course, when it was their turn, the prosecution harped on the fact that Wade Robson admitted to sleeping in the same room with Michael from the time he was age seven. On cross-examination, Assistant DA Ron Zonen tried to insinuate that Robson had reasons to protect the pop star, reminding the jury that Jackson had helped Wade Robson with his career, pointing out that Jackson had put the young boy in a few of his music videos, among them "Black and White."

"Were there times that you actually stayed at Neverland for many weeks at a time?" Zonen asked.

"Not that I can remember," Robson testified. "Like I said, a week to a week and a half. Maybe it was two weeks, but I don't remember any more than that."

"Were there periods of time when you were at Neverland and working with Mr. Jackson on dance routines?" Zonen wanted to know.

"No. I mean, we would mess around and dance in the studio a little bit, every now and then," Robson told him.

"Was there ever an occasion where you were on the dance floor with Mr. Jackson, and he was showing you a routine, and he grabbed your crotch in a manner similar to how he would grab his own crotch while doing these performances?"

"No. That's not true."

"You have no recollection of that?" Zonen pressed.

"No."

"That didn't happen?"

"No."

Zonen was trying to put words in the young man's mouth, but Wade Robson would have none of that. The cross-examination got ugly, and Zonen repeatedly asked if anything inappropriate ever happened between Wade and Michael, but the answer was always an emphatic "no."

To courtroom observers, it seemed that Ron Zonen was trying to badger the witness, and some jurors were beginning to look annoyed.

"I'm telling you, nothing ever happened," Robson testified.

"Mr. Robson, when you were asleep, you wouldn't have known what had happened, particularly when you were age seven, would you have?" Zonen quipped.

"I think something like that would wake me up."

As Robson said those words, certain people on the jury shrugged their shoulders, looking at each other with curious expressions.

"It's a Thriller"

When Brett Barnes was called by the defense as their next witness, the blood left Tom Sneddon's face, and the man turned as white as a ghost. The DA couldn't believe that yet another young man was stepping forward to help Michael Jackson. Perhaps Sneddon felt he had intimidated many of these people. Behind the scenes, it was rumored that people who supported the prosecutor had attempted to contact certain defense witnesses, had wished to keep them away from the trial.

Insiders knew that the prosecution was trying to hound people, people like Macaulay Culkin. Mesereau was informed that Santa Barbara sheriffs were knocking on the neighbors' doors of at least one key witness, which could have had an intimidating effect. Yet Jackson's friends were waltzing into court of their own free will.

Brett Barnes, a twenty-three-year-old man who had flown in from Australia, told the jury that he had to quit his job as a roulette dealer in Melbourne in order to get himself to the Santa Maria court. Brett identified Michael as the gentleman behind the defense table and said that Michael was his good friend, whom he'd known since he was age five.

Barnes told the jury that when he was a five-year-old, he and his mom had written Jackson a letter and had made arrangements to hand that letter to one of Jackson's dancers at an airport in Melbourne. A short time later, the Barnes family received a call from Jackson, and Barnes said the family remained friends with the pop star ever since. Barnes testified that the first time he visited Neverland was in 1991, when he visited with his whole family.

The young man recounted at least ten times that he and his family had stayed at Neverland, telling the jury that he had chosen to sleep in Michael's bedroom on most all occasions. Without hesitation, Brett was comfortable talking about being with Michael in his bedroom, where the problems and concerns of the adult world could be locked out.

"How would you describe his room?" Mesereau asked.

"It's big. It's pretty cool because it's got lots of fun stuff to do there. Video games, stuff like that. That's probably the best as I can describe it," Barnes said.

"Have you ever stayed in Michael Jackson's bed?"

"Yes, I have."

"How many times do you think you have?"

"Countless."

"Has Mr. Jackson ever molested you?"

"Absolutely not," Barnes said. "And I can tell you right now that if he had, I wouldn't be here right now."

"Has Mr. Jackson ever touched you in a sexual way?" Mesereau asked.

"Never. I wouldn't stand for it," Barnes told him.

"Has Mr. Jackson ever touched any part of your body in a way that you thought was inappropriate?"

"Never. It's not the type of thing I would stand for."

Brett Barnes described his times in Michael's room as mini-parties. He told the jury that he could recall his sister being there, along with Michael's cousins, as well as Frank, Aldo, and Marie Nicole Casio. Barnes said there were times when Macaulay Culkin was there playing games with all of them as well, times that he remembered with fondness. Barnes talked about the great fun he had at Neverland—eating all kinds of food, watching plenty of cartoons, going on amusement park rides, playing arcade games, and riding ATV/motorbikes around the property.

"Are you aware of any allegations being made that Mr. Jackson inappropriately touched you when you were with him?" Mesereau asked.

"Yes, I am. And I'm very mad about that," Barnes said.

"You're mad about it?"

"Yeah."

"Why?"

"Because it's untrue, and they're putting my name through the dirt. And I'm really, really, really not happy about it."

Courtroom observers could see that Barnes was quite angry. The young man didn't appreciate any false allegations being made by Neverland employees, especially the allegations made by employees who had been trying to extort money from Jackson. Barnes was acutely aware of the rumors circulating, rumors created by disgruntled employees who claimed they witnessed Brett and Michael taking showers together. Brett Barnes told the jury that nothing like that had ever happened, that employees were spreading lies.

Barnes described Michael Jackson as a longtime friend, as someone who he stayed in touch with throughout the years. It was obvious that Brett Barnes enjoyed his friendship with Jackson, who he said was "like a member of the family."

When Ron Zonen cross-examined him, he wanted Brett Barnes to clarify how often Brett stayed in Michael's room as a guest. Barnes blankly stated that he always slept there, making no bones about it. But Zonen thought it was incriminating, and he wanted Barnes to feel ashamed.

"It's true, sir, that you stayed virtually the entire time in his bedroom. Is that right?" Zonen asked.

"Yeah," Barnes testified.

"And during that time, nobody else stayed in the bedroom with you and Michael Jackson. Is that true?"

"No, that's not true."

"Can you tell us the names of the people who stayed in the room with you?" Zonen wanted to know.

"My sister. Macaulay Culkin. There was Levon and Elijah," Barnes recalled. "There was Frank, Eddie, and Dominick, and his son Prince as well."

Zonen could hardly believe it when Barnes testified that he continued to sleep in Michael's room until the age of nineteen. Brett Barnes told the jury that he stayed in Michael's room with Prince Michael I there, who was age three at the time, and Zonen found this impossible to comprehend.

As Brett Barnes spoke, courtroom observers kept their eyes glued on the young man, struggling to read between the lines. It was obvious that Zonen was trying to do whatever he could to rattle the witness, and people waited to see if Zonen was going to pull the same stunt he used with Wade Robson. With Robson on the stand, Zonen showed the young man a book called *Boys Will Be Boys*.

The book, which Zonen liked to display along with another book called *The Boy*, had been taken from Neverland in an earlier raid, back in 1993. Both books included nude artistic shots of boys, as well as photographs of boys playing on the beach, hanging from trees, and having fun in bathing suits. When Robson was on the stand, Zonen had asked the witness if he would look at *Boys Will Be Boys*, and asked him to tell the jury if he thought it was more than just innocent photographs. Wade Robson looked at the piece of evidence and testified that he'd never seen it before. Robson told the jury that he thought the book was harmless.

Courtroom observers saw that Zonen was gunning for these young men, trying to get them unnerved by any means necessary. Zonen wanted to get the jury inflamed, and he questioned the young men about lewd acts, bringing up sexually explicit materials, throwing accusatory questions at them. The tactic hadn't worked with Wade Robson, but Zonen had the jury on edge, wondering what dark road the prosecutor would try to go down with Brett Barnes. Ron Zonen had become creative with his cross-examination, and people in the courtroom seemed to be bracing themselves for a new form of attack.

"Mr. Barnes, do you consider it disgraceful to have been molested?" Zonen asked.

"Absolutely," Barnes said.

"All right. And why would it be a disgrace for somebody to have been molested?"

Barnes tried to answer the hypothetical question, but Mesereau objected on the grounds that the question called for speculation, and Zonen moved on. He quizzed Barnes about every year of his life, from the time he first went to Neverland at age nine, asking Barnes if he stayed in the same bed with Jackson at age nine, age ten, age eleven, age twelve, and so on.

Barnes testified that he couldn't remember all of his exact ages on the occasions when he visited Neverland. He recalled that he traveled to Neverland almost once a year after his first visit, testifying that he slept in Michael's room whenever he was there.

"Do you still sleep with Michael Jackson?" Zonen wondered.

"No, I don't," Barnes told him.

"How old were you when you stopped sleeping with Michael Jackson?"

"I couldn't tell you that."

"Why don't you still sleep with Michael Jackson?"

"Well, he's got kids now."

It was as if Zonen was using a magnifying glass, scrutinizing instances when Barnes shared a bed with Jackson. He pushed and pushed, trying to frame things in a negative light, but Brett Barnes, from the look on his face, seemed to feel that neither he nor Michael had done anything wrong.

"Did you ever have a conversation with your father about the propriety of sharing a bed with a thirty-five-year-old man?" Zonen asked.

"Not that I recall," Barnes told him.

"Did you ever have a conversation with your mother about that, whether that was a wise thing to do, to share a bed with a thirty-five-year-old man?"

"Not that I recall."

"Did he ever show you any sexually explicit material?"

"Absolutely not."

"Were you aware that he possessed sexually explicit material?"

"No."

Zonen asked Brett Barnes to recount his travels with Jackson, to tell the jury about going on tour with Jackson to exotic places like South America, about traveling with Jackson to cities all across North America. Barnes testified that he felt he'd been "very fortunate" to travel with Jackson and said that it was a thrill, joining the pop star on tour. Barnes told the jury that Jackson arranged for all the travel, paying for other members of the Barnes family to travel along as well.

"When you slept with Jackson, what did you generally wear?" Zonen asked.

"Pajama pants, T-shirt, pajama top sometimes," Barnes told him.

"Always?"

"Well, always pajama pants, always a T-shirt."

"And Mr. Jackson?"

"Exactly the same thing."

"Did you ever talk with Michael Jackson about the propriety of sharing a bed with him?" Zonen quipped.

"Not that I recall," Barnes said.

"At no time, did you ever have a conversation with Michael Jackson, where the subject of the conversation was whether or not you should be sharing a bed with him?"

"Not that I recall."

Zonen tried to get Barnes to say he'd been touched or kissed by Jackson, but the only thing Barnes could recall was that Jackson would often tell him that he was loved. Brett recalled being kissed on the cheek and on the forehead by Michael. And that was the extent of it.

"The Love You Save"

Dressed in a black suit, white shirt, wearing no tie, twenty-three-year-old actor Macaulay Culkin caused a stir when he entered the court. People were whispering about the entertainer's appearance, which seemed to have changed very little from the time the *Home Alone* star had first catapulted to fame. Media people were elated to see Culkin. They weren't sure until the last minute, that Culkin would appear on Jackson's behalf.

Telling the jury that he was the godfather of two of Jackson's children, Macaulay Culkin said that he and Michael shared a unique bond. Each were former child stars, part of a very small club of people who'd been thrust into the limelight before they had the ability to deal with it.

Michael understood Macaulay. Michael knew about the loneliness of the life of a child star, and there were other child stars whom Michael had been drawn to, like Elizabeth Taylor, Liza Minnelli, and Shirley Temple. Michael felt a deep connection to these particular stars, he idolized and adored them. Michael related to them as people who had to fight from being pigeonholed, who grew up under a microscope, who were almost always misunderstood by the public.

Macaulay Culkin testified that he'd visited Neverland more than a dozen times, from age ten to age fourteen, often going to see Jackson with his younger brother, his two sisters, and his mother and father. The actor said that his friendship with Jackson was lifelong, and wanted the jury to know that he continued to visit Neverland throughout his teens, that he had gone to see Michael as recently as a year prior to his appearance in court.

The actor said he spent time with Jackson at other locations, mentioning an apartment that Jackson kept as a hideaway in Los Angeles, where they would sometimes "hang out," watching movies and sharing a casual dinner. Macaulay told the jury that, in recent years, he enjoyed spending time with Michael and his children, whether he'd see them in New York, Los Angeles, or in London.

When Mesereau asked questions about the allegations made by former Neverland employees, allegations that Michael Jackson inappropriately touched the child star, Macaulay Culkin adamantly denied that Jackson had ever done anything offensive, had ever acted sexually toward him in any way.

"What do you think of these allegations?" Mesereau wondered.

"I think they're absolutely ridiculous," Culkin said.

"When did you first learn that prosecutors were claiming that you were improperly touched?"

"Somebody called me up and said, 'You should probably check out CNN, because they're saying something about you.'"

"And did you check it out?"

"Yes, I did."

"And what did you learn?"

"I learned that a former cook had done something to me, and there was something about a maid or something like that. It was just one of those things where I just couldn't believe it," Culkin testified. "I couldn't believe that, first of all, these people were saying these things—let alone that it was out there, and people were thinking that kind of thing about me.

"And at the same time, it was amazing to me," Culkin explained, "that nobody approached me and asked me whether or not the allegations were true. They just kind of threw it out there, and they didn't even double-check it, basically. I mean, if they assumed that I knew the answer, what got me was they didn't even ask."

"Are you saying that these prosecutors never tried to reach you to ask your position on this?" Mesereau asked.

"No, they didn't," Culkin testified.

"Are you aware that the prosecutors claim they are going to prove that you were molested by Michael Jackson?"

"Excuse me?"

From the expression on his face, the jury saw that Macaulay Culkin couldn't believe his ears. He testified that he had "good clean fun" with Michael at Neverland, that his family was always invited anywhere on the property, that Jackson had "an open-door policy" for the Culkin family, that no room was off-limits, including Michael's bedroom.

"Has Mr. Jackson ever hugged you?" Mesereau asked.

"Sure," Culkin said.

"Have you ever hugged him?"

"Absolutely."

"Were you ever suspicious of any of these hugs as being something sexual in nature?"

"No, it was always very casual. It was just the way I hug any of my friends," Culkin said.

"Did you ever see Mr. Jackson hug your sister?"

"Sure."

"Were you suspicious of him hugging your sister?"

"No."

Macaulay Culkin told the jury that Jackson hugged his brothers, hugged his whole family, and there was nothing suspicious about it. They all felt close to Michael, and hugging each other was a way of greeting him. The actor said he'd never seen Jackson do anything improper with any child, and testified that he'd been around Jackson and Wade Robson when they were filming the music video, "Black and White." Culkin believed he had also seen Jackson interact with Brett Barnes, whom he vaguely remembered spending time with at Neverland as kids, when a bunch of people "hung out" and played games in Michael's room.

Under cross-examination, Macaulay Culkin attempted to answer questions that were geared to make it seem like Jackson was trying to buy Culkin's friendship. Culkin acknowledged that Jackson had once given him a Rolex watch but said it was an item that he no longer used. It was an engraved gift from Jackson, kept in a safe deposit box because it was too small for him. Other gifts Culkin described came from Toys "R" Us, the chain store in Santa Maria where he and Jackson would occasionally shop after hours, being let in by the janitor so the two of them could have access to toys without being crowded by fans.

Regarding having conversations with his parents about whether or not it was appropriate to sleep in the same room as Jackson, Culkin told the jury that his parents "never saw it as an issue." The actor testified that his parents came in and out of the bedroom, that sometimes his father would come into Jackson's room early in the morning, waking Macaulay so they could go horseback riding together.

"Did you ever stay at Neverland when Jordie Chandler was there?" Zonen asked.

"I don't know. I'm not sure if I have. I'm not sure who Jordie Chandler is," Culkin said.

"Were you *never* introduced to Jordie Chandler?"

"I couldn't say. I met handfuls of people going in and out. There was always kind of a revolving door of staff and of people, kind of coming in. Sometimes, there would be guests there that I never really met before."

"Were you ever in Mr. Jackson's bedroom overnight while another boy was present in that room, other than your brothers?"

"On occasion, there were other kids that were there. Like I said, some of them were introduced," Culkin testified. "I was introduced to cousins or family friends, or stuff like that. And they'd bring their kids there, the same as me. They would play with me, and we'd fall asleep anywhere. Sometimes in his bedroom, sometimes in the theater, sometimes anywhere."

Before the end of his testimony, reporters rushed out to give the latest "Hollywood" update on the trial. Macaulay Culkin's appearance was expected to draw a news audience, and it did, even though much of what he said in court was innocuous. On that particular day, the media reported detailed testimony from the *Home Alone* star, virtually ignoring the rest of the witnesses who came forward, witnesses who offered testimony that would help exonerate Jackson.

It was eerie to watch the media machine in motion: everyone was using the same buzzwords, no one thinking independently, no one reaching out to report the real meat of the defense case.

Just prior to Macaulay Culkin's testimony, Jackson's defense called five Neverland employees who testified that they never witnessed the pop star acting inappropriately with children. Joe Marcus, the ranch manager who worked at the ranch even before Jackson purchased the property, testified that the Arvizo family seemed to enjoy their time on the estate, telling the jury that he had driven the family to nearby Solvang, recalling that the Arvizos never complained about being held captive, nor did they hint that they needed help.

And there was Violet Silva, a security guard at Jackson's ranch, who told the jury that Gavin Arvizo was "rambunctious" and that his mother, Janet, was "unstable" and seemed to suffer from mood swings. Ms. Silva testified that Gavin had gotten himself into all kinds of trouble at Neverland, including crashing a golf cart into a cart driven by Marlon Brando's grandson. Most importantly, she detailed an incident involving thirteen-year-old Gavin driving a van on the property without permission.

The fact that Gavin was driving vehicles around Neverland, that the accuser could have easily driven off the property, was another major blow to the prosecution's conspiracy case. But media didn't report anything about that.

It wasn't that news reporters didn't care about important testimony, it was that, behind the scenes, TV news producers were the people who made the decisions, and producers wanted to hear about the child star. They didn't want their broadcasts to be bogged down with facts. It was the Hollywood glitz that sold. And telling people about Macaulay Culkin admitting to sharing a bed with Michael Jackson was all that mattered.

"Ask Me How I Know"

The Voice of Michael Jackson:
Exhibits 5009-A, 5009-B, 5009-C, outtake footage with Martin Bashir.

All through the outtake footage of Bashir's documentary, which the jury viewed for two-and-a-half hours, there was an overwhelming feeling of intimacy. Michael had his own personal videographer taping simultaneously, which allowed for candid moments, enough to get a sense of the pop star's true self. It was strange, watching Jackson sitting on a pillow on the floor—from the waist up, looking regal, from the waist down, dressed in comfortable slip-on "house" pants.

When the interview begins, Bashir tells Michael that he's a musical genius, asserting that his documentary will convey two things: Michael's genius and the charity work that Michael has done throughout the world. Bashir doesn't want to embarrass Michael with too much praise, but insists the world should know about Michael's efforts to help children.

Michael complains that the media only reports "negative things" about him, and Bashir responds by calling tabloid reporters "scum." While the tape focuses only on Michael's face, we hear Bashir insisting that the reportage he's seen about Michael is "disgusting" and "it's getting worse."

Michael complains, tired of stupid rumors.

Bashir promises that he's not going to produce that kind of "rubbish."

Just as Bashir's cameras are about to roll, Bashir plays on Michael's affinity for the British, asking Michael to "do an English accent," but the pop star is shy. Michael just smiles, looks away from the camera, and politely declines.

Bashir begins the questions by playing up to Jackson's love for the inno-cence of children, then quickly turns the conversation to Jackson's musical genius, asking if Jackson's success makes people jealous.

Michael tells Bashir that "success does that" and claims that jealousy is some-thing he's lived with, something he's had to deal with over time. Michael feels like a target, but seems to say that comes along with the territory of being a super-star. He asserts that with each step of success, people create more rumors about him.

To Bashir, the pop icon explains that when he started breaking all-time records for the biggest selling albums of all time, almost simultaneously, he was called "weird." Jackson strains and seems hurt talking about how people call him strange and "wacko," about people speculating that he's a "girl" or a "homosex-ual." Jackson insists that the rumors are untrue, telling Bashir that so much about him is "all completely made up." As Jackson begins to get comfortable with Bashir, he mentions that people would be surprised to see how normal and sim-ple his way of living is.

Bashir tells Jackson that he is "the greatest musical artist alive today" and talks about Jackson having produced "the most successful music that the world, the globe, has ever seen." Bashir wonders if Jackson's success might have turned people turn against him.

Michael is candid about people and jealousy. He talks about artists, histori-cally famous figures who were larger-than-life, and how people around them became jealous. He uses the example of Michelangelo, who apparently had his nose broken by a fellow artist during an argument about who the greatest artist was. "People do that to me, but in a different way," Jackson asserts.

Jackson explains how "opinion" can be mightier than the sword, and expresses his grief over the media going "too far." He tells Bashir that he's human, and insists that it hurts him to hear lies, especially because he knows kids are out there listening to all the rumors.

As for handling the public, Jackson explains that often when he goes out, because of the media, he's in disguise. He says that sometimes, because of an emergency or whatever, he just has to run into a store and run out, and recounts a time when he was in a department store, suddenly surrounded by crowds of people who were shoving and breaking glass, trying to touch him.

For Bashir, Jackson recalls that while he was in this department store, things got crazy, and he became surrounded by security guards. He talks about a little boy who made his way through the crowd and walked up and asked, "Michael Jackson, is it true that you take female hormone pills to make your voice higher?"

Jackson seemed to be hurt by the question and he hated the rumors that were running wild among children. The pop star reminds Bashir that his voice is a natural tenor, explaining that his grandfather was a tenor, and that most successful singers are tenors. "I've never seen a female hormone pill in my life," Jackson says. "I wouldn't know what it looked like."

Bashir is curious about Jackson's interest in Peter Pan, asking why Peter Pan is such an inspiration for the singer.

Jackson explains that Peter Pan represents something that is very special in his heart: youth, childhood, and never growing up. He insists he loves the idea of magic and flying, and admits that wonderment and magic are things "I've just never grown out of."

Bashir wonders if Jackson ever wants to grow up.

"No. I am Peter Pan," Jackson says.

But, "You're Michael Jackson!" Bashir insists.

"I'm Peter Pan in my heart," Jackson tells him.

Jackson talks about the music and dance that he creates, and explains that it "comes from that place of innocence." He tells Bashir about a special tree at Neverland, his "giving tree," which inspired many of his songs, including "Heal the World" and "Will You Be There?" He talks about the tree being a place for meditation and writing music.

Bashir wants to know why, if Jackson is so inspired by Peter Pan, some of his music is "very adult."

"Well, that's true, but my music just comes. I don't think about any of it," Jackson tells him. "That's how I know it's the music of the spirits, it really is."

Bashir asks about Neverland, which he calls "an extraordinary and breathtaking place." He asks Jackson to explain what inspired the creation of Neverland.

Jackson says he was inspired by just anything that had to do with being a kid, saying that Neverland is a place where he collects all the things he wished he could do as a child.

Bashir wonders why, when the gates open, there's music piped throughout the grounds, everywhere in Neverland.

Jackson talks about tree lovers and says that people used to make fun of others who talked to their plants, insisting that there has been more and more evidence that plants respond to other living beings. "Plants and grass and trees respond to music," Jackson asserts. "They have emotion. They feel. They have feelings. When they hear music, they grow more beautiful. The butterflies come around. The birds come around."

Jackson speaks about music being a healing force, having an effect on the human condition, noting that there's a reason that music is piped into department stores and elevators, a reason that music is piped into businesses. Jackson knows that music is there to keep shoppers at ease, to keep everyone in a good mood.

Bashir shifts the subject, asking Jackson about the statues all around Neverland, wondering if Jackson considers mannequins to be his "friends."

Jackson confides that he lives with mannequins in his room because they seem to ease his great loneliness. The superstar tells Bashir that at the height of his career, during "Thriller," he would walk up to strangers and say, "Would you be my friend?" Jackson confesses that all he ever wanted was for someone to love him for just being him. Because he could never find that, Jackson would close himself into his room and be with his animals and his mannequins as a way to deal with the isolation.

Bashir seems puzzled. The journalist can't understand why Jackson would claim that he has no friends.

Jackson tells Bashir that most of the people around him are people in the music business. He talks about when people "see Michael Jackson" and suddenly, "They're not themselves anymore." On camera, Jackson seems to yearn to have a part in simple, everyday life. He tells Bashir that he often reads graffiti, just to discover what "normality" is like, "Because it was so hard to find it. I never had it."

In an off-camera conversation, Bashir tells the pop star that he's amazing and truly inspiring. Bashir assures Jackson that his candid interview will inspire people around the world. As a woman touches up Jackson's face, as the lighting gets rearranged, Bashir compliments both Jackson and his makeup artist, Karen. Bashful, Michael changes the subject.

Jackson wonders if Bashir likes flying.

Bashir claims he hates it, and says that the people on airplanes drink too much because they get alcohol for free (implying that he only flies first class).

Michael says that he loves to talk to the stewardesses, but Bashir doesn't find that worth discussing. Michael continues with the subject, teasing Bashir about flight attendants, mentioning that he likes how women take care of him. But Bashir chooses to ignore the topic.

Bashir reads from a Jackson song, which he claims inspires people: "You are not alone, but I am here with you. Though we're far apart, you're always in my heart." Bashir asks Jackson how he got inspiration to write that type of poetry.

Jackson is humble and in no way condescending when he tells Bashir that he cannot take credit for that particular song, explaining that Bashir is quoting from a song written by R. Kelly. Jackson explains that he helped Kelly put it together, making sure the song was structured properly, putting all the composition together.

Bashir compliments Jackson unabashedly, assuring him that the song is important and has served as an inspiration for millions.

Jackson thanks Bashir and talks about loving being able to see people around the world relate to his music. "From Russia to China to Germany to America, young people are all alike—all over the world," Jackson says. The pop star explains that wherever he performs, the audience cries in the same places, it acts happy in the same places.

"There's a spot in the show where a big army tank comes out, and I stop it, and there's a little girl who comes out with a flower. This army tank comes out, and he points the gun at me. The whole audience boos, in every country we go to," Jackson explains. "Then, when the girl comes out with the flower, everybody cries."

Jackson talks about "Earth Song," another tune that people around the world respond to, always lighting torches and holding them up in the air. He tells Bashir that wherever he sings "Earth Song," the whole stadium is lit. "They know what the song is about—it's about the earth, it's about the planet. It's about conservation and preservation," Jackson says. "And they're with it. They want it. They want to heal the world, they really do."

More than once, Bashir asks if Jackson ever feels lonely.

The pop star tells Bashir that he is often lonely in hotels, even when there are thousands of fans chanting in the street. Even as fans are chanting their love for him, Jackson describes the experience as one which makes him cry: "There's all that love out there. But still, you really do feel trapped and lonely. And you can't get out."

Jackson talks about the few times he does go out, and how he's scrutinized by everyone around him. "Why is Michael Jackson buying this? Why is he reading this?" He mentions that on rare occasions when he does go to a club, the DJs always play his music, and people start chanting for him to dance, which, in a sense, becomes a job for him all over again.

Bashir asks repeatedly if Jackson would ever like to lead a normal life, if he ever wished he could go to the local grocery store.

Jackson says he'd love to go to a market and take a cart and throw some food in it, and laughs when he explains that he's tried to go grocery shopping, but the whole place stops, and everybody wants his autograph.

Bashir wants to know if being isolated makes Jackson "obsessed with things."

Jackson talks about how hard it is to be judged all the time, to have everybody judge him. People wonder why Michael Jackson is visiting their home, people wonder why Michael Jackson chooses particular families to be friends with. "Well, you want to be somewhere! You want to be with someone! And you're watched. And you're judged," Jackson explains. "And it's like, 'Leave me alone. I just want to try to fit in.' (He shrugs.) You know?"

Bashir asks if Jackson ever regrets being famous.

Jackson tells him that what he regrets most is all the lies people perpetuate about him. He talks about people repeating things that are "completely not true" and indicates that it hurts when he's looked at as something that he's not. "You can see it in their eyes. You're being judged. People are looking through you—not even at you, but through you," Jackson explains. "[They're] thinking about all that crap. It's so far from the truth. That hurts."

Bashir asks what worries Michael about his own future.

Jackson says that he hopes that, after his interviews for the documentary, people might be put back on track. It's ironic that Jackson specifically states, "Even after these talks [with Bashir], there will still be some judgment that's so far from the truth."

Off camera, Bashir chats with Michael and his makeup artist. Bashir tells Michael that everything he's revealing is "so important." He tells Michael how much people want to hear what he's saying. As Karen reapplies powder, Bashir goes on and on about the greatness of Michael.

Then, in an aside to the makeup artist, with Michael listening intently, Bashir whispers, "Listen to me, Karen. Three weeks after Princess Diana died, I was invited to a meeting with an internationally famous publisher. I was offered over one million pounds sterling to write a book."

Bashir explains that he was picked up in a limousine and taken to Claridges, a fancy hotel where the Queen Mother used to have breakfast. In a whisper, Bashir confides that when he arrived at Claridges, a publisher asked him to write a book about Diana, and the man pushed a contract in front of his face, as if Bashir would be impressed by the great amount of money he was being offered.

"And I was like, only earning only fifty thousand dollars at the time," Bashir tells the makeup artist. But neither Michael nor Karen respond.

And the tape cuts off.

As Bashir's cameras roll again, the journalist wants to capture where they left off. He wonders about Michael's strange life of isolation. He asks about "the violence of your father" and "the pressure to perform."

Jackson recalls a time when he was really young, about eleven or twelve, and he was under contract with Motown and would have to go to the recording studio to make albums, having a summer tour right around the corner. The pop star speaks about a ballpark that was just across the street from the recording studio. Jackson recalls that he could hear the kids playing and having fun and catching ball. "And some of those times I so passionately just wanted to go over there and play a little bit, and not go to the recording studio and sing. Just, you know, have some fun with the kids," Jackson confides. "And I couldn't. I just couldn't."

Bashir asks if that had any effect on Jackson, not being able to go out and play as a child.

Jackson says the experience made him sad, telling Bashir that as a kid, he used to hide in his house or his backyard. He tells the journalist that his mother used to have to hunt him down because he didn't want to leave home. "I didn't want to go [on tour]," Jackson admits. "I wanted to stay home and just be normal."

Bashir asks what Jackson thinks about his father, wondering if Joe hadn't been as strong, whether Michael would have been so successful.

Jackson says there's truth to that, but repeats that he always enjoyed being on stage, that he loves performing and singing. Still, the star admits that there were times when he didn't want to perform. "I just wanted to have fun, to know what it's like to have a buddy over. Or a slumber party. Or a birthday. Which we never had. Or a Christmas. Which we never had."

Bashir compliments Jackson as the artist "who's written, really, the melody of our lives." Bashir tells Jackson that his music "formed my romantic development." Bashir acts completely baffled, wondering why a person who has brought so much happiness and wonderment to the world would be so overly criticized by others.

Jackson says that he can't understand the constant criticism, explaining that it's painful for him to give so much, to put his heart into giving—only to have people be cruel. Jackson can't understand why people are so mean, especially when all he wants to do is give people some bliss and escapism. "Why hurt the guy who wants to bring a little sunshine in your life? Why?" Jackson asks. "I don't understand."

Bashir mentions that Jackson is harshly judged for everything, including things like having plastic surgery. Bashir notes that all kinds of people have "that sort of thing," wondering why plastic surgery has become such a public issue for Jackson.

Jackson tells him that celebrities have plastic surgery all the time and seems miffed that the media presents him as someone who's obsessed with plastic surgery. Jackson asserts that he hasn't had the amount of surgery that people claim, insisting that his eyes have never been touched, his cheekbones are his own, his lips are his own.

Bashir wonders if Jackson can ever do anything that's right.

Jackson says that no matter what he does, there's always somebody who'll say something negative about it. He says that no matter how good his intentions are, there's always some mean-spirited person who will try to bring him down.

Bashir asks about something that's a "secret." It's called International Children's Holiday, and it's Jackson's vision, something Jackson hopes to help materialize.

Jackson talks about the fact that we celebrate Mother's Day and Father's Day, and says we should celebrate Children's Day. Jackson's vision is to see this holiday celebrated all over the world. He sees it as a holiday, a day off from school, where the parents spend the day taking their child to the park, to the beach, to the toy store, and just doing whatever the child wants to do.

"If I had that one day as a child, growing up, my relationship with my father would be totally different," Jackson confides. "I never played a game with him. He never played a game with me. Not a game. If he was forced, even through a holiday, if he had said, 'Okay, Michael, it's Children's Day, would you like to go to a toy store?'—my feelings for him would be totally different."

Jackson talks about the crimes that people see in the schools today, and asserts those crimes are an outcry for attention, saying that too often, children are neglected. He insists that if the kids were shown more love and attention in their lives, there would not be such tremendous rage inside them.

Bashir mentions that one of the things they plan to do is go to Africa, to a particular region where many children don't reach their fifth birthday because of AIDS. He wants to know what an international children's holiday can do for those dying African children.

"Those kinds of children in Africa?" Jackson asks, "Oh, man, it would bring a lot of joy to a child, if they had just an hour. I've seen dying children light up with joy. I've seen children who've been pronounced to have a week to live. They've told me they have cancer all over their body. And I said, 'Let me take care of that child, just give him a little time with me.' And they come to Neverland."

As people study Jackson in the video, courtroom observers are mesmerized. Some members of the jury seemed stunned when they hear Michael say that he'd seen cancer patients turn completely around. Jackson makes reference to a little boy who gained all of his hair back, completely ridding his body of cancer, after visiting Neverland.

Jackson tells Bashir about the power of love and prayer.

Then Bashir says, "Cut."

Off camera, Bashir takes Jackson's hand to thank him for being so "special." He promises Michael that he will tell people the story of Michael's life. Bashir praises Jackson for caring about neglected children and continually wonders why the media only shows negative things about the pop icon. Bashir carries on about how wonderful it is to have watched Michael lift children's spirit.

As the two men wait for the camera and makeup to get adjusted, Michael asks Bashir if he enjoys living in England. Bashir says he prefers to live in Rome, and Michael says that he loves Rome, though he can't handle the paparazzi, who follow him around on bicycles. As Michael sits quietly, waiting for the cameras and lighting to get set up, the pop star says something about Pope John Paul II, wondering about his health. The mention of Pope John Paul II spurs this conversation about the history of the pope and the Catholic Church:

Jackson: They're not married right? They're married to God?

Bashir: Yes. But of course, the problem is, look at what all the priests have been doing.

Jackson: Yeah, with kids. They're in trouble.

Bashir: They're in big, big trouble.

Jackson: Oh, yeah.

Bashir: Big, big trouble.

Jackson: 'Cause I know the women, the nuns, are married to God. The men are too.

Bashir: You know, it's estimated, *Vanity Fair* did a study recently, and they estimated that sixty percent of the priests of the Catholic Church have sexually abused at least one child. Sixty percent, you know what I mean?

Jackson: Really?

Bashir: Hiding behind the Church. And do you know there was this guy [who] had been moved to so many churches, and those bishops, nobody took responsibility.

Jackson: Where was he—in Rome?

Bashir: No, he was in America. And he got moved to different states.

Jackson: That happens a lot with the Mormons.

Bashir: Oh, big style!

Then, Bashir's cameras begin to roll again, and the subject is dropped.

Bashir wants to talk about "a very special day at Neverland," when Jackson hosted a hundred children who were not charged any money, who were given no restrictions, who enjoyed the facilities at Neverland for the day.

Jackson explains that he's done charity work for children for many years, even when he was a little kid. Jackson says that he was always told that true charity meant that you give from your heart, and says he loves making children smile. Jackson feels he's doing what he's supposed to do, telling Bashir that everyone is supposed to be helping children.

Bashir wants to know more about Jackson's "special connection" to children.

Jackson says that he sees God through children, explaining that everything he does—from the performances, to the song writing, to the choreographing, to the directing—is all inspired by children. "I've said this before and I'll say it again: if it wasn't for the children, I'd throw in the towel. 'Cause I wouldn't care anymore. I really mean it. I wouldn't care, I would feel that I don't have any reason to live," Jackson confides. "Everything, in my heart, is for them."

Bashir asks about Jackson's animals, wondering if they also have an impact on the star. Jackson talks about his love for his pets, and Bashir asks Jackson whatever happened to Bubbles, the chimp.

Jackson explains that he had been told by his trainers that Bubbles had to be taken away from Neverland when he reached a certain age, because chimps become mean. Apparently, they're very strong and can become harmful. Jackson tells Bashir he regrets having to let go of Bubbles, who he said could live to be sixty years old. In describing his closeness to Bubbles, Jackson brings up the strange idea of wanting to have a "celebrity animal party" for Bubbles. Jackson tells Bashir about his plan to invite Cheetah, the chimp from *Tarzan*, as well as Benji, Lassie, and animal stars from other TV shows, to attend his party for Bubbles.

The idea of a celebrity animal party would later provide much "inside" laughter for the media. But, like the rest of the outtake footage, none of those details would reach the public. It was odd that no one said anything about Bashir's tactics, which were laid bare in the courtroom. When people reported their newscasts, the subject of Bashir and the exonerating outtake footage just never came up.

Bashir asks Jackson to go back to the subject of children, and claims he saw "a very special interaction" between Jackson and his own kids, stating that "it was a privilege" and "an education," just to watch Jackson being a dad.

Jackson talks about his relationship with his kids, whom he can talk to "one on one, because they don't judge you." Jackson says he connects to kids because they're just out to have fun, which is something he can understand. Jackson says that once he began to realize that he missed out on "so much" as a child, he also began to develop a strong love for children.

Bashir asks Jackson if he has found the kind of friendship with children that he hasn't been able to find with adults.

Jackson admits that, yes, he prefers children to adults because he hasn't been betrayed or deceived by a child. "Adults have let me down. Adults have let the world down," Jackson asserts. "It's time for the children now. It's time for us to give them a chance. Like the Bible says, 'A child shall be leader of them all.'"

Bashir repeatedly asks why people criticize Jackson.

Jackson says people who criticize him are ignorant, explaining that they have not educated themselves about the truth. He says there are people who have corrupt minds, who can't think about him having a wonderful time with children as something that's just pure. Jackson feels sorry for those people.

Again, Bashir wants to know what children mean to Jackson.

"The stars, the moon, the universe. But all children do, not just mine. I'm not territorial," Jackson tells the journalist. He gestures his hands in a circle, telling Bashir that he's always felt it was his responsibility to take care of others. He explains that he takes his children to hospitals with him all the time. "I do as many hospitals as I do concerts, you know? And I don't expect the press to print it, but they don't want to print it, you know? I reach out, I've done it for years," Jackson says. "I take the toys, and I pack up everything, and I surprise them."

Bashir, off camera, tells Jackson that what he was just saying about taking care of the world's children is "the jewel in the crown." Bashir commends Jackson for expressing himself so beautifully. The journalist reminds Jackson why it's so important to get this documentary done, telling the pop star, "People are scum, and there's so much jealousy. The problem is, nobody actually comes here to see it. But I saw it here yesterday, the spiritual … And what I've wanted to convey is the musical genius and also what we saw [here at Neverland with children] yesterday."

The tape ends.

When Bashir's final interview with Michael Jackson takes place, it's months later, and the two men are in a Miami hotel room. Michael appears to be in somewhat of a hurry, on his way to a funeral for a musical legend. Bashir offers write him a "little something" to say for the sad occasion, and Michael politely accepts the idea, though it appears that the star does not plan to take Bashir up on his offer.

Michael seems solemn. He directs his videographer to get footage of Bashir asking questions. Bashir jokes that if he's in a single still photo, it will cost Jackson $5,000 apiece. As Michael applies last-minute powder, all cell phones and hotel phones are disconnected, and just as the cameras are about to roll, Jackson softly sings a melody.

Bashir asks if Jackson can remember the words to the song, "With a Child's Heart."

But Jackson says he can't quite remember recording it. He was too young, and there were so many songs. As Michael speaks, he shakes his head back and forth, adjusting his rich satin maroon shirt. Even though he's highly stylized, Michael is clearly self-conscious, and he continues to fidget off camera, adjusting his shirt and his hair.

Bashir asks Jackson why he thinks he's qualified to lead the cause for an international children's holiday.

Jackson tells Bashir that the children's holiday has been a dream of his for many years. Jackson explains that there hasn't been an outcry for the rights of children, and says he feels that the family bond has been broken. Jackson talks about the age of technology, lamenting the fact that kids spend too much time with video games and computers. Jackson wants International Children's Day to be a time when people come together (he clasps his hands) and make the whole day about kids.

Jackson says that he thinks he's qualified to call for a children's day by default, because nobody else is doing anything about it. "That's our future, and I love 'em to pieces," Jackson insists. "I want to fight for them—to be the voice of the voiceless."

Bashir brings up the 1993 allegations that were made about Jackson and a young boy. Bashir wonders what people will say, hearing Jackson call for an international children's holiday, when they still have questions about what happened in 1993.

"They don't know me. All that was false. I would never do that. (Holds out his arms.) I would slit my wrists before I would hurt a child," Jackson tells Bashir. "You can't judge somebody. How can a person look at a picture of someone on the news and say, *'I hate him!'"*

Jackson talks about being raised in a world with adults and explains that when kids were playing games, or at home tucked away in bed, he was up performing in clubs at 3:00 in the morning, and the striptease show would come on after his act. Jackson tells Bashir about not having friends as a kid, about how he and his brothers worked and worked and worked.

Jackson believes that because he was raised as a very strict Jehovah's Witness, he has been compensating for never having any Christmas or birthday celebrations. He says that Neverland is a place where people can see animals and all kind of funs things that Jackson was deprived of.

"There's candy everywhere," Jackson says, laughing. "It's fun."

Bashir mentions Jackson's wealth, but asserts that the pop star never seems to be able to truly enjoy it.

Jackson tells him he enjoys his wealth through his children. He says he can only enjoy his wealth behind his gates, explaining that when he tries to go out and enjoy himself, "It becomes work all over again."

Bashir wants to know if Jackson finds his performance to be work.

Jackson says it's not work, and says he becomes "one" with his music, with his dance, explaining that a performer who's "thinking" all the time is not approaching his art the best possible way. He explains he can tell when a dancer is counting (he makes his trademark dance moves), and says that counting and thinking are the wrong concepts for dance. Jackson says music and dance are about feeling, about becoming one with the musical instruments. "You need to feel. Become the bass. Become the drums. Become the guitar, the strings."

Bashir tells Jackson that after all the time they've spent traveling together, he feels the star is really lonely. Bashir says he's "worried" for Jackson and wonders if Jackson is ever happy.

Jackson confides to Bashir that many things that make him sad, which is why he wants Neverland always to be a happy place. Jackson says that it hurts him to see news reports about children killing each other, about children using guns, about violence in public schools, telling Bashir that he won't watch the news because he can't stand to hear reports about children being abducted and killed.

"That just kills me, that kind of stuff. So I try not to watch the news," Jackson says. "I feel that pain. I feel that. (He holds his hand to his chest.) I feel it."

Bashir implies that performing is the only thing that can make Michael happy.

Jackson says he loves performing more than anything. "It's probably because I've spent all my childhood on stage."

Bashir notices that Jackson has surrounded himself with "yes" people. Bashir wonders if that's healthy. The journalist gives an example of the time when they were together in Germany, pointing out that no one there told Jackson not to dangle his baby over a balcony.

"My governesses were up there. And I was holding that baby strong and tight. And I know better," Jackson insists, telling Bashir that he's seen parents fling their kids up the air and catch them, assuring Bashir that there was nothing wrong with what he did. Jackson complains that he was just trying to say hello to his German fans, who were asking to see the new baby, and says he decided to show them "Blanket" for a minute, so they could get a sense of the baby, and asserts that the media slowed the tape down, purposely, for dramatic effect.

"I got caught up in the moment. I was holding on tight. And it happened for like, two seconds. But, when it gets on the news, they slow it down," Jackson says, moving his hands in slow motion. "They make me look like I'm this eccentric idiot, dangling this baby over a balcony, like a nut. They don't show you the whole story."

Bashir quotes a newspaper, stating, "After what happened in Berlin, people should be concerned for the welfare of Jackson's children."

"They don't know me," Jackson says. "How can they say that when they don't know me?"

Sarcastically, Bashir wonders if Jackson is actually "happy" that he dangled his baby over the balcony.

"I'm not happy that I dangled the baby over the balcony, no. But I'm happy that I let the kids give a wave to him," Jackson tells him. "I didn't realize that he was over the balcony. But I had him tight. I was not going to let that baby fall. I'm not a nut. I'm very smart. You can't come this far in success and be stupid. (He smiles.) You can make mistakes. But that wasn't a mistake," Jackson tells Bashir.

Promising Bashir that there was nothing wrong with what he did, that there was nothing wrong with going out on a balcony and giving a wave with his child, Jackson insists that if anyone else had done that, if it had been any other star in the world, "Nothing would have been said."

Bashir asks again about what happened in Berlin. The journalist mentions that Jackson's baby was covered, thus the fans really didn't really get to see the baby.

With that, Jackson raises his voice, telling Bashir, "I don't want a Lindbergh baby. Somebody took Lindbergh's baby, Charles Lindbergh's baby. Took him in the forest and burned him to death. I don't want that to happen to my children, so I put veils over them. I don't want people seeing them. The press, they can be very mean. I don't want them to grow up psychologically crazy because of the evil things they [the press] can say to them."

Bashir moves to a softer subject and reminds Jackson that when they were in the Berlin hotel, the pop star threw pillows to his fans.

Jackson tells Bashir that he always sends fans blankets and pillows, because people sleep outside, and it's cold. Jackson says he asks his security people to buy ten or fifteen pizzas, and he sends snacks down to his fans because he cares about them. As Jackson speaks, he taps his hand on his knee, like he's moving to the beat of the music inside his head.

Of course, Bashir doesn't stay on this "cheery" subject very long. Instead, he brings Jackson back to his adolescence, mentioning pictures of Jackson as a teen that show his face with lots of spots.

"Being shy as I am, and was, and it was even worse then. It was terrible. It was like a disease [the spots on my face]. It was so bad, I couldn't walk in a door," Jackson admits, telling Bashir that, back in those days, he could hardly go to a meeting without crying behind a closed door. To Bashir, Jackson confides that he didn't know how to approach people at formal business meetings and would always feel like "a fish out of water."

Bashir asserts that what Jackson has done to "overcome" his shyness and his embarrassment about his looks is to change his appearance.

To Bashir, Jackson denies that his appearance has changed drastically, saying what people see as a change is "called adolescence."

"It's called growing and changing. I've had no plastic surgery on my face—just my nose—it helped me breathe better so I could hit the higher notes," Jackson insists. The pop icon tells Bashir that the media has made up lies about him, repeating that he's had nothing surgically done to his eyes, his chin, or his cheeks. He mentions other stars who've had nose jobs, among them, Marilyn Monroe and Elvis Presley, and wonders why the press singles him out, when there are others who've had much more work done.

"They just want to pick on me," Jackson says, raising his hands. "Cher has had so much stuff—her bottom, her nose, her teeth. Nobody bothers her, and I love Cher. I love her. We used to take care of our skin together."

Bashir can't believe that Jackson is honestly saying he's only had one operation.

"No, no, no," Jackson clarifies. "I was severely burned, and I had surgery for that. But on my nose, I've only had two surgeries."

Bashir mentions Jackson's photos from the past, stating that they look very different.

"No, no, no. I look just like my grandfather," Jackson says, raising his voice again. "Plastic surgery wasn't invented for Michael Jackson. Everybody gets it." As he speaks, Jackson taps his hand to a musical beat and seems aggravated.

Bashir asks about Jackson's eyelids, suggesting something was done to give Jackson a more kind of feminine look.

"Nothing's been done to my eyes, ever," Jackson says, explaining that because he had his nose done, because he had his nose pulled in, it made his eyes look bigger.

Bashir asks about his cheeks.

"These cheekbones? No. My father has the same thing," Jackson tells him. "We have Indian blood."

Bashir asks about Jackson's dimple.

"Can we get on beyond this plastic surgery garbage?" Jackson asks, exasperated. "This is tabloid stuff. You're beyond this. You're a respected journalist. You're being tabloid. (Pause.) It's stupid."

Bashir changes the subject back to Joe Jackson, reminding Michael about his childhood and the way Michael once talked about wanting to run away from his father.

"I hid, I used to hide. He doesn't know it to this day, but I'd walk into a room, and his presence would be there, and I would faint," Jackson confides, telling Bashir that when it comes to Joe, he doesn't think his father realizes how much he frightened and hurt him. Michael calls his father a genius, but somehow, seems scared to death of him.

Bashir reminds Michael that Joe injured him when he was a child.

Michael tells Bashir that perhaps he wouldn't have the level of affection for kids, had he been raised differently.

Bashir hints that some people think that, maybe what came out of his distressed childhood, was a man who is obsessed with his face.

"Well, I know what's inside my head," Jackson says quietly. "That's all."

Bashir wonders if Jackson thinks people go too far with plastic surgery.

Jackson says that it's fine, that he has no real opinion about it, asserting that practically everyone in Hollywood, practically every star, has had work done.

As Bashir carries on about the topic of plastic surgery, he wonders why Jackson is singled out by the media on this subject.

"Barbara Walters just tightened her face again. She never mentions it. You can see it, just look at her," Jackson tells Bashir, as he lists a few other people who recently had face-lifts, including Mick Jagger and Paul McCartney.

Bashir wants to know why Jackson is so defensive.

"They pick on me," Jackson says, "like I'm the only one that does it."

When they take another break, Bashir tells Jackson, "have some water, boss." Bashir again promises Michael that he's doing the best job he can, suggesting that he's giving Michael a perfect platform to set the record straight by cooperating with this documentary.

Jackson reminds Bashir to interview Elizabeth Taylor, and Bashir acts like he knows all about Michael's relationship with Liz. However, when Jackson asks if Bashir has talked to Liz, Bashir admits that he only knows things that Elizabeth Taylor has said about Jackson in public.

Just before Bashir's cameras roll again, Bashir promises to arrange an interview with Miss Taylor, but it never happens.

Bashir asks Jackson to describe his friend, Elizabeth Taylor, and hints that the public sees Jackson and Liz Taylor as "two crackpots" who are great friends.

"That's not nice. Why can't a younger guy be nice to an older lady? We had the same childhood. We have so much in common. We have the same lives. We had to go through the system the same way," Jackson confides. The star tells Bashir that he relates to Liz because she's like a little girl inside, saying that he loves her to death.

Bashir asks Jackson to talk about Paris and Prince, and the way Jackson's children are being brought up.

Jackson says they laugh all day and cuddle. He says he has wonderful children.

Bashir wonders why Prince once said he didn't have a mother.

"How many, many mothers have kids with no fathers? That gets switched around, and that seems more okay," Jackson says defensively. "A father should have that opportunity too."

Bashir asks if Jackson knows what role Debbie Rowe wants to have with her children.

"I don't want to open up the whole subject," Jackson explains. "But, she [Debbie] did it for me. Paris is named Paris because she was conceived in Paris. Prince was conceived in LA, but, she said, 'They're yours, take 'em.' She wanted to do that for me as a present."

Bashir asks Jackson to explain the marriage to Debbie Rowe.

Jackson tells Bashir that it's hard to be married, as an entertainer, asserting that he'll get married again at some point, after he gets over the two divorces he's been through. "I'm married to my fans. (Pause.) I'm married to God. I'm married to children."

Bashir ends the interview by telling Jackson that when he sees him with Prince and Paris, "It almost makes me weep."

"I'm crazy about 'em. I would die for them," Jackson says. "And I would like to have more children, of course."

To courtroom observers, the Bashir footage seemed to go on forever. There was so much outtake footage, all left on the cutting room floor, and as the jury watched Jackson being interviewed, they were clearly moved by his candor, by his honest spirit, by his down-to-earth demeanor. It was obvious that they seemed to think that Martin Bashir was unfair. By choosing to omit important details, by choosing to insert his own biased comments over innocent footage, Bashir had presented an unbalanced portrait of Jackson to the world.

It was interesting to note that throughout the outtake footage, when the pop star became highly emotional, at least three jurors had tears in their eyes. An Asian juror, a woman in her forties, literally burst out crying when Jackson spoke about being battered as a child.

As for the media, none of the people seemed touched. None of them were newcomers to "the Jackson saga." The media was jaded. Even though they could see though Bashir's bait-and-switch tactics, oddly, no one in the media really spoke about it. It was strange that not one reporter revealed anything about Bashir's unfair tactics in their newscasts.

Out of twenty-two hundred credentialed journalists, only two papers made mention of the unfairness of the Bashir piece, *USA Today*, which described Bashir's interviewing style as "unduly intrusive," and the *New York Times,* which referred to the British journalist's "callous self-interest masked as sympathy."

"WILL YOU BE THERE?"

Judge Melville threatened to issue an arrest warrant on the day that Hollywood attorney Mark Geragos decided that he would not appear in court to testify as scheduled. Geragos, Jackson's original defense attorney, had been subpoenaed to testify on Friday, May 13, but because of a conflict in his calendar, the famed attorney sent an associate to the Santa Maria court the day prior, asking that his testimony be postponed.

"There's no special consideration for lawyers," Melville announced. "It's the same with any citizen who has been subpoenaed. It's no different than a subpoena for a deputy sheriff, a mechanic, or a child victim. This is a subpoena he has to obey. The subpoena says Friday, and I want him here at Friday at 8:30 AM."

Michael Jackson had waived the attorney-client privilege in order that Mark Geragos, who represented the pop star from February 2003 through April 2004, could testify that there was no conspiracy. Among media, it was anticipated that Geragos would tell jurors that he hired a private investigator, Brad Miller, to confirm suspicions that the Arvizo family, particularly the mother, was looking for a payday.

On Friday morning, when the high-profile attorney arrived to Santa Maria, wearing his trademark sunglasses and talking on his cell phone, the media watched him swagger into court. Highly anxious to hear what "Mr. Hollywood" was going to say, courtroom observers found that the attorney was personable. As for the media, Geragos spent years creating relationships with TV journalists, relationships that had propelled him to fame. The media knew that Geragos was comfortable being in the spotlight.

As he responded to Mesereau's questions, Mark Geragos made a few self-deprecating comments. He made fun of his legal background, which had everyone in the courtroom laughing. People knew Geragos, because for a number of years, the American public had been inundated with images of the attorney who represented Susan McDougal, a politico involved in a Clinton scandal, actress Wynonna Rider, convicted of shoplifting in Beverly Hills, and Scott Peterson, convicted of murdering his wife and unborn child. The Peterson case had become so infamous, the American tabloids and cable TV news shows were seeing their highest profits and greatest ratings from it—ever.

Because of the tabloid murder case, Geragos had become a star. People asked for his autograph. Some compared him to Clarence Darrow. But if there was anyone who should have been compared to Darrow—one of the greatest trial attorneys of all time—it should have been Tom Mesereau, whose success rate was so high, not even the best criminal attorneys could compare to him.

Unlike Mesereau, who kept a low profile, Geragos loved the attention. Geragos was a "regular" on CNN's *Larry King Live*. He had a vested interest in seeing his name in lights and looked forward to being the subject of countless *People* magazine articles. The media attention brought him celebrity clients, and Geragos loved fame.

Media folks were aware that Geragos made an attempt to have his own show on CNN, an attempt that failed dismally just after he lost the Scott Peterson murder trial. Though the Mark Geragos TV pilot never made it to the air, that didn't stop the celebrity lawyer from pontificating about every crime in America. A much-welcomed guest of Larry King, he had "insider connections" at *FOX News* as well. The lawyer was media savvy, using his clout and well-heeled clients to control interviews on numerous networks, to slant the media in his favor.

"At some point, did you ever hear the name Janet Arvizo?" Mesereau asked.

"At the very [beginning]," Geragos said, "probably before I heard the name Gavin.

"Initially, there was a rundown of exactly what the situation was," Geragos testified. "I was told about the Arvizos. I was also told that the first thing that had an urgency, there was *60 Minutes* taping that was scheduled, and they wanted me to be up there to make sure that Michael didn't make any statements, or questions weren't asked that were inappropriate."

"And this was at Neverland?" Mesereau asked.

"Yes," Geragos told him.

"Did you see Janet Arvizo on that day?"

"I remember seeing Gavin at Neverland that day. And then we were there for, I don't know, maybe twelve hours or so. And during that time there, I was getting downloaded with information as well, from a number of people at the ranch itself."

"And what was your role as far as your representation of Mr. Jackson on that occasion?" Mesereau asked.

"Well, that was really, they just wanted me, I guess, as a backdrop for the interview," Geragos explained. "And ultimately, after sitting there for twelve hours, it was my decision, I told them that, look, if I was going to be involved, I didn't want him doing the interview, and I pulled the plug on it."

"So ultimately, that interview with *60 Minutes* did not take place, correct?"

"On that occasion in February of 2003, it did not. I said that it was not going to happen, and politely asked Mr. Bradley and another producer who was there, I told them that it was not going to happen."

"Mr. Geragos, just directing my question to your state of mind at the time, did you have any understanding whether or not Janet Arvizo and the children were supposed to appear in a *60 Minutes* documentary?"

"Yes."

"Did you talk to Janet Arvizo on that day?" Mesereau asked.

"Briefly, I believe, but I know that I didn't talk to her," Geragos said. "I watched her interact or converse with Mr. Radotsky, who was the producer, and I believe Mr. Bradley."

Geragos told the jury that he'd been asked to go to Neverland that day, on February 7, 2003, so he could monitor the *60 Minutes* interview. He testified that he knew that the Arvizos were going to be there, and insisted that he didn't give any advice to any of the Arvizos, recalling that he hadn't spoken to Gavin at all.

Mark Geragos told the jury that CBS had arrived to Neverland early in the morning that day, bringing a "cast" of thirty to forty people, with all kinds of production staff, along with CBS top brass, Jack Sussman, who was personally accompanying the team.

The famed attorney testified that after the *60 Minutes* debacle, after turning Mr. Ed Bradley away, he focused his attention on the Bashir documentary, looking at the various allegations Bashir made against the pop star. At the time, in February 2003, there were rumblings that Tom Sneddon was starting an investigation of Jackson, but nothing official had yet been filed.

Geragos explained that he decided to launch his *own* investigation of the Arvizo family, because the information he was discovering about them gave him great pause. The famous defense attorney had taken a look at the JC Penney file, and, given what was going on with the media swirl, he was concerned that the Arvizos might use the situation to manipulate Jackson.

Between the whirlwind of media around and the litigious history of the Arvizos, Geragos started a database search—to see exactly what happened with the JC Penney lawsuit.

"And what was your reaction to what you learned about that suit?" Mesereau asked.

"I was gravely concerned," Geragos said.

"Why?"

"I thought that, given the situation, and I was given the information that they were attempting, there were rumors that the family was attempting ..."

The jury wanted to hear what Geragos was about to say, but Geragos was cut off. The prosecution objected to him speculating about rumors, and Mesereau took another tack.

"Did the investigation into the Arvizos continue?" Mesereau wondered.

"Yes. I asked him [Brad Miller] to please find out where they were and to document what they were doing, who they were meeting with, and whether or not they were either trying to sell a story to the tabloids, or meeting with lawyers, or anything even more grave than that," Geragos testified.

In open court, Mr. Geragos said he was concerned that, perhaps, the Arvizos were going to try to extort a cash payment from the superstar.

On cross-examination, Geragos said that he had a "jaded view" of the Arvizos after reviewing the JC Penney lawsuit, asserting that he didn't exactly look at the family as being pristine. Rehashing the Brad Miller tape, Geragos confirmed that he'd asked Brad Miller to record his interview with the Arvizo family. When asked questions about the rebuttal film the Arvizos had taped, which prosecutors were implying was a "forced" effort, Geragos said he was unaware that there had been any script. He informed the jury that he'd asked for a copy of the videotape but had never received anything from Jackson's videographer.

It was a few days later that Larry King arrived to Santa Maria. Winking at journalists with a big smile on his face, he made his way past the flashing light bulbs and into the court. The TV giant had brought a small entourage with him—his producer and three attorneys—one of whom was Hollywood legend Bert Fields.

Out of the presence of the jury, the defense called Larry King to the stand, and one of King's attorneys addressed the court, stating that he was representing a nonparty journalist, submitting a short memorandum outlining the Shield Law.

Through his attorney, Larry King was requesting that a short hearing be held to determine the scope of the direct and cross-examination to protect King's rights under the California Shield Law.

In front of the media and the public observers, Tom Mesereau conducted the hearing, asking Larry King questions pertaining directly to the case. Without going into King's complete background, Mesereau asked if Larry King knew the attorney Larry Feldman.

Larry King said he'd known Feldman for about ten years, adding that he'd interviewed Feldman on his TV show. King testified that, at some point before the Jackson trial, perhaps some months prior, he'd arranged a meeting with Larry Feldman at King's Beverly Hills breakfast haunt, a place called Nate'n Al's.

The talk show host said he was sitting at a booth with a few other people, one being his producer, Nancy Baker, and because seating was limited, King's breakfast guests made adjustments so Larry Feldman could sit next to King when their meeting took place.

"Did Mr. Feldman express any interest in working with your show?" Mesereau asked.

"Very much," King told him.

"How long did the meeting last?"

"About forty-five minutes."

"Okay. Did Mr. Feldman say anything to you about the Michael Jackson case?"

"He did."

"What did he say?"

"He said that the case of ten years ago, when he represented the other person when there was a settlement, that was a definite good case," King testified. "But he thought the woman in this case, the mother, was a wacko, was the term he used. And he thought she was in it, just for the money. He had met with her. He didn't want to represent her. He advised her to see someone else, and he informed the authorities. He didn't tell me which authorities."

"Did he say this woman told him she wants money?" Mesereau asked.

"No, I think he said *he thinks* she wants money," King said.

"Did he say what he based his opinion on?"

"No."

"Did you ask him?"

"No. He just said she was a wacko. He said 'wacko' a couple of times. And he said, 'She's in this for the money.'"

"Okay. Did he say anything else about Janet Arvizo?"

"He thought that she was just in it for the money, and [that] she was a little erratic, or wacko, as he said. And he didn't want to represent her."

"Did he say anything else about the Michael Jackson case that you remember?" Mesereau wanted to know.

"Other than that, that he would like to be a regular on our show," King testified.

According to Larry King, during the meeting in Beverly Hills, King's producer told Feldman that they would call him to pick a date for him to appear on the show and agreed that Feldman would be a regular panelist during the course of the Jackson trial. Larry King told the court that when one of his producers called Feldman about a week later, Larry Feldman didn't respond.

A few weeks after that, Mr. King said that he ran into Mr. Feldman at another Los Angeles restaurant.

"What's going on?" Larry King asked.

"Something came up," Feldman allegedly told him.

King testified that after their brief chat, he never heard from Feldman again. Larry King told the court that some time later, by reading it in a newspaper, he learned that Larry Feldman had decided to represent Janet Arvizo.

That being the bulk of King's testimony, when the hearing was over, Judge Melville ruled that he didn't find that Larry King's testimony would impeach Larry Feldman. Based on the offer of proof, the judge decided to disallow Larry King's testimony.

For the prosecution, Judge Melville's ruling was a gift. Larry King's recollection of his conversation with Feldman could have destroyed the DA's case. Earlier in the trial, Larry Feldman had testified that did not speak about Janet Arvizo in Larry King's presence.

But the Larry King testimony was not something the jury would be allowed to hear. As for the media, the fact that Larry King had legitimate information but had been prevented from testifying in the trial didn't seem terribly important. If the judge was acting in favor of the prosecution, not one TV sound bite reported that.

Instead, newscasts diminished Larry King, disregarding his comments as hearsay. That Larry Feldman had allegedly described the accuser's mom as a "wacko" who was "out for money"—was something that became an inside joke.

"I Want You Back"

Jurors were riveted as they watched the host of *The Tonight Show*, comedian Jay Leno, walk into court early in the morning. The defense had called the TV star, well known for his Jackson humor, to talk about something quite serious. Over the years, Jay Leno had been a big supporter of children's charities. He'd done work with children's organizations, among them, Phone Friends and Make-A-Wish.

Mesereau asked Leno to describe the types of calls he received from sick children, from kids in the hospital who needed some cheering up, and the comedian described getting phone calls from kids who asked simple things, questions about Britney Spears, questions about other stars they they'd seen on his show. Leno explained that there was no procedure he followed. If he received a request from a legitimate organization, he'd make a list of kids who wanted to get a call. Each week Leno placed about fifteen or twenty calls to children who wanted to hear from him.

Leno told the jury he made calls to kids all across the country, usually following the call with a gift of hats, photos, and other goodies from the show. He mentioned that he had an assistant who screened the calls but said that he was "pretty accessible," either through the main *Tonight Show* number or his own personal number at the show.

"How many years have you been dealing with children's organizations like the ones you've described?" Mesereau asked.

"Well, I've been doing *The Tonight Show* about thirteen years, and—certainly that long. And before that, more informally," Leno said.

"And does your work with children involve simply talking to them on the phone, or do you make visits and things of that sort?"

"Any of those things," Leno said. "Sometimes with Make-A-Wish, you'll have a situation where—those are especially sad, because sometimes they're terminally ill children. They'll say, 'Oh, this kid is fifteen, and he's always wanted to go [on] a ride in a Lamborghini,' or something like that."

Jay Leno described many things he'd done for children, holding auctions to raise money, having celebrities sign items, making donations to charities, giving away tickets to his show. Leno said that sometimes he'd bring a child to his garage to survey his car collection, sometimes he'd bring a child backstage to sit on the set of *The Tonight Show* and to hold the microphone and pretend to be a host. The comedian said it varied, on an individual basis, and testified that most of the time, he would just make a phone call. It seemed most kids were very happy with that.

"Do you sometimes reject requests from parents or children?" Mesereau asked.

"I don't know if 'reject' is quite the right word. If it goes through a legitimate organization, no, you don't reject them," Leno told him. "But sometimes you get the odd, you know, 'I'm a farmer. Our crops are bad, our tractor's broken, our fields are not doing well,' and the return address is Brooklyn, New York. So you go, 'Hmmm. That seems a little suspicious.' So you know, you take them on a case-by-case basis."

When Mesereau asked Jay Leno how easy it was for people to reach him directly at NBC, Leno told the jury that people could place a call to his show, and sometimes he'd pick up the phone, and then have to spend ten minutes convincing the person that it was really him.

The more Leno talked about how easy it was for people to call him directly, the more the comedian had everyone in the courtroom laughing.

"They call the studio to reach you directly?" Mesereau clarified.

"Yes, and I'll probably get a lot more calls after this!" Leno said. "My phone will be ringing tomorrow. Thank you for that!"

"If they call the studio, do they get right to you?"

"Sometimes they get right to me, actually. Yes, they can. Up until today, they could get right to me. Up until a few moments ago, you could reach me quite easily!"

Leno had everyone in the courtroom cracking up.

But Mesereau and Jackson weren't interested in jokes.

Jackson wasn't laughing, not a bit.

Jackson wanted the jury to hear about the phone call that had been placed to Jay Leno from Gavin Arvizo, he wanted Mesereau to ask Leno about his connection with the owner of the Laugh Factory, Jamie Masada. It was Masada who initially told Leno about a little dying boy who had a strange form of cancer.

"Do you remember a couple of years ago receiving a call from a child named Gavin?" Mesereau asked.

"Yes," Leno testified.

"And approximately when did that happen?"

"Well, let's see. It's quite a few years ago. I guess 2000, maybe."

"And was it your understanding that Gavin had cancer?"

"Yes."

Leno recalled that he'd been told about Gavin's cancer, he said the circumstance was a little confusing, explaining that some of his conversations about Gavin seemed to run together, but he remembered speaking to Gavin's mother. Leno said that he placed a call to the hospital, and was put through to a room, and said he spoke to Gavin, possibly to his brother, and to his mother.

"Now, how did you learn about Gavin?" Mesereau asked.

"I had gotten a number of voice mails from him. That's how I'd been made aware," Leno said.

"And you've indicated, Mr. Leno, you think you talked to Gavin's mother, right?"

"I think so. Yes."

"Okay. And do you recall whether she called you or you called her?"

"No, I called. I called the hospital room. I had gotten a number of voice mails from the child, and I called the hospital room."

"Do you recall what Gavin said to you?"

"The conversation in the hospital? Or any of the voice mails?"

"Well, let's start with the voice mails."

"Okay. The voice mails I got were, 'Oh, I'm a big fan. You're the greatest.' [He was] overly effusive for a twelve-year-old."

"When you say overly effusive, what do you mean?" Mesereau asked.

"[The kid said] 'Jay Leno, you're the greatest.' You know, 'I think you're wonderful. You're my hero,' this type of thing, which seemed a little odd to me at the time, for someone so young. Why a comedian in his mid-fifties would be—you know? I'm not Batman. You know what I mean? It just seemed a little bit unusual. But okay."

Jay Leno told the jury that most times, when he talked to children, it was very hard to get them to say much. In essence, Leno said it was difficult to get kids to say anything of substance over the phone. Oddly, he recalled that the messages he got from Gavin Arvizo sounded like they were coming from an adult.

"This was—it sounded like—very adultlike conversation. It just, you know, perked my interest at the time," Leno testified.

Leno said that he got three or four similar messages from the child, that he called the hospital and spoke to a boy who was "a little groggy" at the time. On the stand, the comedian remembered that he did speak to Gavin Arvizo, that he also spoke his mother, recalling that he asked them to come visit *The Tonight Show* studio when the boy got better.

Leno said the mother was very grateful for the call, and testified that he subsequently spoke to Louise Palanker, a Laugh Factory comedian who'd taken an interest in the Arvizos, who told Leno that Gavin and his family were so very thrilled to hear from him.

"Okay. At some point, did you complain to Louise Palanker about messages you were getting from Gavin?" Mesereau wanted to know.

"It wasn't so much a complaint," Leno explained. "I just said to her, 'What's the story here? This—this doesn't sound like a twelve-year-old. This sounds like an adult person.' I think the words I used [were], 'It seemed a little scripted in his speech.'"

Leno said that comedian Louise Palanker tried to explain the "scripted" sound of Gavin's calls, telling Leno that the boy wanted to be a comic, that Gavin "writes everything down before he says it, then he kind of reads it."

For Leno, Palanker's explanation seemed to "sort of" make sense. Jay Leno wasn't giving it too much thought at the time.

"This was just another typical day at the office, up to this point," Leno said.

"Did you ever ask Louise Palanker who was writing these questions out for Gavin?" Mesereau asked.

"No, I don't think I said that. I think I just said, you know, it sounded real scripted. It sounded like—it didn't sound like [a child]...." Leno paused. "And she said, 'Well, he's very mature, and he wants to be a comic, so he's very careful in what he says,' and I said, 'Oh, okay.'"

"Did that seem unusual to you?"

"Well, it was just unusual for a child to contact me directly, because usually, as I said, at the very least, a parent, a doctor, or a nurse, a teacher, Phone Friends, Make-A-Wish, those people will call and say, 'You'll be getting a call from this young boy or this young girl.' To get a call out of the blue was a little unusual."

"When you say scripted, do you mean coached?" Mesereau asked.

But the question was objected to.

"At some point," Mesereau asked, "did you ask that Gavin stop calling?"

"I asked Louise, I said, you know, 'I've been getting a lot of these calls,' and she said, 'Oh, I'll take care of it. Don't worry about it.'"

"And when you said that to Louise, was it your desire that those calls stop?"

"Yes."

"And why was that?"

"Because it was kind of the same call, sort of over and over again."

"Did the child seem to call more than most children do?" Mesereau asked.

"Well, most children don't call," Leno explained. "You call them, and you do follow-ups, and things like that."

"Do you recall the mother being in the background of your call to Gavin?"

"I remember someone in the background, but I couldn't say it was the mother. It could have been a nurse. I remember hearing someone talking as he was talking."

Mr. Leno reiterated his conversation with Gavin, which he said was very brief. He recalled asking Gavin how he was feeling and told the boy, "Hey, listen, keep your hopes up."

As jurors studied Jay Leno, hearing the sincerity of his voice, they each had a strange look on their face. It was apparent that every one of them remembered Gavin sitting on the witness stand and telling them that he never spoke to Jay Leno at all.

"Leave Me Alone"

As Michael arrived to court, on the star-studded day that Jay Leno and comedian Chris Tucker testified, he was flanked by his parents, Katherine and Joe.

Katherine seemed confident, but Joe looked concerned, perhaps wondering how the jury would react to seeing more movie and TV stars. People had been distracted by George Lopez and Macaulay Culkin, and there was anticipation that Elizabeth Taylor and Stevie Wonder might appear to testify.

Courtroom observers couldn't help staring at Michael and the Jackson family, but with more stars appearing, it was human nature to become distracted, to fixate on a celebrity's clothing, on their gestures, on their "real" persona. From the look on Joe's face, there was an anxiety that the stars might be outshining the testimony, and Joe Jackson didn't want that.

Out of the sixty witnesses the defense called to the stand, perhaps the most compelling was *Rush Hour* star Chris Tucker, who testified that Michael Jackson was a friend of his, whom he'd known about three or four years. Ironically, the two had met through their efforts to help Gavin Arvizo. Chris Tucker told jurors that he first met the Arvizo boy at the Laugh Factory, the famous comedy club on Sunset Strip. The comedian recalled that David Arvizo approached him to say that his son, Gavin, just loved him. It was David Arvizo who told Tucker that the Laugh Factory was hosting a benefit for Gavin, who told the comedian that Gavin was dying of cancer.

"Okay. So the father told you there was going to be a benefit to raise money for medical bills for Gavin?" Mesereau asked.

"Yes," Tucker said.

"Okay. And you attended that benefit, right?"

"Yes."

"Who else did you see there, if you remember?"

"I met a lot of kids, and I met his brother, Star. And it was kind of dark in the club, but from what I can recall, that's where I met Star. I think it was Star and his father, and that was it."

"And do you recall whether you contributed money on that occasion?" Mesereau asked.

"Not that night. But I did contribute some money, yes," Tucker testified.

"And explain that, if you would."

"I was asked, a few days later, to give some money, because they didn't raise any money, they didn't make any money," Tucker explained. "So I did. I wired some money to their foundation."

"Who told you they hadn't raised any money at the benefit?"

"Gavin told me."

When Chris Tucker told jurors that he wired $1,500 to the Arvizos after Gavin approached him for money, after Gavin complained there wasn't enough funds raised from the benefit—people looked perplexed. They already heard from numerous witnesses who had come forward to talk about being railroaded by the Arvizo clan for money. Some people had written checks to the Arvizos for thousands of dollars. Others brought toys and Christmas gifts to their home.

So many private donations were made from LA celebrities, the Arvizos had received so much money, that at one point, Janet Arvizo had gone out and plunked down $23,000 for a Ford SUV. The defense entered Janet's cashier's check into evidence, written to Hollywood Ford, showing jurors what Janet was trying to do with the money. Regarding the car—Janet lost her nerve and backed out of the deal. But she banked the $23,000 just the same, all the while receiving welfare checks and looking for other forms of assistance.

Jurors heard from a newspaper editor who was begged to place a free ad in a local paper asking for donations on behalf of Gavin—only to later find out that Gavin Arvizo's medical bills were entirely covered by his dad's medical insurance. One woman who raised money for the family testified that she brought the Arvizos a giant turkey for Thanksgiving, but she was sent away by the mother, who said she would have preferred to have cash instead. It seemed any of the little things that people did—the Arvizos just didn't feel were good enough.

Chris Tucker testified that he "hoped" the money he'd sent to the Arvizos had gone to pay medical bills—but his tone seemed to say otherwise. He described a day when he took the Arvizo family to Knott's Berry Farm, where they enjoyed a day of free amusement rides, meals, and all the candy they could eat. The movie star tried to downplay his good nature, mentioning that he'd taken the Arvizo kids to the mall a few times, buying them a few sporting goods, without going into details. But Mesereau didn't let the subject drop.

"Now, you said you bought clothes for the Arvizo children at a mall, is that correct?" Mesereau clarified.

"Yeah," Tucker said.

"And explain what you did, if you would?"

"We went to, like, a sports store. They liked the Raiders, and I bought them some Raiders stuff. Shoes and hats and stuff like that."

"And who was with you when you bought these clothes for the Arvizo children?"

"The father, David."

"Did you ever meet the mother?"

"I met her in—the first time in—Las Vegas."

Chris Tucker explained the circumstances under which he met Janet Arvizo, telling jurors that he was filming a new movie in 2001, that he didn't have much time to chat with the Arvizos, who had taken a road trip there, having been invited on the set by the star.

"They came to the movie set, right" Mesereau asked.

"Yes," Tucker testified.

"You met them there?"

"Yes."

"To your knowledge, did they stay very long?"

"To my knowledge, I heard they stayed awhile. And they were, they were trying to get them to leave, but I didn't know because I was so busy. They did stay a couple of—a week or two."

"Did you see them again in Las Vegas on that trip?" Mesereau asked.

"Yeah, I saw them in and out several times," Tucker testified. "I definitely saw the kids because they'd come to the set. I think the mother came a few times too, and the father. So I saw them. But I was so busy."

Chris Tucker told the jury that he was "friendly" with the Arvizos, and said that when he got back home to Los Angeles, a few months after his film finished shooting, Gavin called him, looking for Michael Jackson. Gavin was hoping to visit Jackson at Neverland, but Jackson couldn't be located at the time. Chris Tucker said he received numerous calls from Janet, who was crying and crying about the health of her son. Janet Arvizo was so distraught, telling Chris that she felt he was like their "brother." Somehow, Tucker felt obligated to help the whole Arvizo clan.

From the moment they first met, Gavin had asked for Chris Tucker's phone number. Tucker said he gave Gavin the number because he wanted to be accessible. He wanted to do anything he could, he wanted to help the boy. Tucker testified that he'd received countless calls from the Arvizos, mostly from Gavin and his mother. The comedian tried his best to befriend these people, doing little things, like giving them Nike shoes, and playing basketball with them, but he also wanted to keep some distance.

Over time, the *Rush Hour* star invited the Arvizos to his LA residence. They were there on at least three occasions. While visiting his home, Gavin approached Chris Tucker for money. Apparently, the boy put on a sad-puppy-dog face, and Tucker agreed to place money into the Arvizos' account.

At some point, the Arvizo kids began calling to ask for the keys to one of his cars, an SUV that Tucker wasn't using much, and Tucker offered them the car but later got "nervous" about it, especially when the Arvizo children kept calling, badgering Tucker's girlfriend.

Tucker told the jury that he became suspicious about the number of calls. When he later discovered that Michael Jackson had already lent the family an SUV, he told his girlfriend not to turn over the car keys. Mr. Tucker said that he did not turn over the truck keys to the Arvizos because he thought he was "doing too much" for this family.

And it was true.

There were many perks the Arvizos enjoyed at Chris Tucker' s expense. The star had taken them on numerous trips to Neverland, even at times when Michael wasn't present. Among other things, Chris Tucker had flown the Arvizo kids, with their dad, in a private jet to watch a Raiders game in the San Francisco Bay area.

"Did anything else they did make you suspicious?" Mesereau asked.

"Well, I think they did a lot of things that I didn't see, that my people were telling me to watch out," Tucker told him.

"Who were your people?"

"My brother, a few of my assistants that were on the set with me, were watching everything, you know. Gavin's behavior, Star's behavior. And they were telling me. But I was working. And they were telling me, you know, it was time for them to leave."

"Were your suspicions based on what you observed, or what other people told you?"

"I observed a lot of stuff, but I always gave them the benefit of the doubt. I felt sorry for Gavin, and I always wanted to try [to] help him, and I let a lot of stuff just go by. But I knew what they were talking about."

Chris Tucker told jurors that he was made aware, on the set in Las Vegas, that the Arvizo family was trying to upgrade their accommodations, that they wanted the producers to move them to the star's hotel. The Arvizos wanted to be put up in a suite comparable to Chris Tucker's hotel room, which the movie star was paying for out of his own pocket.

"Do you think they were taking advantage of you?" Mesereau wondered.

"I was hoping they weren't, but when it got back to me, yeah. That's what it looked like," Tucker said.

"Did any member of the Arvizo family ever refer to you as part of their family?"

"Yes."

"Who?"

"The mother, and Gavin, and Star."

"And what was your reaction to that?"

"I was—you know—getting a little nervous, because my whole thing was to just help the kid, not get attached to the whole family. Not like that," Tucker testified.

"I just wanted to make his life a little bit easier, so I said, you know, I need to watch myself because I'm high profile," he explained. "You know, I got to be careful, because sometimes when people see what you've got—they'll take advantage of you. So I tried to be careful and tried to pull back a little bit."

Chris Tucker told the jury that Gavin always referred to him as his "big brother" and would tell him, "I love you" on a regular basis. Star Arvizo also referred to Tucker as being "like a brother" to him. All three children pulled at his heartstrings, telling Chris Tucker how much they loved him.

It was no surprise that when the Bashir documentary aired in England, when the media first came pounding at their East LA door, that Tucker was the person the Arvizos called to complain about all the hoopla. They wanted Chris to locate Michael. They wanted to get away from the media. They wanted Chris Tucker to help them.

"The media was following them around, and they wanted to find Michael. They wanted to get out of town and find Michael," Tucker testified. "And I said, 'Okay.' I was trying to help them to get out of town, so they could, you know, be left alone."

"And Gavin told you they wanted to be with Michael?" Mesereau confirmed.

"Yeah, he was looking for Michael, and they wanted to find him. They found out he was in Miami some kind of way, and they wanted to go to Miami."

Tom Mesereau put phone records up on the screen, showing jurors the calls made to Chris Tucker from the Arvizos on February 4, 2003. He asked Tucker to clarify that the calls were placed from the Arvizos to him—and not the other way around.

Chris Tucker was sure that the phone numbers and times matched his recollection, and told jurors that he offered to fly the Arvizos out of town, that he offered to charter a plane, to take the Arvizos to Miami.

As this information came before the jury, heads were spinning.

People just couldn't believe their ears.

For months, prosecutors had argued that the Arvizos were virtually forced to go to see Jackson in Miami. The Arvizos—Janet, Davellin, Gavin, and Star—had each testified that it was not their idea to fly to Miami. On the stand, each one of the Arvizos acted like they were coerced into doing Jackson a great favor, coerced into boarding that plane with Chris Tucker, into taking that trip to the resort in Miami, at Michael's expense.

"Did you ask Gavin how he knew Michael Jackson was in Florida?" Mesereau wondered.

"I can't remember. I'm pretty sure I did, and I think he was calling Michael's people and he found out, some kind of way," Tucker said.

"Now, at this point, given all the conversations you'd had with Gavin, his requests for money, the talk about automobiles, what you'd seen on the set, did you consider Gavin to be someone awfully sophisticated for someone his age?"

"Yes."

"And explain what you mean by that."

"He was really smart, and he was cunning at times, but I always overlooked it because I felt sorry for him. I knew he was a little kid—but I knew he was cunning. And his brother, Star, was definitely cunning."

"When you say 'cunning,' explain what you're saying."

"Always stuff like, 'Chris, let me have this. Let me have this. Let me get that. Come on, I'm not feeling good.' Stuff like that. And I knew he was going too far, but I always said 'He's sick,' you know, 'He's got a lot of problems, family problems,' so I just overlooked it."

Chris Tucker told the jury that on the night he chartered the plane to take Janet Arvizo and her kids to Miami, the Arvizo clan looked "relieved to get out of California," and they were all excited to make the trip to see Jackson. While they were in flight, Janet convinced Chris to let her borrow his SUV, and Tucker agreed to give her the keys once they got settled in Miami.

Tucker recalled that just after the flight took off, before the kids fell asleep, Gavin was happy, just absolutely elated, that he was going to see Michael Jackson again. This was February 5, 2003, just a few days after the Bashir documentary aired in England, when none of the Arvizos really knew what had been alleged in the Bashir piece.

"Did anyone in the Arvizo family give you the impression that they were going to Miami against their will?" Mesereau asked.

"No," Tucker said.

"Now, when you got to Florida, what did you do?"

"I met up with my brother at the airport, and we went straight to the hotel."

Tucker said his brother had a car waiting for them at the executive airport, and testified that, rather than check into his room, the Arvizo kids insisted that they find Michael, so they all went up to the top floor to just briefly say hello.

"Do you recall saying anything to Michael in his room?" Mesereau asked.

"Just said hello and was happy to see him," Tucker said.

"And did you discuss the Arvizos with him?"

"I did."

"What did you say?"

"Later on, I did. I just told him to watch out for Janet because I felt suspicious about her."

"And did you tell Michael Jackson why you were suspicious of Janet Arvizo?" Mesereau asked.

"Yeah, because—and she even made me more suspicious later on. But first, like I said, I gave her the keys [to the SUV], and at that point, I knew something wasn't right. And then I was trying to talk to Michael, and she was always inter-rupting. And I was like—I didn't know why she was doing it.

"And then I just—I tried to pull Michael in the room, and I said 'You need to watch out. Just be careful.' And then, that was really brief, and then I left."

"Now, why was that conversation brief?" Mesereau asked.

"Because the phones were ringing, the kids were all over the place, and it was, you know, Michael's very busy. So it's always somebody pulling at him," Tucker said.

"Do you recall whether or not Michael responded when you said, 'Be careful of these people'?"

"Yes, he did. He was listening. And we talked about other stuff, and then I left."

"Do you recall Janet saying anything about Michael Jackson being like a father to their family?" Mesereau asked.

"Oh, yes. Oh, yes. That was right before we went in the room," Chris Tucker told jurors. "She was frantically saying Michael's the father. I'm the brother. And that's when I told Michael. I took him in the room, and I was trying to talk to him, and I said, 'Something ain't right.' I said, '*Mike, something ain't right.*'"

"Moonwalk"

Following Chris Tucker's appearance, the defense rested their case. As Mesereau sat down behind the defense table, he could see the blood rushing from Sneddon's face. Tom Sneddon had asked to play the tape of Gavin's police interview, and the judge granted him that right for the purpose of the state's rebuttal case. Sneddon and his team had been waiting for months, certain that the police interview of Gavin Arvizo would prove to be the biggest day of testimony at the trial. For the prosecution, their most critical moment had arrived.

Behind the scenes, Tom Mesereau had argued that the police interview was inadmissible hearsay, but Judge Melville ruled that the jury could view it, not for the truth, but to show Gavin's demeanor. With that, Mesereau requested that the Arvizo family be brought back to Santa Maria. Mesereau insisted that the Arvizos be present to be questioned in a surrebuttal, an option the defense rarely asserts.

Tom Sneddon beamed when he showed jurors the police interview, and people watched carefully as the boy gave a chronological account of his time spent with Jackson. People were sympathetic as they watched Gavin talk about his cancer. Gavin said he first stayed in Michael's bedroom when he had no hair on his head. Gavin seemed enamored with Jackson, and told detectives that over the years, he tried to keep in touch with the pop star, but Jackson always had new phone numbers and was hard to reach. Gavin recalled that he once visited Jackson at the Universal Hilton in Burbank, having been brought there by his father while he was still receiving cancer treatments.

In September of 2002, Gavin said he got a call from Jackson, asking him to come to Neverland to tape a video about his cancer being cured. After the Bashir interview aired, Gavin said he was upset about seeing his name in the news. CNN mentioned his name often, and Gavin claimed that prompted him to fly to Miami to hold a press conference with Jackson. Gavin told detectives that he got drunk in Miami, that Jackson had given him wine so he would "relax."

Much to the chagrin of the jurors, Gavin was vague as he detailed alleged acts of molestation he said happened "four or five times." The boy was being evasive. As jurors watched Gavin claim that he'd been inappropriately touched by Mr. Jackson, some of them had quizzical looks of their faces. Many of the things he said seemed orchestrated. The boy looked like he was choosing his words, almost acting. Moreover, it was difficult to determine how much Gavin was being maneuvered by police.

"Gavin, buddy, you're being really brave," an officer told him.

"Gavin, we want you to do this. You're doing the right thing," the officer cajoled.

The eighth grader told police that he was drinking alcohol at Neverland often, insisting that, after their return from Miami, he drank wine or liquor with Jackson every day. Additionally, Gavin claimed that Jackson licked his hair on the plane ride from Miami to Santa Barbara, something he never mentioned while on the witness stand.

Gavin told detectives that "everything happened after Miami," and yet he didn't have a hint of quiver in his voice as he spoke. Gavin blankly said that he never saw Jackson's private parts, that he wasn't positive about what happened during the alleged sex acts, and that he wasn't sure what an ejaculation was. Some people wondered how a thirteen-year-old boy could be uncertain about something like that.

Nonetheless, mainstream media thought the police tape was damning. They ran to their news tents to report the accuser's allegations, this time, choosing their words carefully. After viewing the police tape, mainstream media felt that conservative Santa Maria jurors would convict Jackson. Some people reported that Jackson's defense team was sunk.

As the state wound up their rebuttal case, the Arvizo family had already arrived to Santa Maria. They were being lodged at a secret home, and insiders learned that the Arvizos had been prepped by the DA's team the night prior, and were ready to address the jury again.

Media folks were hyped to hear Mesereau question the Arvizos one last time. People were teasing with each other, saying how much they looked forward to a new version of the "Arvizo show." But at the last minute, the defense attorney changed his mind. As Sneddon ended his rebuttal, resting the state's case against Michael Jackson, Tom Mesereau announced, "The defense rests."

With those words, Tom Sneddon turned white. The DA looked dumb-founded and was staring at Judge Melville. It looked like the man was having a hard time trying to compose himself. Sneddon couldn't believe that Mesereau had pulled the plug on the Arvizos. Mesereau had thrown his final punch to the prosecution.

The DA was devastated to have lost the opportunity to cross-examine the Arvizo family. The prosecution needed to alter the perception of the Arvizos, and the DA could have done that by allowing the Arvizos to re-explain things, by hav-ing the Arvizos fill in the gaps and holes in their prior testimony. If Sneddon could have turned the Arvizos into credible witnesses, he seemed to think he would get a guilty verdict on something—whether it be for conspiracy, for serv-ing alcohol to a minor, or for lewd acts.

Even without the Arvizos, it was clear that DA Sneddon and his team felt the jury would convict Jackson of some charge. They were looking forward to Jack-son serving prison time, and they held a private victory celebration days before the verdicts were in. Sneddon knew that if he won the trial, he and his team would be known around the world. They all would become instantly famous.

The prosecutors could ride on that fame forever.

During the closing arguments, presented first by the prosecution, then by the defense, and again by the prosecution—the media was busy fretting over posi-tioning for the verdicts, trying to predetermine how long the jury would deliber-ate. There were specific locations set up for closing argument "analysts." The media pool coordinator, Peter Shaplen, wanted to avert a media stampede, as evi-denced in the Martha Stewart verdict, and he was dealing with hundreds of media people who were vying for the limited media seats in the courtroom. Even the overflow room, with its closed-circuit TV, was going to be crowded and would not have enough room to afford every wire, paper, radio, and TV station a runner per count of the indictment.

As the jurors deliberated, media people were becoming frantic. They weren't really concerned about Jackson, they were concerned about sound bites and cam-era shots. The media had to deal with beefed-up security, which included the Santa Maria Police, Santa Barbara sheriffs, the Santa Barbara Mobile Field Force, SWAT teams, and bomb-sniffing dogs. For the verdicts, additional security was provided for trucks and gear outside the media pens, all of which posed more complications for tired journalists and producers.

There were so many rules to follow, there was so much hassle for media to get anywhere near the courthouse, people were aggravated. There were very specific instructions about "site credentials," and all members of the media had to display official court credentials, a rule that was enforced by deputies at all times.

All media people were subjected to weapons and recording device screening, and tensions were high. No members of the media were permitted beyond the railing that separated the court gallery from the litigation area, so there was no chance to get near Jackson or any of the key players. The list of procedures and regulations was staggering, and the rules had gotten on everyone's last nerve.

As the media learned that Judge Melville had set aside two days for jury instructions, people made anxious pleas to allow cameras into the courtroom to carry the verdicts—*live*. In the meantime, four pool cameras were set up in the courtroom walkway, fifty-two camera positions were mapped out for TV crews, and fifty still-camera positions were assigned slots, given to media who paid a "County Impact Fee" for the privilege of covering the trial. There was preparation for a jury news conference, for prosecution and defense news conferences, for a helicopter pool, and for jail sites—if applicable.

On the day Judge Melville read the jury a complex set of instructions, Melville re-read the specific counts against Jackson, explaining the specific law that had to be followed. Judge Melville told jurors that they could consider alleged past acts only if they tended "to show intent" on Jackson's part, regarding the crimes with which Jackson was actually charged.

Jackson was eligible to serve concurrent sentences, and legal experts were predicting that, if the forty-six-year-old pop star was convicted on all charges, Jackson was facing a possible prison sentence of eighteen years and eight months. It was serious, and depending on aggravating circumstances, the total amount of time Michael Jackson was facing behind bars could have been equal to a death sentence—adding up to fifty-six years. For viewers, TV pundits described the exact charges Jackson was facing, and the sentence each charge carried:

* **Count One**: Conspiracy involving child abduction, false imprisonment, and extortion. The count carried a minimum sentence of two years, a maximum of four years, and a $10,000 fine.
* **Counts Two through Five**: Lewd act upon a child under the age of fourteen. Each count was punishable by a mandatory prison sentence of three to eight years.
* **Count Six**: Attempt to get a child under the age of fourteen to commit a lewd act upon Mr. Jackson. The count carried a prison sentence of three to eight years.

* **Counts Seven through Ten**: Administering an intoxicating agent—alcohol—to assist in the commission of lewd acts upon a child. Each count carried a sixteen-month to three-year prison sentence.

TV pundits explained that Judge Melville also gave the jurors the option, regarding the last four felony counts, of finding Jackson guilty of four lesser-included offenses for providing alcohol to minors, a misdemeanor.

On the day that Michael Jackson was found "not guilty" fourteen times, many people were weeping silently in the courtroom. There was a shock wave that hit everyone, and the media folks who expected a guilty verdict seemed to be in a state of disbelief, with their jaws dropped.

After Jackson and his family left the room, after the public spectators filed out in order, the media went outside and saw the world in a new light. The fans were spreading joy and love, hugging and kissing each other, and jumping up and down. The world looked colorful, with banners, and horns honking, with hundreds of people dancing in the streets.

As for the media, many of whom had predetermined a guilty verdict, people realized they had spent months reporting only one side of the story, and had to admit they had been wrong.

As soon as the gag order was lifted, the media wanted to hear from the jury, and a short press conference was held at the Santa Maria court.

Identified only by numbers, the jury, ages twenty-nine to seventy, had witnessed a trial filled with salacious testimony, dramatic moments, and celebrities galore. As the eight women and four men talked to reporters, they tried to explain why they found Michael Jackson "not guilty" on all counts.

They answered countless questions, many about Jackson's superstar status affecting their judgment, which seemed to insult them. The jurors insisted that they hadn't treated Jackson any differently because of his celebrity, saying they spent a lot of time seriously studying the evidence and looking at the testimony. They told media that not one piece of evidence stood out above any other, claiming that they considered all the evidence to be equally "important." However, jury foreman Paul Rodriguez later confided that Gavin's police confession was critical, saying that jurors watched it numerous times.

Some jurors publicly admitted that they found the Arvizo family to be con artists who were trying to frame Michael Jackson. Others felt there was no smoking gun, that the prosecution simply had not proven their case. Still, the prosecution, with no physical evidence, had been able to publicly humiliate Jackson—they had successfully made fun of his skin, his sexuality, and his lifestyle, all the while presenting a bunch of junk evidence and false testimony.

After the jury press conference, jurors were followed to their cars, being hounded by media who were offering limo rides and plane tickets to New York, begging them to appear on popular morning talk shows. But most jurors weren't interested. They felt exhausted and overwhelmed, and they just wanted to go home. Jurors had spent many sleepless nights pondering the case, and they seemed to want nothing more to do with the public spectacle.

But two months later, two jurors crawled out of the woodwork to try to sell their own books. Hoping for book deals, they appeared on MSNBC network, and both jurors publicly stated that they felt forced into voting for "not guilty" verdicts, throwing a black cloud over the veracity of the jury system.

Viewers found it outrageous that these American Citizens, who had promised to serve their country, had the audacity to come on television to claim that they had been coerced. People found it offensive that jurors were trying to cash in on Jackson, not by telling the truth, but by smearing the American justice system.

Jury Foreman Rodriguez would later insist that the two isolated jurors' version of the events was inaccurate. Rodriguez made it clear that nobody twisted any-one's arm, that behind closed doors each member of the jury acted with a clear mind and came to the "not guilty" verdicts of their own accord.

Inside the courtroom, some members of the media made attempts to mask their surprise about the outcome of the case. Many reporters couldn't believe the verdicts were true, that Jackson was a free man and had slipped away from public scrutiny. Of course, for the most part, the media still wanted to report the dirt, and were already speculating that Jackson was fleeing the country.

When Tom Mesereau and his team walked out of the courtroom victorious, they initially declined to hold a press conference. However the next morning, Tom Mesereau agreed to appear on all three network morning shows, telling viewers that there was nothing phony about the defense's case, asserting that there was "a lot that was phony" about the DA's case. That same evening, Mesereau would do an interview on *Larry King Live*, offering his thoughts on the trial for a full hour.

Mesereau would later appear on *The Tonight Show*, telling Jay Leno, "If you know Michael's philosophy about life, you know that he would never hurt a child." Not long after the trial was over, Mesereau was deemed "one of the most fascinating people of the year," and he taped a prime-time segment with Barbara Walters, insisting that the case against Jackson "was built on sand."

After all was said and done, after the tears, the glee, the prayers, and the public farewell to Jackson, one journalist would study an obscure element of an exhibit entered into evidence. It was a note handwritten by the superstar, etched inside one of his books. And it was this permanent etching that would forever capture the essence of Michael Jackson. In the book, the superstar had written the words:

"Look at
    the true spirit
        of happiness and
            joy in these boys
                faces,
            this is the spirit of
                Boyhood, A life
                    I never had and
                        will always
                            dream of."

Acknowledgments

Michael Jackson Conspiracy would not have been possible without the help of many people. I have to thank Tom Mesereau, Jr., for believing in my honest spirit, and Judge Rodney S. Melville, for allowing me access to the trial exhibits and transcripts, as well as Court Clerk Carrie Wagner and Judicial Assistant, Darla Rodriguez. I must also extend a special thanks to Jury Foreman Paul Rodriguez, and to veteran trial observer Iris Crawford, both of whom made astute observations about the trial that were invaluable to me.

I wish to thank Peter Shaplen, the top-notch media pool coordinator, who found a place for two authors at the Jackson trial, myself being one, and in addition, I thank TV star Bill O'Reilly and *FOX News*, for allowing me to cover this trial for them. Others at FOX were good to me, among them, Geraldo Rivera, David Tabacoff, Roger Friedman, Jim Hammer, and the list goes on, including all the camera and sound people who kept things rolling.

I must also thank Susan Driscoll, the CEO and president of iUniverse, for trusting in the value of this project, and to all the iUniverse associates who moved heaven and earth to get the book done, especially Janet Noddings, Laura Beers, Lynn Everett, Lisa Chen, Katie Bose, Monika Lin, Joe Steinbach, Sarie Whitson, Lori Kaser, Scott Manning, Wenyan Bian, Fiona Wang and Steven Zhang. In addition, I thank media manager and promoter Melanie A. Bonvicino for talking me into writing a self-published book, especially when I didn't feel I had the strength, and I thank Pearl Jr., who talked me into taking a risk on a pro-Jackson effort, even though I had attacked Jackson on television many times. Without Pearl's advice, I probably wouldn't have been so bold.

I thank the TV, radio, and print journalists who truly befriended me during the trial, especially Jane Velez-Mitchell, Frank Swertlo, Jim Moret, Linda Deutsch, Howard Breuer, Tina Sussman, Nick Madigan, Steve Penna, Ann Bremner, and Valerie Harris, as well as courtroom artists Vicki Ellen Behringer, Mona Sha-fer Edwards, and Bill Robles—these folks will always be close to my heart.

I give a special acknowledgment to author J. Randy Taraborelli, who also became a friend to me during the trial. I believe that no understanding of Jackson would be complete without reading his book, *Michael Jackson: The Magic and the Madness.*

As always, I thank my readers, who are more important to me than they will ever know. And I'm eternally grateful to my assistants, Louis Flores and Kristal Mize, both of whom I love dearly, who make things run more smoothly for me.

I also thank my friends and family for being understanding and supportive of the writing process, even if they don't always like the subject matter. And I espe-cially thank my love, John Faltings, for his tireless devotion and support. I could not have written this book without him.

As I wrote this book, I also thanked God, every day, for giving me the will to persist.